# LA SCALA

Lorenzo Arruga

# La Scala

*With an Introduction by Paolo Grassi
and Testimony to Times Past by
Mario Labroca*

**Praeger Publishers
New York**

*Design: Diego Birelli*
*The photoreportage on opera in today's Scala was done by Pepi Merisio*

Published in the United States of America in 1976
by Praeger Publishers, Inc.
111 Fourth Avenue, New York, N.Y. 10003

© Copyright 1975 by Electa Editrice, Milan, Italy

Library of Congress Catalog Card Number: 72-91252
ISBN 0-275-53680-7

Printed in Italy

# TABLE OF CONTENTS

# INTRODUCTION

*There was a generation of men in love with music and the theater in the 1930's and 1940's — men like Silvio D'Amico and Mario Labroca, Alfredo Casella and Guido Salvini — who, even in the face of Fascist hostility and indifference, did everything in their power to keep Italian musical and theatrical culture in a European context and dimension. It is to men of this caliber that the members of my generation will always be grateful, for even in the grimmest days of Fascist obscurantism they stimulated others to believe in the values which the Fascist regime's ethic rejected but European culture in its ideal form still strongly affirmed.*

*Indeed one of the most moving moments for me soon after taking the job of Superintendent of La Scala in February 1972, after twenty-five uninterrupted years as the director of Milan's Piccolo Teatro — twenty-one of them in collaboration with Giorgio Strehler, and four alone — was the meeting with my dear old friend Mario Labroca who told me about this book, which was to be published by Electa and of which Labroca had written a first draft, sadly never to be completed because of his illness and greatly lamented death. Soon after, a man of the younger generation, Lorenzo Arruga, took over the task and placed Labroca's precious contribution in a more ample and organic context, combining it with a well articulated historical and photographic documentation, thus putting "La Scala's image through the ages" in a framework that does honor to his brilliant and lively intelligence — intelligence, that is, in the original Latin sense of a continuous search to understand the reality of artistic events.*

*I have the pleasant task of introducing this volume and La Scala of today. Since Arruga has rightly insisted on a history of La Scala which is identified with the choice of new operas and of those authentic composers that can be assigned a place in history, I wish to say right off that today's La Scala describes itself and wishes to be described as the theater which, though it has not yet been able to bring to fruition a new opera-ballet commissioned from the deeply mourned and tragically deceased composer Bruno Maderna, with choreography by Béjart, has, however, commissioned the following: a ballet by Virgilio,* Specchio a tre luci, *presented last September and to be presented soon again; a new work by Luigi Nono* Al Gran sole carico d'amore, *to be produced on April 4th of this year; and a new opera-ballet by Luciano Berio, to be produced within two years. The Teatro alla Scala is also arranging for a new composition by Sylvano Bussotti, which we hope to present during the 1975-76 season, and also a new work composed by Gerolamo Arrigo,* Rorogigasos, *which we hope that Maurice Béjart will agree to stage for its world première with his original choreography.*

*The rigorous custodian of the great values of the past and the alert witness to the authentic values of modernity, La Scala of today wants to make its own organic contribution to the public of the best living Italian musical talents, thus achieving the status of an institution which performs its task in a dynamic musical and cultural situation. This does not alter the fact that (both in the opera and ballet as well as the symphonic seasons), a large space is set aside at La Scala for modern and contemporary foreign music, though without forgetting our job of making better known the most important creations of the past. Arruga objectively emphasizes that particular aspect of La Scala, which is becoming more and more open to a new audience, a popular audience, and an even larger group of workers, student-workers, and young people, all those citizens who have traditionally been excluded (because they lacked the price of a ticket, or simply did not have the habit of enjoying music) from permanent contact with the ideas of culture in general and music in particular. Confronted by the ever greater demand for culture, art, theater and music which rises imperiously from the broad popular masses of a society in the process of transformation, La Scala has tried to give ever more advanced and concrete answers to the problem. Though well aware of an immense gap between that demand and an inadequate supply, a public corporation like our theater must rigorously and ethically carry out its social duty, since in fact it spends the public's money. Today's great opera theaters on the various continents are all facing serious economic, financial and organizational difficulties, and La Scala is no exception to this international rule, which in Italy at this very moment is more serious than elsewhere: there must now be an end to the long delay of putting into effect law 800, of August 14, 1967, the indispensable reform which would provide a new and modern system for all musical activities in Italy and would represent not only now but in the future a more progressive relationship between music and society in our republic.*

*I think that I can definitely state that La Scala will never agree passively, slavishly or weakly to lower the highest possible standard of its activities, a standard, moreover, which is even now difficult to attain due to the objective contradictions afflicting opera houses throughout the world. While we remain convinced that the esthetic and artistic standard established by our choices and productions will constitute a firm reference point for the history of yesterday, today and tomorrow, it is especially necessary to affirm that the transformation of La Scala into a "theater for everyone" (in a society which, though struggling against hardships and conflicting pressures, is now changing its character) we regard as irreversible. So what we want is clear: a theater tied to the history of yesterday, today and tomorrow, a theater proudly committed to the defense of artistic values, a theater intimately bound up with the new social reality. This is the reality of La Scala at the moment in which I write these lines, and this is the desire of all of us who work at La Scala. Only time will tell whether we have been able concretely to defend the presuppositions of our work, whether La Scala of the 1980's will be the just, rightful and living heir of two centuries of our institution's history.*

*Paolo Grassi*

*Milan, March 7, 1975*

# TESTIMONY TO TIMES PAST
*by Mario Labroca*

One day an out-of-towner who was staring at the façade of La Scala asked me where he could find the theater. When I told him it was that very building, he appeared very disappointed and murmured to himself: "So small!" Obviously, in his imagination that name had assumed gigantic proportions.

In fact, from the very start, La Scala was a "different" sort of theater from all the others. Stendhal realized this at the beginning of the 19th century. His first contact with La Scala was downright frenetic. "I arrived", he tells us, "at seven in the evening, limp with exhaustion. But I ran straight to La Scala. My whole journey was repaid. And all this despite the fact that my senses were so worn out that they had nearly lost the capacity for pleasure. Tonight I have seen everything that can be imagined by the most Oriental fantasy as regards the strangest, most striking and richest of architectonic scenic beauty, everything that can be concocted in the line of magnificent draperies and of characters who not only wear the costumes but also have the faces and gestures of the country in which the dramatic action takes place." And the very next night, Stendhal was again at La Scala: "On the stage there appeared without a single pause at least one hundred singers and supernumeraries in such splendid costumes that in Paris they would be reserved only for the prima donnas and the star performers." And we know Stendhal is telling the truth, since this is all testified to by the drawings of 19th century costumes preserved in La Scala's museum — utterly truthful testimony, besides, since these are the patterns used by the dressmakers who made the costumes — where one can see not only meticulous drawings of the costumes for all of the leading roles but also of those worn by the extras and members of the chorus. "My first impression", Stendhal concludes, "is one of complete and utter enchantment."

So this enthusiastic Frenchman from Grenoble had found his ideal in Milan's theater: beautiful music, splendid costumes and scenery, lovely female singers with "manners instinct with naturalness and enchanting gaiety", and he will be quite happy to hand over a *zecchino* every evening of his stay to reserve a box on the third tier; though he will leave Milan with a feeling of deep disgust for the French opera theaters. "If my journey to Italy has one drawback", he remarks sadly, "it is actually this." "I say that La Scala", Stendhal continues, "is the first theater in the world, because it is the theater which purveys the greatest musical pleasure. There are no chandeliers or lamps in the auditorium itself; the theater is illuminated only by the light coming from the stage." One should underline this last observation. At that time theaters were lit by candles and, since they could not be repeatedly extinguished and lit during the performance, the auditoriums where always lit up and so the spectators were in a constant state of distraction. The semi-darkness remarked upon by Stendhal at La Scala was a distant prelude to that modern concentration which is demanded in a theater during the course of the performance.

If a reader who is not an opera expert looks over the list of programs for La Scala from its inauguration down to the advent of Rossini, he will find very few opera titles to arouse his interest, and though he may come across the names of a few familiar composers, they are usually the sort confined to the pages of music encyclopedias — and not always with complete justice. There were so many overwhelming geniuses in the 19th century that the opera-goer has tended to forget what happened before these great artificers arrived on the scene. But that is not all. Like society, opera was having its own special difficulties, making the transition from the neatly logical stylistic modes of the 18th century to the violent and perturbing frenzies of Romantic poetics.

If we wish to understand fully the function that lyrical opera fulfilled from the time of its birth, we must remember that at one time it resembled a great deal what the movies are for us today. Like the movies, operas had to be created and produced in a short time, getting them quickly to the distributor (that is, the opera house) within a fixed, unavoidably firm deadline — in other words, before the fashion had changed. Moreover, lyrical opera was the only spectacle that, like the movies today, enchanted people because of the grandeur of its scenic means and the pleasures of its singing voices, which also had a rhetorical and suggestive effect, not to mention the joy of liberating laughter. And, as we well know, God in his infinite wisdom sends us masterpieces very seldom, so that we shall not lose our faith in art and our love of it — indeed, as seldom as those great miracles which keep lazy believers trudging down the road of true faith.

La Scala has always engaged in a much broader range of activities than other Italian theaters. It staged a great number of operas, had the possibility of giving them the breathing space of several performances, and could permit the best of them to make those periodic returns which help to establish comparisons between what has already entered life and what, from day to day, is being born into it. This continuity also fostered a precious and opportune loyalty and led to the ripening of the major operas by prolonging their existence, endowing them with an unexpected contemporaneity and contact with the various forms of expression gradually being tested and accepted, the changing operatic idioms. Besides this, we should not forget that the Milanese theater, thanks to the nature of its management, was not only at the center of local civic but also national life (of course, I am speaking only of music), owing to the ties it had with the history of the entire country. Perhaps this was the reason for its lack of interest in what was happening in other theaters, especially foreign ones, the new things that were appearing in them and the revolutions bursting into flame here and there throughout the world.

*1. La Scala at night.* ▷

La Scala looked upon itself as a kind of affectionate mother to the operas which its public had adopted, and for years cradled and nursed them as though they had no legs of their own to stand on, while at the same time putting off the production on its stage of creations which were different from the customary ones. In the floodtide of its activity, La Scala also became a sort of museum of Italian operatic life (and it is not by chance that it is the only theater which possesses a rich museum open to all those who want to delve deeply into the subject). Its choices have not always been felicitous, nor have its preferences always been justifiable. Yet the principles upon which they were arrived at, the protective and conservative objectives La Scala has pursued, certainly helped to strengthen both its structure and means so that La Scala acquired the character of a *living* museum. To us, this type of museum is not the tomb of artistic opera but rather the place where operas of the past are brought back to life. The contact with an alert and intelligent audience ensures their continued journey on the path to immortality.

The history of La Scala is replete with encounters, personalities and incredible combinations. First of all there is the presence of the musicians — both composers and executants — who somehow come together in an extraordinary fashion for certain decisive appointments. There are remoter presences who generate special events in which the theater can recognize itself. This is what happened with Shakespeare and the two *Otello*s: Rossini's *Otello*, which was assiduously presented at La Scala for more than fifty years, as in no other Italian theater, and Verdi's *Otello*, which was one of tnose strange appointments with destiny when the history of the theater could be felt as a living presence.

The appearance of Verdi's *Otello* was a sensational event. The opera was born from the collaboration of Verdi and Boito, though everyone was kept in the dark until the very last moment. The meetings between the composer and his librettist took place in the utmost secrecy. Now we know all the details of this miraculous conception, but during that period, when Verdi had entered his seventieth year and was behaving with much greater prudence, any indiscretions about his life or work irked him tremendously. As a consequence, *Otello* ripened in a hothouse atmosphere of silence and discretion. The press was not as strong as it is now, photography was still in its experimental stage, and the telephoto lens which today can so often profane private life and the domestic household was not even remotely imaginable. It should also be added that in 1886 a new agreement had been reached between the impresario and La Scala's Directing Council which absolutely prohibited anyone not connected with the theater from attending rehearsals, so that it was very difficult for rumors to filter through the studio walls.

Yet as soon as the program for the 1886-1887 season was announced, the crowd took the box offices by storm and the regular subscribers occupied whatever places were available. Because of this, posters soon had to announce that all seats and boxes were sold out, no standing room was available in the orchestra and the small lobby was closed to the public. Seats in the orchestra, boxes and balcony cost five lire, which in those days was a small fortune. For the occasion, Arturo Toscanini, who had already made his mark as a conductor, played the cello again, being a fine instrumentalist, and was part of the cello "quartet" that introduces the enchanting duet between Otello and Desdemona at the end of the second act. Many years later, when talking about it to me, Toscanini recalled with deep emotion how at a certain point in the rehearsal he felt his arm being touched, turned and saw Verdi, who said quietly to him: "Please, play it just a bit softer." Toscanini added that the sonority was a trifle forced because of the extremely ambitious cellist, who wanted to star even when he should have muted his instrument in accordance with the passage's meditative, softly penetrating tone.

The opera, conducted by Franco Faccio, astounded from the very first moment. The sudden storm with which the action opens, the noise of the tempest mingling with the scene's livid lights, startled the audience, which found itself confronted by a new and unexpected spectacle. The auditorium had been hermetically sealed during the rehearsals, and the lack of gossip and critical anticipations only increased the audience's amazement, for in the swift, dense passage of about twelve minutes of music they witnessed a hurricane, a woman's desperate supplication to the sea, the calming of the storm and the joyous cry of "Victory!"

At the opera's première, the part of Otello was sung by Tamagno, one of the greatest operatic tenors, and when he burst out with the word "Esultate!" the audience burst into a round of applause which, it seemed, had never resounded so loud and prolonged in La Scala's auditorium. All of the acts were applauded with the same enthusiasm and during the season the opera was repeated for a grand total of twenty-five performances. And Toscanini, who of all the names that have been listed on La Scala's billings throughout its history is one of the most decisive, in his future career faithfully carried out Verdi's most intimate artistic concepts and took to heart his essential lesson.

Benvenuto Franci, the baritone, famous during a long and happy career which ended only a few years ago, remembered that Scandiani, having heard him sing in *Trovatore* at the Dal Verme theater, invited him in 1924 to La Scala so that Toscanini could hear him. "You're a bit of a shouter", Toscanini told him. "But when we do *Trovatore* here at La Scala I'll handle you personally because, for example, when I heard that *'Leonora è mia!'* you let out a 'sol' like a punch in the stomach. What are you doing with that 'sol'? This is a count who is talking, a hero, not some beggar, much less a shouter. That's why you must sing it as Verdi wrote it, without that 'sol'." Franci explained that the aria, which he sang a trifle loudly, Toscanini wanted sung just a little below his normal voice. "Remember," Toscanini always said, "Verdi wrote it that way and that's the way it must always be executed — not a quarter tone less, nor a quarter tone more. And you must never go slowly; you must always be in the right tempo. My stick is so precise that you can never go wrong!"

This should be said since his lessons were an example to everyone and brought about a new situation — after him, all Italian operas began to be presented in terms of their actual scores. From then on, and even today, the large opera houses — at least the best of them — have tried to keep faith with this standard of inexorable precision and taste. Only if the conductor is mediocre and the theater is managed by people who lack sensitivity is it still possible to revive that sad past. Fortunately, Toscanini put an end to an equivocal situation which had been produced by long-standing musical abuses and contamination.

The history of the Milanese theater often reflected the history of the city in which it stood and even, in certain obvious instances, the history of Italy. La Scala was the first theater in Italy which could boast of a serious management that presented programs demanding great commitment, and chiefly because it never gave the impresarios the power which they had acquired in nearly all of our large opera houses. On the contrary, La Scala, from its very inception, was run by a governing board composed of the city's eminent men, who formulated the programs and entrusted their realization to an impresario who, hedged about by all sorts of obligations and tied to specific, fixed tasks difficult to overlook or neglect, was limited in his functions and therefore lacked overwhelming prestige. Besides, La Scala was aimed at the tastes of the boxholders and had gathered them together with the wise objective of forming a real association, which thus helped to ensure considerable financial support and rather handsome cash gifts for each of its seasons.

Furthermore, Milan was the city in which resided that bizarre population which roved all over Europe from the second half of the 17th century down to the close of the last century — I refer to the world formed by opera companies, together with their orchestras and choruses, which went on tours that reached almost all of the Italian and continental theaters. These creators of operatic spectacles constitute a true caste, which has brought all the way down to our day indestructible habits consolidated by the centuries — nomads who put on operas, strange nomads who no longer travel in wagons or the barges on Venetian canals and have even gone beyond the train and ocean liner, rocketing about the world in supersonic planes. Yet apart from the speed of their journeys, nothing else has changed. In Milan

are still located the largest agencies for singers and for all the other crafts associated with the production of operas, from the musicians in the pit to the stagehands behind the set, and they all can be found in bare, squalid offices in the buildings that huddle around the Cathedral. And then the famous Galleria Victor Emanuel, one of those curious, iron-ribbed, glass-domed constructions housing shops and cafés which was inaugurated around 1880, immediately became the place for meetings, discussions, and the usual petty, back-biting gossip that has always been an integral part of theater life. For two shifts — from eleven o'clock in the morning until twelve noon; and from five o'clock in the afternoon until eight o'clock in the evening — there gathered under the glass dome a bustling swarm of people from a restless, anxious, insecure world, almost always looking for a job, even a temporary one, to help tide things over. Both great and small artists were on hand and among them circulated impresarios who had come from every part of the world, together with agents of every caliber, rank, capacity and moral standard. Here milled about the veterans of thousands of failed auditions, and maniacs who poured in from everywhere, each convinced that he had the most beautiful voice in the world. During those hours, the Galleria sounded like a huge bird-cage, for many of its habitués emitted those sharp, intermittent sounds which insure the singer of good vocal health, that series of *mi mi mi mis* which imitates the sweet call of a little bird and over which at times rose the "trills" of a more adventurous singer trying to arouse the curiosity and interest of the agents who might be there. The weirdest, tallest, most improbable tales were being told; failures were being transformed into triumphs and the triumphs of others into colossal fiascos. At twelve-thirty and at eight o'clock on the dot the Galleria would suddenly empty, and one saw the opposite phenomenon to that of the pigeons which, at meal times, converge on the Piazza San Marco from all the districts of Venice. I am sorry that I never looked down on the piazza from the top of the Cathedral during those long-ago years, watching the spectacle of men suddenly propelled from the exits of the Galleria to every corner of Milan: it must have been a fascinating sight and was perhaps quite amusing to those — and there were certainly many — who happened to see it by chance.

When the bombs fell on Milan, city life did not come to a halt, despite the many deaths and the great piles of rubble. It did not halt even during the dark months of Fascist and Nazi criminality. La Scala, which had suffered badly, transferred its scenery and costumes, its orchestra and chorus to the Teatro Lirico, the old theater formerly called the Cannobiana. Performances were often interrupted by air raid alarms. Carlo Galeffi, who was thought, mistakenly, to be dead, was taken to the morgue; and the baritone Armando Borgioli was tragically killed by a burst of machine-gun fire. Even if everyone's thoughts

were turned to the end of the war and the collapse of the tyrants, the performances continued with truly Lombard technical competence. Over the years, chiefly during the period of Verdi and after Toscanini, La Scala had greatly improved the concentration and discipline of its audiences. But the unleashed passion for opera continually led to the creation of what may be called "fans", similar to an analogous situation in sports.

Even in recent years some episodes have occurred which hark back to the bad old times of the impresarios and the bad taste of starting brawls when what were really needed were silence and attention so that the audience could listen intelligently. Yet one must realize how difficult a singer's life can be, and how each performance becomes a danger to be confronted and overcome. The slightest break in a breath, a minute clot of phlegm that mists the clarity of a voice — such things were indelibly etched on the memories of La Scala's public. On the other hand, major artists must tread warily when they have reached that delicate region known as "success"; and I can recall quite vividly one of the most famous tenors of some years back, a man loved by the public right down to the last performances of his career, who carried with him wherever he went a fanatical believer in his greatness as a singer. This believer had only one duty — as soon as the applause seemed to die down, he would shout from the upper tier the singer's first name followed by the words "You are an angel"; and the applause would flare up again like the fire in a stove doused by a timely bath of gasoline.

Ah, dear old La Scala — how many times we have hurled words of dissatisfaction and reproach at you because of the obstinacy and inadaptability you showed at certain moments of your life toward the great composers of the past and, even more, toward our contemporaries. For us, who were then very young, you seemed, at the première of Pizzetti's *Fedra* in 1914, the ideal milieu for the renaissance of a whole new musical world. We hoped this would be the prelude to something that would slowly mature over the years. And we have waited for many, many years, often without results, but finally we are witnessing today the arrival on La Scala's boards of the time we had for so long dreamed of. La Scala is no longer the immobile museum which many have wanted it to be, with its head turned only to the past and its eyes blindfolded against the future; it no longer stands at the periphery of life, echoing with regret and nostalgia for its many faded glories.

Today La Scala is as alive and new as on the evening of August 3, 1778, when it revealed itself for the first time to the people of Milan and the world. To have reached this goal is due to Ghiringhelli, its director, and to all those who have collaborated with him in the formulation and realization of its programs. Today Paolo Grassi, a man born in the theater and of the theater, has recently taken Ghiringhelli's place. I have known him

for many years and I am sure that both he and his collaborators will show excellent judgment and taste in their work; he is marvelously fitted to conduct La Scala toward a luminous future, as luminous as the present now being concluded.

The new opera theater has certain difficulties in being born out of the new musical trends, and it is often hard to say what the public of today wants or aspires to. In the past, opera was the most beautiful and imaginative of spectacles; today we are not quite sure what spectacle the public actually prefers. The distractions offered by art are infinite and are welcomed with enthusiasm, especially by the young; for them, music is only jazz and pop, with all the nuances that exist today between these two poles.

Perhaps it will be sufficient to keep faith with the most characteristic aspect of opera, which is its ability to send us on enchanting, untrammeled voyages through the world of the imagination. Such superlatives can only commit La Scala to great goals, otherwise they will become the first step toward the ponderous and the rhetorical. But we are certain that this will not happen.

*To Franca*

*Two hundred years of La Scala's history in a few hundred pages: the author finds himself facing a difficult task. What choices should he make? What aspects should he emphasize? What should his basic theme be?*

*It has seemed to him appropriate to develop his discussion with the reader chiefly around two fundamental themes.*

*The first theme will be a meditation on why La Scala is La Scala. What has it done to make its myth endure for so long, so uninterruptedly and so splendidly? Why, though always argued over, even at times deprecated and yet boundlessly loved, has it carried forward its history and so had its effect on the culture of Milan and Europe at least as deeply as it itself has been affected? What contributions has it made, what composers and interpreters has it welcomed and favored, with whom has it been closely linked and, as it were, identified in so changeable and tumultuous a history and city? This of course is a fascinating problem; and just thinking about it one begins to see a different La Scala from the official one: a theater which aims to reconcile tradition with the new ideas coming into existence, but in the meantime makes precise, clear-cut choices, even at the cost of having troubled relations with the artists and the public.*

*The other fundamental theme is the vision of two centuries of theater and music as seen through the focus of La Scala. For if one wants to imagine accurately and concretely what happened in La Scala, what spectacles, operas and ballets were chosen and how they were staged, what techniques and styles characterized the singers, what interpretations were offered, one must follow the history of the theater as if it were a spectacle that is being sung, played and acted, with its scenery and costumes, and try to grasp the significance which all these elements assume at different times. So the chief concern of this account has not been that of judging and classifying, nor even that of giving the specific interpreters or composers the emphasis and bold relief that they would deserve in a balanced evaluation, but rather of discussing them so as to make clear the part they played in this history and to show through them the part that was played by that other great La Scala protagonist — the public.*

*These observations, reflections and reportings of facts and events run from La Scala's origins down to the present day; and the author, contrary to the well-tested prudence that suggests an ever more hasty and elusive narration of contemporary events, has given a great deal of space to them as compared with the events of the past. Certainly the material becomes more mobile, uncertain and subject to debate the closer one comes to the present; but it has seemed right to me in this book to carry the reader to the point where he can see the problems from the inside, and also the possible choices, the provisory evaluations, rather than let him wait until history hands down its definitive decision, if one grants that history has the desire and capacity to do this. On the other hand, the author's main aim is to make the reader participate, to put him ideally into contact with La Scala in its multiple and complex life, above all to make him feel that it is a place where the life of art — that is, life* tout court — *can continually be born and is being born.*

*This entire discussion has assumed the aspect of a document and a history because of its rich iconography. The photographic material is often rare and precious; above all it coincides with and supports the intentions of the text. Indeed Diego Birelli's design for the book makes an essential contribution; and the attentive reader can feel here an affection for our theater, which grows page by page without ever becoming a mere glorification and without ever being simply beautiful or striking.*

*So as to make one feel not only La Scala of yesterday — which lives so amply in the testimony of a great man of music and a great critic, Mario Labroca, in the notes with which he opens our book — but also La Scala of today, another testimonial has been inserted, this time in pictures, that of the photographer Pepi Mirisio, who has captured in his own manner and with his own peculiar sensitivity two of the most significant spectacles in recent years, the most representative ones available as the book was going to press — an opera and a ballet. Here too, the logic which governs the images and their order is simply an attempt to make the reader participate in and feel La Scala's life from the inside.*

*A book conceived in this fashion also demands something from the reader; mainly, not to expect something different from what the book actually is. For example, some interpreters have been given many pictures, others few or even none; which does not at all mean that the former were or are so greatly superior to the latter; it was simply due to the fact that to document their contribution seemed more enlightening in a historical sense than handing out the illustrations as if they were diplomas or prizes. The captions underline this function and explain the reasons for our choices.*

*So two hundred years of La Scala are presented in this book in their fascinating, vivid, mysterious life; and the ambition of the author and his collaborators is that this life will come to mean something to the reader, that it will awaken something in him as he reads, that, as can only happen in the theater, he will, after finishing this book return to La Scala and discover it all over again, in all its power and familiarity: this theater which one never finishes discovering, knowing and investigating.*

The great fire that raged through the Carnival of 1776 on its last night burned down the Teatro Ducale in a few hours. At that time, Milan was a city of one hundred thousand inhabitants, all subjects of the Empress Maria Theresa of Austria and members of a society which, after the long years of Spanish domination, was just beginning to regain its political, moral and intellectual dignity and was filled with a powerful, typically Lombard desire to make up for lost time after so many adversities. In short, it wanted to enjoy itself. And so the Empress Maria Theresa, her direct representative in Milan, the Archduke Ferdinand, and the Plenipotentiary Minister Firmin, together with the people of Milan themselves — at least all of them who belonged to the wealthy aristocracy — decided then and there to build an even larger, more beautiful opera theater than the one they had so suddenly lost.

In fact they built two theaters, one of which was La Scala; and two centuries later, during a night of tragic warfare, it took the fire ignited by aerial bombs an even shorter time to destroy it. Milan now had more than a million inhabitants, if such a figure has any meaning after so disastrous and tragic a period, and once again the city was searching for its moral, political and intellectual redemption and nursing an angry, determined desire to obtain redress against the recent violences of hardship, sorrow and destruction. But when the war ended, nobody even suggested the idea of building a larger, more beautiful or in any way different theater. With one accord, the city wanted to get its La Scala back — it was just as simple as that. For by now in its building, its history and its very name, Milan could recognize its own face and life. And so La Scala was rebuilt exactly as it had been, and it has lived and still lives as a symbol not only of art but also of the need for communal encounter and exchange. Its long and eventful history, which will be traced here over two centuries of music and drama, represents to some extent the history of all Italians, both in Milan and throughout the nation.

The Teatro Ducale was located inside the Archduke's palace. And some people maintained that it was perfectly in keeping with tradition for the Archduke to play host on occasion to magnificent dazzling beauty and festive pleasure, thus bringing himself into closer contact with the most influential strata of society. Yet there were others who considered it objectionable for him to mingle in this promiscuous way with the rather vast crowd of nobility which could be accommodated by so large a theater, with its orchestra and three tiers of boxes. Indeed, some people advanced the strange, somewhat improbable idea that, though he might not have personally taken care of it, the Archduke, weary of all the bustle and confusion, must have been very happy when he saw the place finally burn down. At any rate, it was a splendid theater, run in truly ducal style, and if today, when

Piermarini inv., et del.

5-6. In 1717 the Teatro Ducale opened its marvelous hall in the palace of the Archduke of Milan, while under Austrian rule, presenting spectacles and celebrating holidays and special occasions (Fig. 5 on pages 22-23). It burnt down on February 26, 1776.

On July 5, 1776, the box-owners of the destroyed Teatro Ducale obtained from the Empress Maria Theresa the land and a decree to build a more splendid theater.

The architect Piermarini designed the project, whose most significant sections are reproduced here on the following pages. La Scala, built in record time, was inaugurated on August 3, 1778.

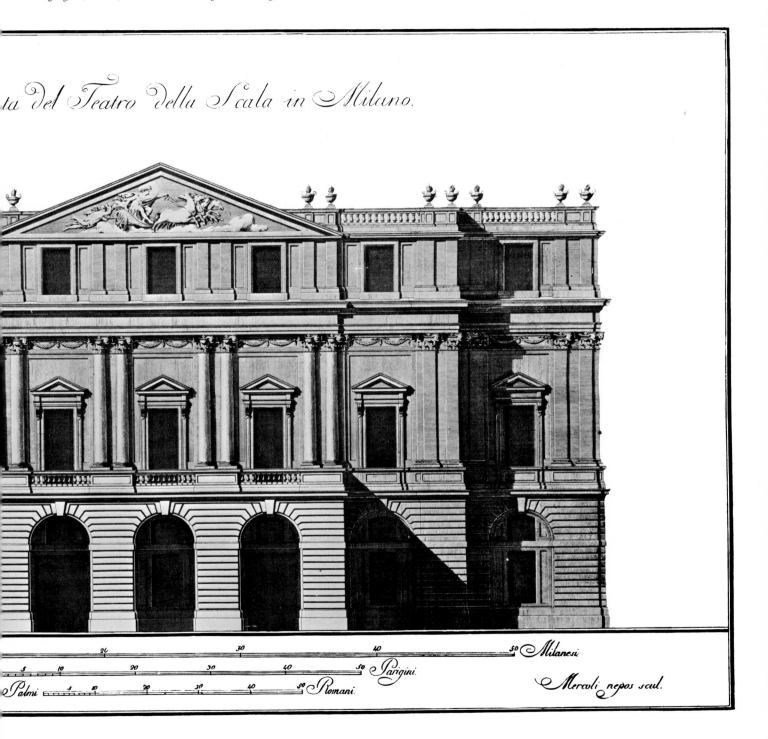

ta del Teatro della Scala in Milano.

Milanesi.

Parigini.

Palmi     Romani.

Mercoli nepos scul.

7-10. La Scala's orchestra was 24.84 meters by 22.01. The height from the floor to the center of the ceiling was 19.88 meters. At the start it offered seats freely arranged in the orchestra and standing room; only in 1891 was the orchestra totally filled by rows of chairs, with 772 seats. At the beginning there were three tiers of boxes, 36 boxes on each tier plus the space for the entrances and for the Royal box; plus two more tiers with 39 boxes each, together with eight boxes on the stage, each with its small wardrobe room. At the very top, the balcony.

The stage measured 39.99 meters in length by 25.33 to 30.75

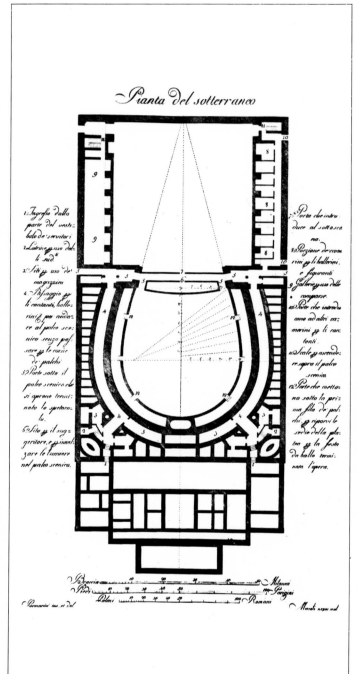

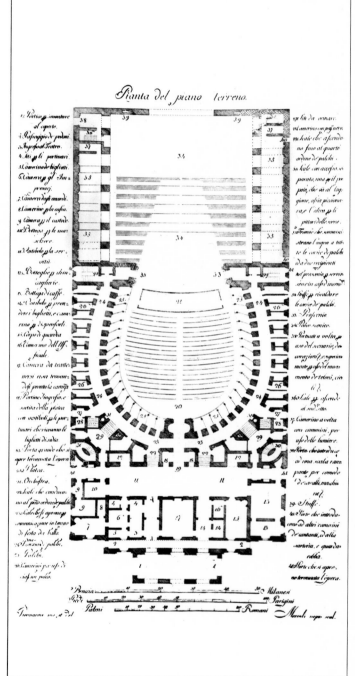

meters in height and 6.99 meters in depth. The front of the stage remained surrounded by proscenium boxes until 1921. The orchestra pit was built as late as 1907. The theater was illuminated by candles. The theater was built on the land once occupied by the church of Santa Maria alla Scala. The construction, which was in the hands of the brothers, Marliani and Nosetti Fé, cost about a million Milanese lire, paid for by the sale of the boxes.

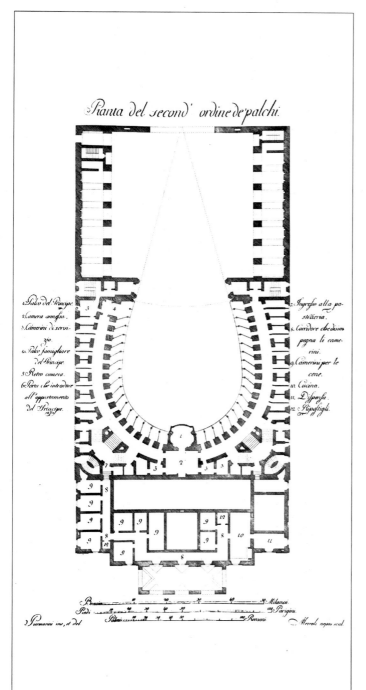

9

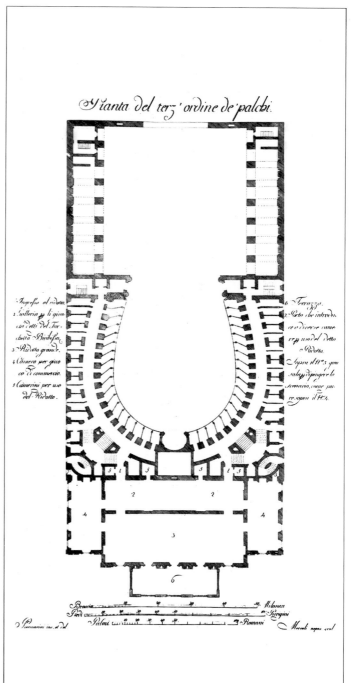

10

11-12. *The theater when completed had an orchestra lobby, to which was later added a lobby for the boxes and, eventually, a lobby for the balconies, and was regarded from the start as important, almost sacred. Destroyed by the war in 1943, it was rebuilt exactly as it had been. The boxes were decorated by each owner in accordance with his tastes; but they gradually assumed a common style; in 1921, bought from their private owners, the boxes' interior walls were covered in red damask. In 1821 a central chandelier was installed. In 1907 the fifth tier of boxes was transformed into a balcony. Thus the theater*

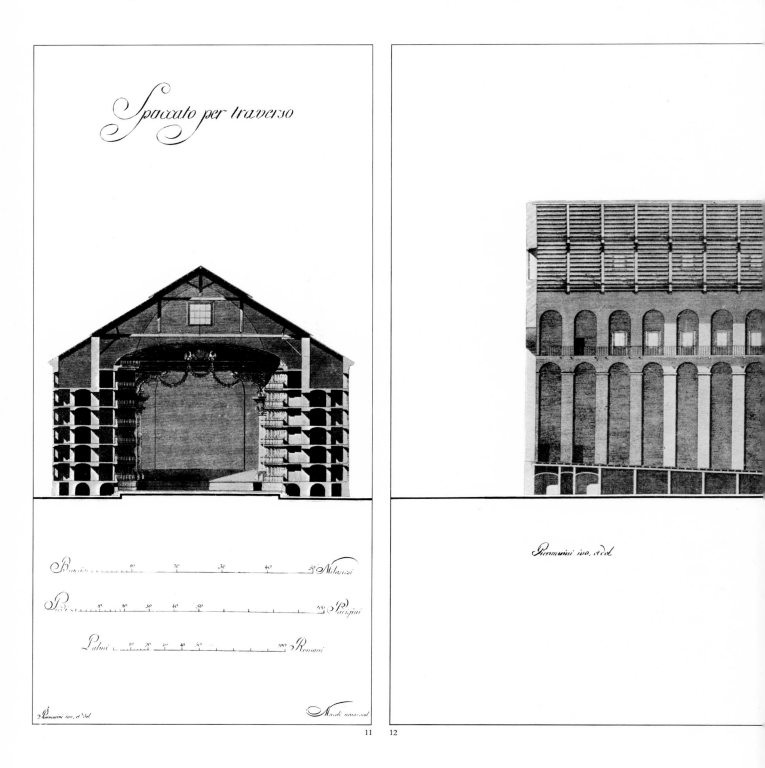

11  12

28

has 155 boxes in four tiers, the central box, 204 numbered seats on the first balcony, 205 numbered seats on the second balcony, together with standing room on the balconies, so that the theater can hold about 3,000 spectators. Besides the building, in which are housed the orchestra, chorus, ballet corps and technicians, La Scala possesses a cluster of warehouses and studios for making sets and costumes in Bovisa, an outlying quarter of Milan.

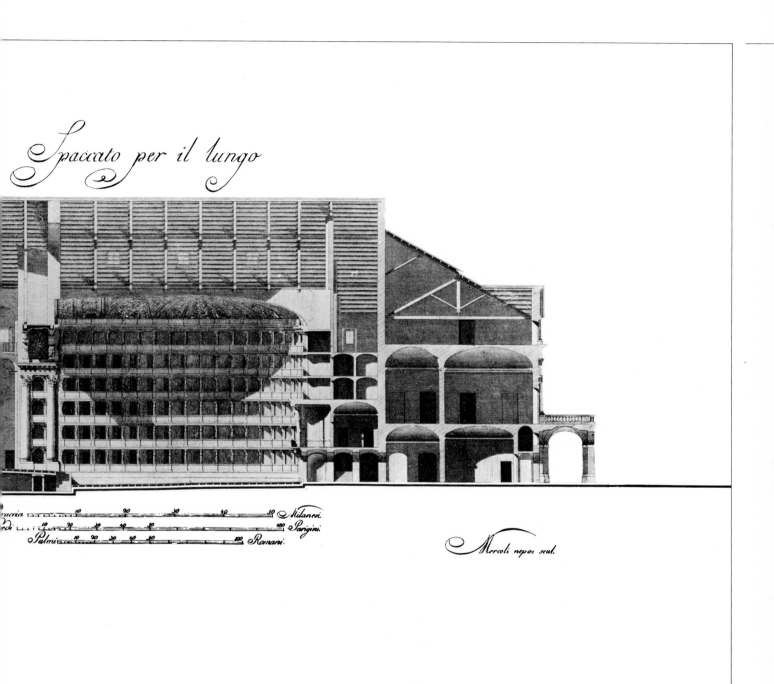

*Spaccato per il lungo*

reviewing its fifty-eight years of existence, one tends to pause admiringly at the names of such librettists as Parini and Metastasio or the glorious name of the young Mozart, who composed three operas which were performed here, in its own time the Teatro Ducale put its main effort into presenting the best performers that could be culled from Europe's stages. Singers such as the male soprano Farinelli or lovely Adriana Gabrielli were engaged so that the audiences could go into ecstasies together with them; dancers and ballerinas were admired with ever-increasing enthusiasm; and galas, costume balls, prose dramas and assorted delights were prepared and presented with that penchant for the aristocratic and majestic which is so exquisitely Viennese and conjures up an atmosphere of elegance and order. All of which was at the same time deeply tinctured with the typically Milanese wish to create and to appropriate the creative feats of others, which is never too far from the mood of a trade fair where the best is sampled and emanates a sense of pride ard supremacy, indeed is liked in advance precisely because it is being offered as the best.

The choice of composers was unquestionably farsighted. Besides Mozart, Gluck was also here at the very start of his career, as were the already famous Hasse, Galuppi, Johann Christian Bach, Piccini and Sammartini. Also, in the repertory of plays in prose, which was much smaller than that of opera, one encounters the first productions of Goldoni's comedies. But the performances in general and those of opera in particular had somewhat the character of a festive anthology immersed in a lively, almost unruly gaiety, with the audiences largely inattentive to what was happening on the stage or, rather, sporadically attentive, depending on the popularity of the numbers being played and the appeal of the famous singers and actors in the prcduction. It was a pageant of torches, flowers and resplendent costumes, with its own peculiar ritual and emotion — brief, melting silences, delirious or even pensive, happy, boisterous acclamations and long stretches of utter indifference. To see the scene, as it were, one must remember the gambling which thrived behind the boxes, the undemanding pleasure of being able, when one wished, to listen to the most ravishing arias or to watch a dancer's most graceful steps; or, finally, the exchange of invitations and late suppers from one box to another, while the orchestra below was packed with chairs and mobs of people milling about freely. Or it may have been something deeper — a love of the theater, a trusting belief in oneself, the sense of a destiny that must be fulfilled. Whatever it was that produced this particular charming and disorderly world, the nobility soon organized itself into a committee of "palchettisti" or box owners for the theater that was to be reborn, pledging to foot the bill for its construction. And for one year they had a temporary theater made of wood, canvas and plaster, risen as if by magic during the three summer months; later they had the theater on

Via della Cannobiana, which was completed and inaugurated in 1779 and would have an interesting history of its own. But most important of all, as early as 1778, long before the scheduled time, they had the privilege of entering the large and far from temporary theater which Maria Theresa, under the auspices of Archduke Ferdinand and the stewardship of Minister Firmin, had graciously allowed to rise on the site of the ancient church of Santa Maria alla Scala.

The author of these marvels, that is, the architect of the three theaters, was Giuseppe Piermarini (1734-1808), the man who was giving a new appearance to the city and who soon after building La Scala and the Cannobiana would be appointed official architect to the Royal and Imperial Crown. Piermarini had come to Milan in the footsteps of his teacher Vanvitelli; in fact it was while working with this great artist on the construction of the Royal Palace at Caserta near Naples that Piermarini had discovered that the Baroque, the imaginative movement of shapes under the light, could preserve not only the lucid rationality of Renaissance architecture but also its special feeling for spaces and proportions. But he realized above all that beyond the Rococo elegance of the whimsical style with which Italians then loved to surround themselves, overly precious and rather deficient in imagination, there existed a further reality which his epoch was inventing. This was the reality of great scenic design expressed by such creators as the Bibbiena and the Galliari — the joy of nimble perspectives, of illusory spaces magnified by a pictorial rediscovery of classicism yet wedded to a concept of space that endowed the protagonists and characters in any and all events with imagination and grandeur. In other words, from 1770 on, when he undertook the task of rebuilding the Ducal Palace in Milan, reconstructed whole sections of the city with the dedication of an enlightened city planner, and designed the public parks, Piermarini knew that his task was to create backgrounds that helped to exalt the life Milan's citizens were intent on living with a new sense of freedom and uncramped space. It was a conception of urban design which long antedated Romanticism and is surprisingly close to the dreams of today's most advanced city planners. But even more profoundly his own, perhaps because of native feeling, since he was born at Foligno in chaste and somber Umbria, was a certain composed severity which appreciates simple ornamentation for its own sake and employs shapes and colors to put harmony within the reach of whoever wants to live in it and respond to it. Nothing could be more neoclassical than Piermarini's well-ordered sobriety, clearcut and severe but never oppressive. And so here again we have the proof that, through the theater, Milan and Italy were trying to find in classicism a foundation for their taste and civilization long before Napoleon, who, believing that this style suited the greatness of his Empire, tried to promote the vogue of imitating antiquity conceived entirely in the key of patrician sumptuousness, but did it in a helter-skelter manner. The Milan which by now had become tired of the austere yet opulent pomposity of Spanish Baroque and which could not find much in common with the prettified but ponderous petit-Baroque dictated by Austrian fashion, immediately recognized itself in the ample spaces and serene stateliness of Piermarini's palaces and milieu. But when 1796 rolled around and, with it, the Cisalpine Republic, Piermarini was dismissed. He was now seen as the man who embodied a period in the city's life which the new ideas of revolutionary intent wished to repudiate, just as later they repudiated the fanciful pretentions of French imperialism. And Piermarini returned to Foligno, but the mark he left on the city still remains as a distinct stratum, a moment, a reality that characterizes it and expresses some of its most attractive qualities.

So, after a very short wait, the theater unveiled its beauties in the summer of 1778. Externally, it was then almost identical to what we now know, save for the addition of two small frontal projections surmounted by balconies which were set at each side of the façade in 1830, several emergency doors opened in the side wall in 1884, and a number of windows that pierced the building's right flank. And the theater was immediately liked — all of it. The sober, elegant exterior with its three-tiered façade and pediment, the central projecting body with three arches supporting a loggia accessible to traffic; and the interior with its five rows of boxes plus an upper, horseshoe-shaped balcony that had a curve permitting good visibility and acoustics, the orchestra with enough room to seat six hundred spectators, a great profusion of equipment, the charm of the foyers, the ceiling vault of plaster over wooden grids (which promised even better acoustics), covered by colorful frescoes by the painters Levati and Reinnini, who also decorated the entire auditorium, and the window roses executed by Giocondo Albertolli; and, finally, the multicolored embellishments of the boxes, which each owner was free to decorate as he wished.

The only part of the theater that came under critical fire was the large portico that welcomed in and sheltered the carriages. Milan's historian of that period, Petro Verri, the famous Enlightenment figure, knowledgeable chiefly in politics and economics, correctly expresses the perplexity of his contemporaries when he finds the portico a trifle cumbersome, since "it covers and obscures part of the edifice". And yet, aside from its functional justification, the large portico carries out a coherent logic, that is, the image of a theater evocatively inserted into the city's life, and thus bears witness to the theater's most intimate *raison d'être*. It does not draw the eye to the façade or to the building in general; it is not an invitation to contemplate the beauty of its architecture; instead it reaches out to gather in the public, inviting it to enter so that the magnificence of the hall and, once inside it, the magnificence of the spectacle may be revealed.

The first production opened on August 3rd, 1778. The program included one opera, *Europa riconosciuta*, and two ballets, *Pofio e Mirra ossia I Prigionieri di Cipro* and *Apollo placato ossia La riapparizione del sole dopo la caduta di Fetonte*. All of the music was composed by Salieri, except for that of the last ballet, a large part of which was the work of a certain Maestro De Baillou; and the librettos were written by Matteo Verazi, assisted in the first by Claudio Legrand, who also danced the part of Pofio, and in the second ballet by Giuseppe Canziani. Matteo Verazi was a man of the theater who could boast of a vast experience acquired abroad; he also had an exceedingly cavalier attitude to literature, even an impudent one. There is no doubt that he thought of the theater more as a parade,

**EUROPA RICONOSCIUTA**

DRAMMA PER MUSICA

DA RAPPRESENTARSI

NEL NUOVO REGIO DUCAL TEATRO
DI MILANO

Nella folenne occafione del fuo primo aprimento
nel mefe d' Agofto dell' anno 1778.

DEDICATO

Alle LL. AA. RR.

IL SERENISSIMO ARCIDUCA

**FERDINANDO**

Principe Reale d'Ungheria, e Boemia, Arciduca d' Auftria,
Duca di Borgogna, e di Lorena ec., Cefareo Reale
Luogo Tenente, Governatore, e Capitano
Generale nella Lombardia Auftriaca,

E LA

SERENISSIMA ARCIDUCHESSA

**MARIA RICCIARDA
BEATRICE D'ESTE**

PRINCIPESSA DI MODENA.

IN MILANO,

Appreffo Gio. Batifta Bianchi Regio Stampatore
Colla Permiffione .

14

15

a gorgeous display, an assemblage of all the things demanded by fashion on great occasions, than as a creative synthesis. As for synthesis, or even a reasonably good feeling for form, Antonio Salieri (1750-1825), the still young but famous composer, was also far from being an inspired contributor to the art of musical dramaturgy, despite the fact that he had made a name for himself in Vienna and Paris and had had the good fortune to be a student of Gluck's as well as a teacher of Beethoven and Schubert. Thus, on that summer evening, while the active, prodigal Milanese aristocracy admired its new and splendid theater and of course itself, there unfolded before its eyes an improbable parade of mythological delights and a multitude of things to listen to and watch. The audience's response was ecstatic. Applause and praise for Maria Balducci, who sang the part of Europa, for Francesca Lebrun Danzi, for Giovanni Rubinelli, for the *castrato* Gaspare Pacchiarotti, and for Lucca Roscio, who "kept time in the pit", as they put it in those days when speaking of the conductor, and for his colleague Giuseppe Perruccone, who eventually became a *personaggio tipico* or "stock character" at La Scala and was given the nickname "Pasqualino". And, finally, wonder-struck admiration for the sets by the Bernadino brothers and Fabrizio Galliari. As is only right for an official newspaper, *La Gazzetta di Milano* expressed enormous enthusiasm, extolled the insuperable "pomp and public gaiety" and described the theater in exquisite detail — "all of it grandiose, with everything that is best suited to its excellent functioning — façade, solidity, forms, organization, vast scope, comforts, ornamentation, proportion, resonance, visibility...".

Thus began the actual chronicle of events at the Teatro alla Scala. Yet even earlier there had been a buzz of gossip, of hopes, intentions and predictions, all magnified by tests of the theater's acoustics and buoyed up by declarations made by Maria Theresa, by the most illustrious groups of the local aristocracy, and by all sorts of people who passed the word around, which was the custom in cities so small in comparison to ours and which, as a matter of fact, is still the custom today. But among all of the omens, one particular omen was greeted with especial emotion. During the wrecking operations on the church of Santa Maria alla Scala, the crews uncovered, unexpectedly and precisely on the spot where the theater would rise, a marble portrait stone bearing the image of the actor Pilades, the great Roman mime. When reporting this discovery, the journalists trotted out the richest rhetorical prose in celebration of so strange an event — and then, without too much conviction, they predicted for the Teatro alla Scala all the things that it eventually actually became.

*16-18. Yet the composers of the music, if they counted for less
in the immediate success than the singers and even the dancers,
were honored by a kind of idealization that consigned their
images to Fame and History.*

So amid happy omens and an even happier reception,
La Scala launched a series of events under the direction
of the so-called "*Cavalieri Associati*" or "Associated
Knights" — Count Castelbarco, Marquis Fagnani, Marquis
Calderara and Prince Menafoglio di Rocca Sinibalda —
who had taken over the concession to run the theater;
and who were being "wisely and tactfully" — to quote
the then current phrase — watched by the Imperial and
Royal government, which regarded a passion for opera
as an excellent antidote to the possible emergence of
dangerous political passions. The irony is, however, that
over the years the exact contrary proved to be the case,
since opera became the perfect focus for intense political
emotions.

The program started out a trifle haphazardly, combining
a little of everything — operas, ballets, dramas, costume
balls, jugglers, entertainments of all kinds. The tables in
the foyer offered the chance to gamble, an activity which
a later edict in 1788 would prohibit everywhere except
in the city's theaters during performances, and the sole
rule enforced there to prevent cheating concerned the
method of shuffling the cards. Yet in this incredible
bedlam we can encounter the names of illustrious composers: Domenico Cimarosa (1749-1801; at La Scala from
1780), who had come to Milan to win acclaim and in
1784 wrote, expressly for La Scala, *I due supposti conti
ossia Lo sposo senza moglie*. Another composer beloved by
the public was Giovanni Paisiello (1740-1816; at La Scala
from 1780), another great contemporary, who was composing comico-pathetic operas in the Neapolitan style.
And besides these rather well-known names, there were
the Bohemian composer Mysliveczek (1737-1781; at La
Scala from 1780) and Giuseppe Sarti (1729-1802; at La
Scala from 1785), while Nicola Zingarelli (1752-1837; at
La Scala from 1785), another Neapolitan of a certain
importance and prestige, became a habitual presence.
The opera seasons soon settled down to a rhythm of
three a year: that is, from Saint Stephen's Day on the
26th of December to February; from April to May; and
from August to September. In 1788 La Scala began to
commit itself publicly by posting announcements of the
works which would be performed. And so it was in
1788, thanks to this prearranged and officially announced
program of operas and performers, that "La Scala actually
begins to be La Scala," as is stated by Franco Armani
and Giacomo Bascapé in their succinct and perceptive
history of La Scala, which they have fondly called a
"biography".[1] Indeed, this was a decisive moment. After
a short period under Marquis Calderara's management,
the theater was entrusted to the impresarios Gaetano
Maldonati, Francesco Benedetti Ricci and Count Angelo
della Somaglia. And from this point on the list of composers showed a marked shift toward the north of Italy.
To be sure, one still heard Paisiello, whose operas *Nina
pazza per amore* and *La Molinara* were often repeated;
and Zingarelli still presented his very popular *Giulietta*

16

JEAN PAISIELLO

*Maître de Chapelle de la Chambre, et Compositeur de LL. MM. Siciliennes, Agregé au Collège des
Professeurs de Musique de Venise, et pensionné de S. A. J. la Grande Duchesse de toutes les Russies*
*Gravé d'après le Tableau original de Madame le Brun de l'Académie Royale de Peinte de P.*

17

AL NOBIL UOMO IL SIG. CONTE CAV. PIETRO GHERARDI

Capitano nel R. Corpo dei Cacciatori Volontarj di Firenze, e Gentiluomo di camera di S.M.Il Re d'Etruria.

e *Romeo* — in short, the masters of the Neapolitan style were still among the theater's favorites. But other important names began to affirm themselves, composers who had not come here to exploit a reputation and language created elsewhere, but whose art was aimed at meeting the changing taste, the new attention to dramatic form in opera and to a certain dramatic logic, and also the first intimations of those Romantic stirrings which were just beginning to run like a thrilling shiver through all of Europe. Thus, Ferdinando Paër (1771-1839; at La Scala from 1793), who was born in Parma but had lived and worked in Vienna, embarked here on that course of experience which, after his return from Vienna, would lead him in 1804 to confront in his opera *Leonora ossia l'Amore coniugale* the great theme which would later become Beethoven's in *Fidelio*. In the same way, Johann Simone Mayr (1763-1845; at La Scala from 1789), a native of Bavaria who had taught in Venice and Bergamo, contributed not only an orchestration in the Austrian manner, a tradition in which the music organizes the performance and dramatic action and provides a coherent continuity to the most involved, farfetched subjects, but also the first works which conveyed the perturbations and excitements of a changing world, such as the resonant, plangent *Ginevra di Scozia* (1803), or, composed specifically for La Scala, the suggestive pronouncement contained in *Amor non ha ritegno* (1804).

Yet during these years of adjustment and experimentation, La Scala itself was probably the main attraction. Diaries, statements, newspaper accounts and memoirs all testify to the vivid impression made by the dazzling array of boxes, their parapets adorned with bizarre and colorful decorations set against the silvery background, their interiors covered along the walls with damask or other precious fabrics and fitted out with looking-glasses and chandeliers which could be glimpsed through the half-gathered silk curtains; and on each box the ever-present coats-of-arms, which were both a decoration and a reminder of the prestige of the box owners' families. The curtains could be drawn to obtain privacy for conversations, suppers or whatever the occupants wished to do, which of course gave rise to all sorts of erotic and spicy legends. And then, the display of handsome faces and elegant attire, the alluring nudity of female arms and shoulders which suddenly appeared at the boxes' edge during the most beguiling moments of the spectacle, to listen to a famous aria or applaud an enchanting ballet... Of course there were still many defects. The lighting was poor, at least until 1788, when the stage was equipped with eighty-four oil lamps and the theater with nine hundred and ninety lamps of different types, which were hung from the ceiling, causing some discomfort due to the smoke and the danger of starting a fire (but it was possible to open sections of the ceiling, and pails and receptacles full of water were placed everywhere, in the corridors to the boxes and on the roof). And it was also rather cold in the theater during the winter season. But all the same, it was the great showcase for the highest society and its beauty and magnificence, not to speak of noble, caressing music, of colors and the changing shadows created by the lights flickering on and off, and of space, the great space which embraced everyone in a spellbinding experience.

Outside the boxes were the people who crowded the

orchestra and the top balcony. Here there were no invitations to dine, no enraptured silences or amorous play behind drawn curtains. In fact it is hard to imagine anything further removed from what we today regard as the behavior of a normal audience. Charles de Brosses, as could be expected from so erudite a gentleman and scholar of philosophy and archaeology, in his *Lettres familières écrites d'Italie en 1739 et 1740,*[2] had already expressed his annoyance with the Milanese audience some forty years earlier:

"The people in the orchestra are either insane or drunk, or both; not even in the marketplace does one hear such noise; everyone carries on a conversation, shouting at the top of his lungs. When the singers come on the stage he greets them with deafening screams and then goes right on talking while they sing, not even bothering to listen to them. But that is not all: the gentlemen in the orchestra express their admiration by rapping on the benches with their long canes; at which signal the audience in the top balcony flings down millions (*sic*) of printed leaflets containing sonnets that praise the leading male or female virtuoso."

The young Scala, too, for several years resembled the Teatro Ducale when it came to disorder and noise. As the seats filled up, the theater gradually began to stir and hum, waiting for the beautiful ladies to arrive, carrying on conversations as they sipped a cup of coffee or munched a sherbet. It is of course quite possible to listen to an opera in this way — one has only to think of the atmosphere in a cabaret. But, inevitably, certain hierarchies will become established with regard to roles and singers, in fact to such a point that from those days on and for a good part of the century, the less important arias were called the "sherbet arias". Singers were obviously offended at being confined to the "sherbet" section of a work. Today, as we read the scores we can find in such secondary parts qualities even superior to those of other, more important passages, but on the stage at La Scala, in the year of the Cisalpine Republic, rather than sing a sherbet aria, Genoveffa Canevassi Garnier preferred to be put in jail for twenty-four hours. The performances therefore became a struggle on the part of the singers to capture attention as often as possible. Opening nights have characteristics that became quite typical of La Scala, not only the atmosphere of wonder and prestige but the fact that the works are presented with skillful and imaginative means, as Pietro Verri wrote to his brother: "The pomp of the costumes is unequalled, the extras fill the stage with a crowd of more than a hundred figures, the singers in the choruses change their costumes several times. The cost is enormous.... The singers in the choruses are actors rather than statues, the extras do their job properly, the scenes are set without stage hands in full view toting columns and light boxes, everything is arranged beforehand. The actors do not mangle the recitatives, the libretto has neither

Roberto Focosi dis.

Luigi Rados inc.

# DOMENICO CIMAROSA

Nato in Napoli nel 1754. Dopo avute in giovanile età le prime nozioni di musica, entrò nel conservatorio di Loreto ove attinse alle lezioni di Durante. Dedicato con istraordinaria cura allo studio musicale, in breve tempo si fe chiaro con opere nelle quali splendono i lampi del suo fertile ingegno. La di lui fama sempre più progredendo per l'incontro felice delle sue produzioni, fu chiamato a Pietroborgo da Catterina 2.ᵈᵃ Imperatrice per comporvi opere serie e buffe, delle quali l'estro, la fecondità d'immaginazione e l'originalità le distinsero sempre da' suoi coetanei, risuonando delle sue opere i più accreditati teatri d'Europa: Fra le tante sue composizioni si hanno maggiormente a pregio: L'Italiana in Londra, Le Trame deluse, Il Matrimonio segreto, Gli Orazj e Curiazj, Il Convitato di pietra, Le Astuzie femminili ecc. Egli fu onorato da primarj personaggi d'Europa e da Sovrani stessi che si compiacquero distinguerlo. Spirò in Venezia il giorno 11 Gennajo del 1801.

Dedicato all'Illustrissimo Signor Marchese

## FEBO D'ADDA

Vice Presidente di Governo, Cavaliere dell' I. R. Ordine di Leopoldo

head nor tail, but the show is successful because it is always varied, the arias are short and frequent: duets, trios, full ensembles, blending with or interrupted by the protagonist. One's eyes are always busy and one's ears are not bored by monotony.

"Do you want to know how the opera begins? As you are waiting for it to start you hear a clap of thunder, a burst of lightning, and that is the signal for the orchestra to begin playing the overture. At the same moment, the curtain rises and before you stretches a stormy sea, lightning, trees along the shore buffeted by the wind, sinking ships, and the symphony imitates the rain, wind, the roar of the waves, the screams of the shipwrecked. Then, very slowly, the music quiets down, the sky clears, the actors step off the ship, while the chorus and several solo voices take up the action. Later on there are triumphs, deployed armies, thirty-six horses in a line, battles, fires, hand-to-hand combats, amphitheaters with savage beasts, and Phaeton struck down by a thunderbolt. It is like a magic lantern show of ill-assorted objects, which nevertheless forces you to pay attention."[3]

So it was this idea of what an opera should be, which was formed by the audience, that determined the staging, contents and mood of the score; a balance sought not in dramatic structure and musical unity but in the ability to arouse attention and to grant calculated respites — all in accordance with the Baroque conception which aims at astounding as much and as continuously as possible, and also the Baroque manner of shaping a discourse that proceeds by accretions, by the restless shifting of things, by a kind of perpetual flight from things, if only to attain a higher pitch of enchantment and beauty. However, operas that were alive throughout and had a well-wrought unity were also appreciated, though most of them were composed in a different environment, as, for example, Cimarosa's *Il Matrimonio segreto*, which was created in Vienna, or minor operas by Pavesi or Federici that exhibit a neat professional skill and a certain breadth of style. As a rule, the most autonomous and concentrated work came from the Neapolitan experience of comic opera, the only truly fertile source, together with that of Mayr's work. In short, from Naples and Vienna a lesson of authentic life and living doctrine brought ferments of renewal to La Scala. No precise and authentic operatic truth was born from the alternately boisterous and spellbound approach to listening to opera that turned La Scala, and earlier the Teatro Ducale, into a vast, unrestrained world of fantasy on whose threshold one might innocently linger. Today when one reads the letters in which the very young Mozart speaks about Italian opera and his consuming desire to compose works of this kind himself, we can understand what fascinated him. We can see how this world of heroes and swooning tenderness, of shallow but colorful, larger than life characters who could for an instant become real in the refulgence of melody, the opulence of voices filled with iridescent and hidden hues, combined with the presence of singers who challenged the indifference of the audience or trusted to its readiness to accept them, could have produced the sort of opera that is unknown today. But, after having written three magnificent, youthful scores for the Teatro Ducale, Mozart soon left. In fact, when he was first staged at La Scala in 1807, he had already been dead for sixteen years. The greatness of his

20. *Nicola Zingarelli, another composer typical of the Neapolitan school.*

21-23. *The spectacle took on life because of the sets designed by the Galliari brothers: stupendous classical scenes in which, more than a relationship with the individual operas, there was emphasized the exultant glorification of architectonic values and natural beauty.*

20

21

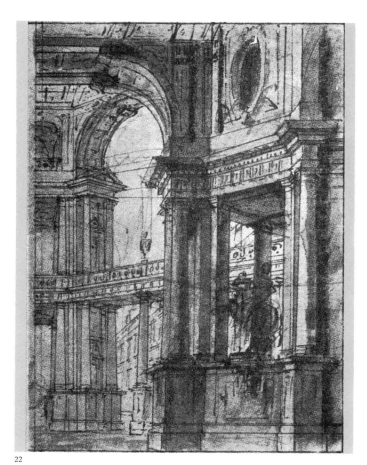

22

23

24-25. *Simone Mayr, portrayed here with his school, including Donizetti, represented the other tendency of the Austrian school, in which singing was more composed and sober and the symphonic role of the orchestra took on more importance.*

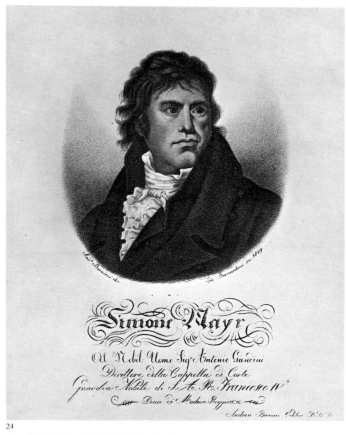

24

25

genius, which was immersed at one and the same time in divine and everyday concerns, had led him to an entirely different structure and form, to the unification of experiences, of entire worlds miraculously and logically contained in a few brilliant strokes of expression. And, as a consequence, although his work was well received, it did not become habitual fare. In 1807 *Così fan tutte* was given thirty-eight performances, and yet seven years went by before *Don Giovanni* and *Le Nozze di Figaro* were presented. Nobody else who had not merely equal genius but also the ability to derive from the musical theater an autonomous statement that contained its own esthetic measure would appear in 18th century Milan. But perhaps we should try to find Milanese 18th century opera not so much in the scores as outside of them — in that alternation of bewilderment and self-reliance, enthusiasm and disappointment, inattention and sudden response to the imperious summons of a moment's beauty; a somewhat haphazard and elusive experience which, nevertheless, had great suggestive power and in its own way began to create the myth of La Scala.

Of course, to varying degrees, all those who participated in the spectacle were part of the myth. For instance, the composer was certainly not among the most important and best known; his name appeared on the libretto (until the middle of the 19th century) buried among those of all of his collaborators, and since in those days the libretto was printed to serve as a program, this unconsciously revealed the official estimate. Indeed the librettist counted for much more; he was listed as the principal author and had the title of "poet". At times the text he had written for one composer would be presented again with music by another; at other times he would write a libretto expressly for a particular occasion. And among the interpreters there did not in fact exist the person we call the orchestra conductor; the orchestra followed the tempo taken or indicated by the first violin. During the rehearsals, above all those of the singers, the composer was deeply involved, helped and sometimes replaced by the "*maestro al cembalo*", that is, the harpsichordist. Among all these collaborators a certain degree of importance could be won by the skill of special conductors, such as Vincenzo Lavigna (1776-1836; at La Scala from 1802), a lively, systematic mind and good musician who later had Giuseppe Verdi for a pupil and who, having come to La Scala with the support of Angelo della Somaglia, worked there successfully until 1831, when he relinquished his post.

Onstage, of course, the best dancers were greatly admired; especially Giustina Campioni and Caterina Curtz, both of whom had danced at the inaugural performance, according to some because of their beauty and according to others because of the wild somersaults and leaps that seemed to characterize Giuseppe Canziani's (at La Scala from 1778 to 1779) concept of ballet.[4] As for many other dancers, the accounts vary considerably, perhaps also because of the controversy, accompanied by a storm of open letters and newspaper articles (the *gazettes* in those days were extremely sensitive to theatrical events), which was generated by the competition between choreographers: the great Jean-Georges Noverre (1727-1820) and the equally famous Gasparo Angiolini (1731-1803; at La Scala from 1780). Actually, since the dispute concerned which of the two could be regarded as the fa-

ther of the *ballet d'action,* it did not involve anything of basic interest, and really was testimony in favor of a ballet in which academic dance, conceived of as a sequence of movements, was being replaced by danced theatrical action. In short, the ballet waters were in agitation and opinions could not avoid being influenced by friendships and antagonisms. At any rate, what remain evident in this period are not so much the names of particular great male and female dancers as a feeling that as time went on success and recognition were distributed in accordance with a variety of preferences. However, Angiolini worked on both the choreography and music of his ballets in a fervor of dedication and elegance destined to last and to produce much more significant results in the future.

But true stardom was reserved for the singers. Still idolized were the "angelic" castrati who, with their agile, flexible, brilliant voices, their appearance equally suited to male and female roles and, above all, their extraordinary technique with its extremely long-held notes, tremendous range and the fantasy of its elegant, expressive coloratura, aroused both ambiguously erotic and purely musical and theatrical passions. This was true of such remarkable performers as Luigi Marchesi, called the "Marchesini" (at La Scala from 1790 to 1805) and Gerolamo Crescentini (at La Scala from 1786 to 1804), who was one of Bellini's teachers. The worship of female singers was even greater: from the beautiful Angelica Catalani (1801) with her somewhat cold yet stupendous voice, to the fascinating comic opera prima donna Elisabetta Gafforini (at La Scala from 1802 to 1811) — the former endowed with a violent, despotic temperament, the latter forever on the watch for excesses in the acting of certain licentious roles. But here, too, the accounts are confused by the usual scrimmage of debates and controversies, though a determining influence was probably exerted by the various political positions taken by the singers during the vicissitudes accompanying the French and Austrian occupations of Italy and Milan. La Catalani was a hot Francophile and La Gafforini just as adamant a Francophobe. As for Marchesini, he was even mentioned by the poet Alfieri in his poem "*Misogallo*" as the only Italian to oppose Napoleon, since the "*Gallo Corso*" — that is, roughly translated, "the Gallic rooster from Corsica" — was in fact unable to expel Marchesini from Lombardy even though he had declined to sing in his presence.[5]

Singers with strong, masculine voices were equally appreciated, but only in later years did they reach the height of their fame and, on the basis of what we have been able to reconstruct from remote clues and picturesque memoirs, the peak of their art.

And all around the characters created by the lyrics and music rose the astounding world created by the stage scenery. The sets of the Galliari brothers (at La Scala from 1788 to 1802) expressed the classical ideal and so were based on ample spaces and sublime vistas, yet one could already sense in them a concern for nature that drew the Arcadian dreamer closer to Romanticism's immersion in it, while the predominance of architectural forms gave a vivid feeling of a revived and viable classicism; or the Venetian luminosity of Pietro Gonzaga's (at La Scala from 1779 to 1791) landscapes, interiors and vast, monumental exteriors, with their intimate emotional resonance; or the wise and solid skills of Paolo Landriani (at La Scala from 1792 to 1817), who gradually laid the foundations for a new kind of scenic design that would respect both physical proportions and a sense of history and would eventually achieve complete maturity in the work of Alessandro Sanquirico. The singers and actors wandered about through these imaginary rooms and landscapes conjured up by painted flats and backdrops without the slightest prearranged acting plan, except for the habit of acting completely according to their own ideas and impulses, or, for some others, of acting together with the others, and somewhat helped by the familiarity that came from rehearsals and repeat performances.

Certainly one has only to think of the type of opera in which the action is continually suspended in the arias to realize that the singers had more ability to entertain the audience by their sheer presence than to perform in a manner that was attentive to psychological verisimilitude. Moreover, if we think of the nature of stage lighting at that period, which made the front of the stage a privileged area, together with the need to sing in time with the orchestra, which brought the singers as close as possible to the orchestra pit, and all this in the agitated conditions we know, it is easy to see that a naturalistic performance, or even a performance that was both natural and convincing, was out of the question. It is indeed almost impossible for us to form an accurate idea of that unique moment when interpreters and audience met, precisely because it was not fixed in a coherent or necessary manner by the dramaturgical event. Nor do the contemporary prints tell us much about the criteria that governed the making of the costumes, dubbed "garments" by the theatrical dressmakers, who were often different persons for the men and women. And so, in the end, we find that this initial period of La Scala's existence is surrounded by the disquieting and fascinating aura of much that is irretrievable.

In all honesty, it would be difficult to maintain that the general atmosphere in the theater was always enthusiastic. In fact it never was at La Scala, partly because of the conservative nature of an audience that grew fond of a certain tradition and wanted it to be observed, or even fonder of a certain level of excellence which it wanted to see preserved, and partly because of conflicting ideas, preferences and exigencies. But this atmosphere was especially a subject of controversy at the beginning, when even the performers themselves made it a point to answer provocations, or yielded to the enticements for greater success or greater gain, thus producing some rather lively and colorful incidents. For instance, in 1791 the two star dancers, Andrea and Antonio Vulcani, gave a wretched performance that set off a tremendous uproar in the theater. When they were hissed and derided, they responded by making indecent gestures and were subsequently forced to post written apologies on the theater's door. When they appeared again on the stage, Count Kevenhüller, who was responsible for keeping order in the audience, issued a proclamation that any booing, hissing and whistling would be punished by fines; so the audience greeted the two dancers by laughing and jeering uproariously. In the end, the two Vulcanis were dragged on stage by the police and forced to apologize in person to the audience. This custom of apologies was rather widespread, at least for dancers, and survived for a long time. As late as 1816, Celestina Viganò and Giovanni Franco-

lini were compelled to present apologies in writing and stuffed their ears with cotton so as not to react to the storm of insults and provocations. In any case, the entire atmosphere that surrounded the relations between performers and audience was as disorderly as can possibly be imagined. A certain Vittorio Ferrari who in 1921 published an elegantly printed but rather vague fifty-page history of La Scala,[6] characterizes the onstage behavior with the following description, which, if not wholly accurate or true of every performance, is nevertheless evocative and significant: "Despite Rules and Regulations, Ordinances and Proclamations, discipline on the stage was nonexistent. Singers and actresses laughed and made merry with their admirers in the boxes, took snuff, insulted the prompter, and if summoned back on stage by applause, showed up half naked with the excuse that they were already undressing; and the singers in the choruses and the ballerinas followed their example by accepting the compliments of their admirers in dark corners of the stage."

This world of La Scala at the end of the century which so naturally joined the pleasures of music and theater with those of the "little suppers" served to the nobility in the back of their boxes by their butlers, or prepared in the "sala dei fornelli" or "charcoal-stove room" chiefly for the audience in the orchestra, and which took advantage of the irregular light of the not too numerous torches to go onstage in search of ballerinas or singers in the chorus and a dark corner in which to make love to them, was no doubt a distracted world, perhaps dissolute, but above all naive. It was the same world that, outside La Scala, could not count on much in the way of public entertainment: a few minor theaters (among which the theater of Via della Canobbiana would soon become pre-eminent), the drawing room, a successful buffet dinner and Luna Park, together with a few ingenious marvels such as shadow plays and magic lantern shows. But ideas and conviviality, ferments, new trends and contradictions all lived side by side at the end of the 18th century, as Leonardo Valente has described in an acute article:

"Europe seemed to be collapsing under the generous weight of new ideas. The old Austrian throne, with its administrative intelligence, its rigid etiquette, its great qualities and grave errors, seemed to totter under the impact of the wind blowing from France. Milan lived in a contradictory world, so that Parini and the dandies, Beccaria and international swindlers and adventurers filled the same drawing rooms and were equally sought after. At La Scala there was talk of new ideas, people ran ahead of the times, and yet in the foyer the gambling continued and quite a few members of the nobility lost entire fortunes in a single night. Somehow, our theater was the symbol of this world."[7]

This disorderly, fervent city, as we know, contained the ideas and the men that would transform order into exploration and fervor into the conquest of a new consciousness. In fact there lived in Milan a revolutionary thinker of the stature of Cesare Beccaria, who would write a world-famous book on criminology — *Dei delitti e delle pene*, 1764 — and would also lay the foundations for modern Italian law. There was also the group of intellectuals around Antonio and Pietro Verri, and there was a poet of great moral stature, Parini (1729-1799), who with his scathing irony flayed absurd conventions and mores in his poem "Il Giorno", which is dedicated to the vices of that emblematic figure, The Young Gentleman. But the relationship between the intellectuals and society was marked by neither clear direction nor steady coherence. The very same Abbott Parini was deeply involved in the most frivolous expressions of 18th century society; he wrote foppish drawing room riddles and shared in that particular mentality which bestowed the classical name of "Symposium" on a hair-splitting coterie equipped with perhaps refined but certainly affected tastes and engaged in a vapid, purely literary game in an atmosphere of erudite complacency. Indeed, when La Scala was to be inaugurated — on whose stage would sing the castrati, a practice Parini considered barbarous and against which he had even written an ode — and he was asked to suggest a subject for the painting on the drop-curtain that would reveal the world of the new opera house, he complied without a murmur, choosing Apollo in the act of pointing out the models of good taste to the four theatrical muses and obliterating the opposing vices by his splendor. For this service Parini was presented with a valuable snuffbox. The theater did not yet represent an opportunity for the ripening of ideas, consciences and responsibilities, since the bond between art and ideas, entertainment and spiritual fulfillment, which would later be discovered and proclaimed by the Romantics, was not even a matter of consideration. Vincenzo Monti (1758-1828), the poet and literary figure who was regarded as the master of the period immediately subsequent to this, when he saw the youthful Alessandro Manzoni at La Scala's gambling tables harshly reproached the future author of *The Betrothed*, commenting ironically on the "beautiful verses" he was sure to write if he continued on this path. And yet, at La Scala, the same Monti listened to the performance of cantatas and hymns set to his verses in honor of both Austrians and French, indiscriminately, as they succeeded each other at the head of the city's government. And in 1796 La Scala calmly heard the *Marseillaise* played in honor of the Franco-Italian troops then entering Milan, and the *Te Deum* in honor of the Austro-Russian troops, and even the reading of Napoleon's victory bulletin from Marengo, which in fact earned the French officer who read it from the stage a thunderous round of applause.

And yet, little by little, La Scala also began to reflect the profound changes taking place at that time in Milan and Europe. The sudden tempest which unsettled habits and emotions with the arrival of the Franco-Italian troops and later led to the establishment of the Cispadana and Cisalpine Republics, brought a gust of madness. Soon after there occurred the unprecedented success of the "Pope's ballet", that is, the ballet entitled *Il generale Colli in Roma* (choreography by Le Fèvre, music by Pontelibero), which on February 25, 1797, presented a mime dressed up as Pope Pius VI who, after mincing and hobbling about the stage, ended up by putting on his head the Phrygian cap instead of the Papal tiara, as a sign of his agreement with French ideas. It is a ballet that, if one reads the plot today, with its hodgepodge of political satire and variety theater folklore, whimsy and banality, proves to be utterly boring, yet at that time it was awaited with great impatience, endlessly discussed, brawled over and acclaimed. For, as the first example of

political ballet, it set out to excite and inflame. There were also repercussions and consequences, quite natural for this type of politicized spectacle: The protagonist, who was also the choreographer, and in fact physically resembled the Pope, was not paid all the money promised him and, by way of reward, was banned from all of the theaters. At least if we credit what he himself wrote in an appeal in which, among other things, he complained of having been blacklisted in "the very houses where, by my profession, I earn my sustenance". To such extremes could a parody of the Pope lead in the Italy of that period. First encouragement and applause, then ostracism. A mentality which, with its mixture of anticlericalism and formal Catholic obsequiousness, will persist throughout La Scala's existence, past and present, even if no Pope's dead ringer has since danced the "*périgordin*" on the stage with a General Colli, nor even with other, less significant generals in history.

In 1797 there was also a "bull fight" which the Harlequin company presented at the end of a comedy entitled *Il giovedì grasso a Venezia*. It featured a live bull which was to be hunted down by dogs, employing part of the orchestra for the show, and the spectators' dogs had the pleasure and possibility of joining in; all of which was offered as "a token of... gratitude to this free public." The Central Ministry of the Cisalpine Republic also kept a watchful eye on the details of this free public's behavior. It forbade calls for encores and was concerned that encores be denied and there be no more demands for them, as can be read in a pompous "warning" issued on November 23, 1797 — which date, in imitation of the French Republic that had tried to change all the names of the months in order to start public life with a clean slate, was called the 3rd of "*Frigifero*" — or, to translate the Latin literally, "cold-bringer" — in the Sixth Republican Year. And precisely this farce of changing the names of things while leaving their substance intact appeared to be La Scala's attitude during those untidy, slapdash years. The coats of arms on the boxes were removed but the audience remained exactly the same. In much the same way, a booklet financed by the French government and entitled *Milan in Republican Uniform or the Renaming of City Gates, Squares, Quarters, etc.*, proposed the following changes: "Visconti Street is to be renamed Tolerance Street, the Street of the Hours is to be renamed the Street of Love Tokens, Saint Sisto Street is to be renamed Street of the Shelter of the Laws, and the Street of Our Lady is to be renamed the Street of the Burgled Labels", and so on. Even after the establishment of the Italian Republic which, with Napoleon as president and Francesco Melzi d'Eril as vice president, followed a brief return of the Austrians[8] and lasted for twelve years with Milan as the capital, La Scala seemed pretty much what it had always been — a different face but the same habits. It was as though the Napoleonic experience had simply exchanged 18th century fashions for the Empire style with its high-waisted peplum. Only the décor of the boxes had been replaced by parapets with balustrades and neoclassical festoons, created by the scene designers Giovanni Perego, Vaccani and Canna; and there was a ceiling decoration painted by Hayez with dancing figures linked to each other by a blue ribbon, which in turn suggested a change to blue silk for the boxes' curtains. Beneath their wide-brimmed hats (a practice that lasted

26. The drop-curtain with the painting of Apollo and the Muses. The subject had been officially decided upon by the poet Giuseppe Parini, the author of the famous satiric poem, "Il Giorno". Despite the cultural and moral development of Milan the men of letters adored this decorative atmosphere. What cannot be reproduced in pictures is the sensation of experiencing La Scala during those initial years: a theater filled with torches, sounds, boxes with drawn curtains that open to allow a glimpse of a woman's arm or face; and the great buzz of talk and excitement...

26

for a long time and, among other things, provided protection against the spitting by which the occupants of the top balcony expressed their disapproval), the men sitting in the orchestra, though picturesque and wearing a look of determination that seemed intent on bringing a new world into being, did not in themselves inspire the thought that the world would really be changed, and for the better. The writer and memorialist Giuseppe Rovani, in his famous book *Cento Anni* (1856-1865), caught perfectly the contrast between the generations: "As they passed by, the older men who still clung to their cocked hats and pigeon-winged perukes, their whiskerless faces and shaved chins, were outraged by the new and peculiar styles affected by the young men. Broad, tall hats, expanded to the size of cauldrons, festooned with velvet ribbons from behind which peeked the large republican cockade, hid those appropriately grim-looking faces, right down to the eyes. Wide, thick whiskers covered the cheeks, suggesting the image of two bristly pears which, descending from the hat, went to hide inside an enormous white cravat that swathed neck and chin and impinged on the rights of the auricular lobes. Only the eyes and nose were given freedom, but, sheltered by the fixed shadow of the hat which grazed the eyebrows, they had a fierce and suspect appearance."[9] And there still prevailed the inveterate habit of listening inattentively and restlessly, of conversing and busying oneself with completely unrelated matters, almost as if opera were mainly a pretext to meet, and ballet an amusing variation on that pretext. This habit did not disappear for a long time, for as late as 1822, in the memoirs of an Englishwoman, Lady Morgan, who attended the performance of Pacini's *La Vestale* at La Scala, her chief praise is lavished on the fact that the orchestra, although occupied by the bourgeoisie and not the nobility, was filled with ladies dressed in accordance with Parisian fashions and wearing delightfully large picture hats (with what pleasure on the part of whoever sat behind them is unknown). And that the men spoke with much liveliness but in low voices and, despite their tall, round hats, had a military air about them. The only sad note was struck by the mention of the glitter of Austrian officers' uniforms in some of the boxes (this was 1822, and the restoration had already taken place). On the other hand, Lady Morgan thought it elegant that the ladies entered their boxes usually after the first act, removed their hats and hung them on the wall, as was done in Paris, and, immediately turning their backs to the stage, devoted themselves to greetings and conversations that were interrupted only when the music warned them that an important aria, duet or *pas de deux* was about to begin.

But in spite of all this, even earlier, at the time of the Italian Republic, and afterwards, during the time of the Kingdom of Italy — a period when Milan made generous attempts to assume great responsibilities and lead an independent social life as an enlightened European center — certain internal realities about the audience were changing. In fact, the new style of performance, which would soon be consecrated by the great Rossinian epoch, with its greater composure and its more recognizable coherence, was beginning to assert itself. The praise for operas and composers began to be heard more clearly, supplanting that bestowed on the individual singers. Of course lovers of librettos and poetry may be saddened to learn that on December 9th, 1811, the then greatest poet in Milan, Ugo Foscolo, the author of *Sepulchures* and *The Last Letters of Jacopo Ortis*, had a total fiasco at La Scala with the production of his noble tragedy *Ajax*. But the truth is that *Ajax* was a considerable bore; and one shouldn't be too outraged if during the last act the Milanese, already pretty worn out by the preceding acts, answered Teuco's invective by shouting "*Oh, salamini*", or "Oh, small salamis." After all, the inhabitants of Milan, whether bourgeois or aristocrats, were more familiar with the Lombard lexicon for cured meats than with the historical events on the Greek island of Salamis, and a knowledgeable playwright ought to have been aware of this. Yet tragedies by Monti, Pindemonte and, above all, by that foremost writer of tragedies, Vittorio Alfieri, had great success. In 1803 Belli Blanes played in Alfieri's *Orestes* and, around Belli Blanes, Salvatore Fabbrichesi, engaged by the Viceroy Eugène de Beuharnais, built his company in 1806, with a theatrical organization and a style of acting that presupposed an attention that was far from superficial. People also began, now and then, to attend concerts, and at this point the name of Niccolò Paganini comes to the fore. In sum, despite the many cabaret-style attitudes, the many extraneous interests and peculiarities, now so far from our attitudes and mentality that we cannot help but be scandalized or amused by them, one gets the impression that during the first thirty-seven years of its life La Scala also acquired a sense of how to gather people together and unite them, a sense of theater, which can exist side by side with a desire to be sociable, to meet and put oneself on display, but of course means so much more than just those things. So, slowly, in its own fashion, La Scala also learned what in the particular instance mattered and still matters most: to listen. So much so that as early as 1812 it was a shock, a revelation, an event, when suddenly from Venice, at the age of twenty, Gioacchino Rossini arrived at La Scala with one of his operas.

27

27-28. *La Scala participated in the enthusiasms for the victories of the various political forces, whether they were French or Austrian. The French (here a soldier reads a victory dispatch) were favored by the majority because they encouraged Milanese autonomy. In these politico-theatrical events the ballet entitled* The Pope's Ballet, *presented in 1797, was famous, and it is here reconstructed in a 19th century print. The mime, who was also its choreographer, had a great success, impersonating a blatantly caricatured Pope who supported the French, but he was later fired.*

28

*29-31. Rossini's dazzling arrival was the arrival of irresistible,
extraordinary youth. The singer Malanotte was reputed to have
left Lucien Bonaparte's regal bed to go and live with him...
(Here are shown Malanotte, Bonaparte and Rossini).*

And so Rossini (1792-1868; at La Scala from 1812) arrived
during the final period of the Napoleonic Kingdom of
Italy. The opera theater was an important concern of
the state, perhaps also because Napoleon was fond of
opera, which was another reason to keep up the old
traditions of the Teatro Ducale and to try to obtain
the services of the best composers of the moment, and
while they were still young. It was also a matter of
prestige in that somewhat makeshift court which, though
prone to mistakes in etiquette and organizational lapses,
yearned for pomp and magnificence, as is so often the
case with revolutionaries who decide to become the
builders of a new empire. Thus, on January 24, 1812,
Monsieur Brentano de Brianti — formerly Citizen Brian-
ty — the representative of Minister Vaccani at La Scala,
wrote to the minister that he had received from Venice
"excellent reports about a certain young Maestro Rossini". Immediately there followed a rapid exchange of
official documents between ministers, sub-ministers, pre-
fects and representatives of the official censorship, who
passed along secret information, until a decision was
reached: Rossini was worthy to compose for La Scala.
Soon the rumor began to circulate that the young man
would presently appear, that he was indeed twenty years
old, that he was witty, that he was born in Pesaro and
had established a reputation chiefly in Venice, that he
was protected by a certain lady of the aristocracy, or,
at any rate, that there was another lady in Milan who
was willing to do the same, and that the singer in one
of his operas, La Malanotte, had most certainly slipped
out of the hospitable bed of Lucien Bonaparte — the
Emperor's brother, no less — in order to be with him.
And people wondered whether he would be up to composing for a theater where one was accustomed to the
excellent, most worthy qualities of a Giuseppe Nicolini
(1762-1842; at La Scala from 1794) and a Stefano Pavesi
(1779-1850; at La Scala from 1805), the sort of composers
about whom sensational mistakes could not be made.
It was, however, a justifiable curiosity and the doubts
were also justifiable, though none of those involved in
the events could possibly have imagined the final results
and consequences. Yet, listening to the opera of his
debut, *La pietra del paragone*, on September 26, 1812, it
became possible to guess that something quite important
was indeed taking place. The libretto was by Luigi Ro-
manelli (1751-1839; at La Scala from 1779), one of the
most prolific poets in the theater, whose librettos would
eventually fill eight large volumes, and who knew how
to refine the operatic vocabulary and give it literary
dignity, while at the same time keeping an eye on the
need for theatrical brilliance, the changing times in Europe, and the fact that the text must always be subordi-
nated to the music.
In *La pietra del paragone* we find a curious state of affairs
surrounding a certain Count Asdrubale, who is very rich
and is being pursued by three young widows. First the

29

30

32. *After having had his first success, Rossini (here in a suggestive, famous portrait by Camuccini) had to prove that he could compose a serious opera. The result was a period of difficult relations between him and the Milanese public.*

count and later his beloved dresses up in disguise, provoking outlandish situations in order to prove the sincerity of their budding, mutual love. All the characters enter with great élan, as if carried (or driven) by the music, which invests each of them with a full-blown personality. The poet Pacuvio, oafish but pretentious, imagines the most absurd subjects, casting a light of parody on a world that is living its last glorious hours:

I pretend that Alceste while making love in bliss
To Arbace's shadow thinks somewhat like this:
Oh, disdainful little shadow of the Mississippi
Don't be so shy and stay here awhile with me.

A passage which became widely known and remained in the Lombard tradition, so much so that in Fogazzaro's novel *Piccolo Mondo Antico* (1895), Uncle Piero sings it, only slightly changed, on the shores of Lake Como to his little granddaughter. Then there is Macrobio, the journalist, who comes onstage and pompously proclaims: "A thousand prophets to the ground I strike/With a single swat of a newspaper", and who, in a round of duels in which he has become involved, reserves the last for himself, declaring: "With the man who is killed/I will then cross swords". There is the lovers' declaration through a feigned play of echoes, a hunting scene, a thunderstorm, and the becalmed, deeply moving atmosphere of the finale, in which a long phrase by repetition gathers together and embraces all the characters in the fading light of dusk.

The opera was a success, indeed a triumph — it was given fifty-three "sold-out" performances, and the public affectionately renamed it "*Sigillara*", the ridiculous word which dominates the opera's most astounding and comical ensemble. So this little opera was a prolonged joke, like so many others which had preceded it; but it reached the public in a different way: it was enthusiastically welcomed not so much for its amusing situations as for its being as a whole, the revelation of a daring, unbridled composer who answered La Scala's wish to have "its own" composer. So Rossini, with this play set to music, gained the public's attention and made that attention more constant, even expectant; and he entered custom, too, so that literature preserved the echo of his first encounter with Lombardy and La Scala. Soon what was happening all over Italy also took place here, as *La Gazzetta Piemontese* reported:

"The beautiful musical phrases of this Italian genius insinuate themselves with such ease into the listeners' ears that a few months later they are on the lips of every idler in the street. But that is not all, for you can hear them sung at private concerts, played at balls, and as intermezzos and symphonic interludes between the acts, and by the year's end alarm clocks and barrel-organs repeat them incessantly all through the winter on every street."

Rossini's arrival at La Scala was one of the most decisive events in the theater's history. For many years after, the theater was identified with him and never again abandoned him. For the first time, there was a composer who remained in the repertoire uninterruptedly. La Scala presented only five of his operas in their première performances, yet in a short time almost all of Rossini's operas were produced and with an insistence and frequency that only great popular favor could support. In three years — 1823, 1824 and 1825 — out of the fifty-two operas that were staged by La Scala, thirty-two were by Rossini. In 1905, when an accounting was made as to which opera was given the greatest number of performances at La Scala and the Canobbiana, *Il Barbiere di Siviglia* was clearly first, with three hundred and nineteen performances. Yet, if from the very start the public was overwhelmed by that rhythm which, as Rossini himself said, embodies the force of expression, and which was neither the elegant and profound equilibrium of Mozart's lofty imagination nor the set arrangements of Cimarosa's brilliant and seductive fantasy, but rather a methodic, captivating procedure that enclosed the opera's theatrical and musical parabola in a perfect circle, not all the relations between the public and the composer, the composer and the theater were happy ones.

Anyone who is familiar with the history of opera theaters in Italy during the 19th century and above all during the period that runs from Rossini to the early Verdi, knows that all the theaters confronted the composers with serious problems. The demand for new works, especially right after a great success, was too pressing; the stars' exigencies that had to be satisfied were too complicated, not to mention the fact that usually the great singers, abetted by the audiences that wanted to listen to them, insisted on certain customary formulas, for the new works not to contain compromises, patchings and tired passages. And the same public that wanted operas written immediately and established the conditions which embarrassed the composer, soon grew tired of him, or even deserted him when it did not find the results congenial. From this point of view La Scala was just as ruthless as the other theaters, yet the commissions it gave to composers afforded them a bit more time and leisure, at least a few more months; and the companies had a number of weeks in which to rehearse. But for Rossini, who furiously overturned difficult circumstances, making them into occasions for invention, there were few advantages. Another kind of problem remained: the encounter with an audience that wanted to adopt him in its special way, while he naturally invented his art and life in his own manner. Thus, through the story of his five premières, there will be told the story of La Scala's relations with Rossini, which is a kind of secret profile of the official celebration: somewhat different, but not too much, from what will happen later on to other great composers, Verdi included.

So, after the great success of *La pietra del paragone*, Rossini was commissioned to write an *opera seria*, and, on December 26, 1813, with Felice Romani coming to La Scala as a librettist, *Aureliano in Palmira* was produced. It was akin to an official act of approval — both because of the date, which inaugurated the season, and because an *opera seria* was regarded, due to its classical subject matter and stately proportions, as an important, very difficult undertaking, so much so that from 1778 to 1814 La Scala presented 244 comic operas as against 84 *opere* serie. The *Aureliano* did not turn out very well, at least if one goes by its subsequent history, since it was never revived. Certainly, it was received coldly. So Rossini had to return, during the summer, with the sole aim of entertaining, and on August 14th he presented the delightful comic opera *Il Turco in Italia*. But this time, too, things did not go at all well. Two important and significant reactions had come into play. The first was in Rossini himself, who, having the previous year in Venice composed *L'Italiana in Algeri,* with its delicate interplay of musical proportions and its wild, unleashed comicality, carrying both Turkish-style antics, which were then in fashion, and comic opera itself to their extremes, had exhausted his interest in such mad, untrammeled *Commedia dell'Arte* buffoonery and had moved away from it. The second reaction came from the audience which, having generously forgiven the young composer's semi-failure, now demanded a work that would in effect be a pleasant reparation, as befitted the foremost opera house. So Rossini set to music Felice Romani's libretto of yet another Turkish frolic, but more subdued and consciously constructed, where actually the emphasis falls on a detachment from the subject matter and which is embroidered upon by a poet who observes the world and comments on it. This character, not usually seen on the boards, wonders at every step how one can make an opera out of the comical scenes he witnesses, which are the normal scenes of Rossini's comic opera. Today such a character would be the occasion for modern directorial patterns, dramatic conceptions of an "epic" kind — to use the Brechtian term — or at least of a generally lyrical type; but in those days its use was unknown. Though it actually did not know *L'Italiana in Algeri,* the public somehow became convinced that Rossini had used sections of the Venice opera or had followed its model, decided to make it an issue of Milanese prestige, took offense and condemned the work. So once again, there was an icy chill. The fourth work of Rossini's to have its première at La Scala was presented in 1817. In the meantime, *L'Italiana in Algeri* and *L'inganno felice* had been produced elsewhere and began the rehabilitation of his fame outside of Milan.

This time, however, Rossini chose neither a serious nor a comic opera but rather a semi-serious one entitled *La gazza ladra*. The librettist was no longer Romani but the young Giovanni Gherardini, a man of letters and a philologist. The subject is meaningful, even if we find it difficult to grasp the peculiar balance of taste and language when confronted by the story of a poor girl accused of having stolen some silverware and sentenced to death, pursued by the town mayor's lust, and finally vindicated in a happy ending. The plot is scarcely credible and completely alien to our present concerns and ways of thinking. Bur Rossini's emotions and attitudes in approaching the work are certainly of great interest. A humorous reference to the opportuneness of the choice and the difficulties attending the composition of the score can be found in a letter of March 19th to his mother: "I am writing an opera entitled 'La gazza ladra', the libretto having been versified by a freshly minted poet, and so it drives me crazy. The subject is very beautiful and I hope (God willing) that we'll have a tremendous fiasco — and the two of us, out of tender affection, will share this first-class fiasco."[10] But a much more extended

indication of his feelings can be seen in a bad-tempered letter which he wrote the month before[11] to his friend Leopoldo Cicognara:

"Here, my dear Leopoldo, are my thoughts on the present state of music. Ever since the five notes were added to the harpsichord, I said that a baneful revolution was developing in our art which had at that time reached perfection, for experience has shown that when we wish perforce to achieve the best, we fall into the worst. Haydn had already begun to corrupt the purity of taste by introducing strange chords, artful passages and daring novelties into his compositions, but he still preserved so much loftiness and ancient beauty that his errors could seem forgiveable. But after him, Cramer and, finally, Beethoven, with their compositions devoid of unity and spontaneity, redundant with peculiarities and the arbitrary, totally corrupted the taste in instrumental music. At the same time, in the theater the simple and majestic styles of Sarti, Paisiello and Cimarosa were supplanted by Mayr's[12] ingenious but worn-out harmonies, in which the main melody is stifled by the accompanying parts; and all the young theater composers became followers of this new German school. Many of our singers, born outside of Italy, renounced the purity of musical taste which never existed outside of Italy and adopted the impure style of the foreigners to please the capitals of Europe, and when they returned to their country they brought back with them and spread these germs of bad taste. And so the divine Pacchierotti, Rubinelli, Crescentini, Pozzi, Banti and Babini were set aside for the likes of Marchetti, David, Antani, Todi and Billington. And the corruption already seemed to have reached its culmination with the help of the singer Velluti, who more than any other abused the supreme gifts bestowed on him by nature when (lo and behold) La Catalani's appearance on the scene made it clear that a wicked thing does not exist that won't leave room for worse to come. Warblings, leaps, trills, jumps, semitones, notes all botched together — these characterize the singing that now prevails. Hence measure, the essential element in music, without which the melody cannot be heard and harmony lapses into disorder, is ignored and violated by the singers. They startle rather than move the public, and whereas in the good old days the musicians sought to make their instruments sing, our singers now endeavor to make music with their voices. And meanwhile the populace who applaud this abominable style do to music what the Jesuits did to poetry and eloquence when they preferred Lucan to Virgil and Seneca to Cicero.

"These are my ideas on the present state of music, and I must confess to you that I have little hope of seeing this divine art rise above the corruption in which it is now submerged, without a total overthrow of existing social institutions; so, as you see, the cure might then be worse than the disease. Farewell G.R."

(This letter, generally thought apocryphal by many au-

Isabella Colbran to Maria Malibran and Giuditta Pasta (shown here in two prints) as Desdemona, with the tenor David, and Lablache and Tamburini, both as Figaro.

Two characters became almost mythical: Desdemona playing the lyre or harp to accompany her willow song, and Figaro. Desdemona represented a rediscovery of Shakespeare and the new, already Romantic world. Figaro represented the unbridled vitality, elegant yet robust felicity of a new epoch. At La Scala Il Barbiere di Siviglia also became a typical vehicle for baritones, for singing as well as sharp, agile acting.

33

GIUDITTA PASTA

*L'aura tra i rami flebile*
*Ne ripeteva il suon.*

Otello Atto III Sc.I.

*Venezia Carnovale 1832-33.*

36

34

L. Lablache

als Barbier von Sevilla.

38

35

37

39

thoritative scholars, was considered authentic for a long time; in any case, it gives a good idea of Rossini's views.) One should not expect a reliable and comprehensive theoretical exposition from the letter of a young, enraged composer worn out by fatigue who is, besides, not yet twenty-five years old. And it would be all the more difficult to look for it in this scrap-heap of arguments in flat contradiction to his development and his life, since he had actually been formed and developed by the Austrian school (as a young boy he was often called the "little German"). As for Beethoven's orchestral works, he did not know the scores, and later in life he always spoke of "Papa Mayr" with affection and gratitude. But, on the other hand, it is interesting to ask ourselves what was on his mind, what was his goal, as he thought about *La gazza ladra,* which was to be staged three months after this letter. And here, too, it is perhaps possible to explain more clearly his opposition to the singers of his time. Apart from the *castrato* Giovanni Battista Velluti (at La Scala from 1810 to 1813), who sang for the last time in Rossini's *Aureliano,* disgusting him by the absurd and disorderly liberties he took (but this was the last season for the *castrati,* since they were outlawed by a decree which put an end to the horrendous custom in Milan), and perhaps with the exception of David, who had a secondary part in *Il Turco in Italia* (and yet, according to contemporary accounts, Giacomo and Giovanni David, father and son and both tenors, were considered excellent musicians with finely trained voices), Rossini's accusations had no connection with the lack of success of his two works presented at La Scala. On the contrary, Rossini had always had first-rate interpreters, beginning with Filippo Galli, first a tenor and later a bass (1783-1853; at La Scala from 1812 to 1840), who was a friend and whom he considered the ideal protagonist for his comic operas, right down to Marcolini and Maffei-Festa. The fact is that the exceptional singers he mentions are all from before his time, a period which, from his perspective, seemed to be surrounded by myth. In other words, Rossini is recreating here the mythical Scala at its origins, a manner of singing with its own peculiar "purity", a way of producing opera that consists in relying on singing as music and only on that, not permitting the intrusion of harmonic complexities, the richness of counterpoint, or the sonority of the orchestra. It is undeniable, however, that here too he runs into a contradiction. *La gazza ladra* is a complex opera with many levels; harmonically it has some remarkable passages, while instrumentally it can hardly be considered light. Indeed, a certain Pezzi, a music critic and sworn enemy, complained bitterly about the beginning of the opera with its thundering drums and the end accompanied by trumpets and cymbals; in his opinion, the only thing lacking was a cannonade. Yet reaching out for a myth is not rank imitation, but rather a kind of devout impulse, an act of faith, or at least an orientation, an effort. Also, a dream, or the creation of a new form that embodies the present while addressing itself to the irrevocably lost past.

*La gazza ladra* opened on May 31, 1817, La Scala saw itself perfectly mirrored in it, and the result was a resounding triumph. It conquered all along the line. Rossini's operas took over La Scala. Two years later, to honor his contract for the inauguration of the season, Rossini, listless and exasperated because the public refused to

*40-42. At the end of his life, Rossini (portrayed here in an etching which he sent to Liverani) saw his most celebrated characters take their place in the popular imagination. A fan (see next three pages) preserved at La Scala's Museum portrays some of them, among whom can be seen the pathetic and delightful Ninetta, the protagonist of* La Gazza ladra.

40

GAZA LADRA.

follow him on the innovating path of such works as *La donna del lago,* which was tepidly received in Naples, threw together *Bianca e Falliero* on the basis of Romani's libretto and never again returned to La Scala.

Ever since the restaging of *L'inganno felice,* Rossini's operas were always mounted with sets designed by Alessandro Sanquirico (1777-1849). From the beginning, Sanquirico's fortunes were tied to Rossini's, since, as a newcomer to La Scala (1805) he had done the sets for *La pietra del paragone,* and actually from 1817 to 1832, the most important Rossinian period, he was the theater's only scene designer. The scene of the trial in *La gazza ladra,* as one sees it in the drawing (43) would by itself be sufficient to give an immediate sense of this significant encounter: the spacious hall with its high ceiling, the huge bench of the judge seen in perspective at the back, like a distant event, and poor Ninetta, approaching it and looking utterly foreign to the scene (this is an imaginary presentation of the acted scene), surrounded by the bustle of sparse, indifferent onlookers. It would be difficult to conjure up anything more closely related to the tragic nature of the incident and its inner sense of something that can take place quite routinely; and yet, at the same time, the proportions of the great gaps, perspectives and spaces are bereft of any sort of realism, as if everyday images could not be viewed realistically and everything tended to a meaning beyond the pathetic and dramatic, in a synthesis of perspective effects and lights that transfigured these emotions without contracting them and went beyond events and misfortunes to achieve a severe and noble harmony. La Scala found in Alessandro Sanquirico not only a perfect scene designer but also a kind of hallmark or master-image which was as easily wedded to the spaces of its auditorium as to the opera for which it had to provide the settings. At times this master-image presented typical scenes in the Baroque manner: a garden, a large reception hall, a bleakly terrifying landscape or ruin (though always neat and composed), all based upon formulas that can still be found in so many operas constructed in this fashion. And quite often it participated in the action by interpreting, summarizing, almost inventing the operas' world hand in hand with the composer. Sanquirico's technique was precise and enormously conscious, as Elena Povoledo has succintly described it in her article on him in the *Enciclopedia dello Spettacolo:*

"Perfectly trained in the architectural articulation of masses and the understanding of scenic depth as a dramatic space (rather than a place), he interpreted it positively with an intense and very lively chromatic sensitivity, fond of the pictorial effects of deeply accentuated lights and shadows. He used architectural sketch plans that were assymmetrical but not excessively so, for he preferred perspectives with a single central, or slightly off-center, axis, without, however, going so far as to use the diagonal of an angular perspective. He frequently adopted the 'proscenium arch' (a sort of closeup principle that often framed a majestic scene, whose perspective, however, was resolved on the backdrop); in both his architectural interiors and natural exteriors, in conformity with the neoclassic-romantic origins of his iconography, he showed a predilection for ample rooms and vast, evocative spaces. Typical of his repertory are his 'pavilions', with their rich curtains, draperies, friezes, and

*43. The set for Rossini's* La Gazza ladra *was designed by Sanquirico. This study reveals the stage director's imaginative strategy. At the back, the somber, dark judges are sentencing the poor, innocent young girl, accused of a theft actually committed by a magpie.*

Alessandro Sanquirico was La Scala's only scene designer from 1817 to 1832. Through him and his work, La Scala hit upon its hallmark, which was a kind of reconciliation between an inherited Baroque style, the classicism in the air and the aborning Romanticism. Sanquirico's sets, with great naturalness, put the opera's characters and events in ample, stupendously theatrical spaces, as if their significance were to be sought beyond the subject, in the transfiguration of the images which in turn reflect the music.

44-47. Sanquirico's artistic level, even in the large productions, was always very high. The decorative element, which embraces architectonic and natural aspects in a perspective that has a single axis shifted assymmetrically, was vast in its scope. During Sanquirico's years, the stage was illuminated by oil lamps with protected glass spouts. The lights could be regulated with striking effects of contrasting areas. Usually in Sanquirico's sets the background is luminous.

That the relations between Sanquirico and Rossini were not always pleasant, given the distance between their two worlds, can be

44

45

46

47

seen in these three scenes, painted for two operas which were not very successful *Ciro in Babilonia (1818) and Aureliano in Palmira (1813). The set (the large illustration) painted for Rossini's* Ciro in Babilonia *in 1818 reflects not only the personality of this excellent artist but also the taste for the* grandiose and precise that animated La Scala *during those years of great culture and style.*

*48-50. Here in three scenes (the first two for the ballet* Otello Ossia il Moro di Venezia, *the third for the ballet* L'alunno della giumenta) *are the typical settings of Baroque scene design—drawing room, garden and ravine, composed in a classical manner and animated by an almost Romantic taste.*

*51-52. Another Sanquirico set. The scene for the ballet* Jesostri *testifies to the establishment of a manner which will remain valid and recurrent at La Scala right down to the present, a manner of approaching the exotic which links operas all the way from* Semiramide *to* Aida.

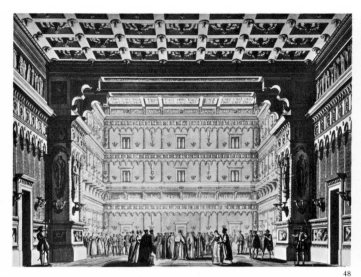

48

49

50

51

On the following two pages the real imagination of Sanquiri-co, amplifies, for Meyerbeer's Il Crociato in Egitto in 1828, the taste for the grandiose, the complicated and highly animated, which will become the next path for this designer. This set offers us a fascinating image of how spectacles were presented dur-ing those years. From the very start the attention paid to details was very great, as we know from the testimony of writers like Verri and Rovani, and great amounts of money were spent on this part of the production.

53-55. *A whole long procession of operas about Rome was given a style and tone by Sanquirico's sets: here Pavesi's "opera semi-seria"* La gioventù di Cesare *(1817), Mozart's* La Clemenza di Tito *(1819), and Pacini's* L'ultimo giorno di Pompei *(1827). At times, as in these three sets, La Scala's Romanticism seems to reflect the ideal of an urban order which Milan — Piermarini's Milan — had just experienced and, together with this, its rather Arcadian dream of escape, which smacks of the poet Parini and the academies which flourished all over Italy.*

*Sallustio*
eletto alla prima Magistratura

*Ottavia*
sua consorte

53

54

*Clodio*
figlio di Pubblio

*Fausto*
liberto di Sallustio

55
56

56. *Side by side with Sanquirico, whose sketches drew the characters in costume, a collaborator supervised the "wardrobe", and here, for* L'ultimo giorno di Pompei, *the supervisor was Rosa Cervi. This style has its own elegant coherence, rare in the theater of that period.*

Menenio
*loro figlio*

Appio Diomede
*Tribuno*

Pubblio
*custode delle pubbliche Terme*

Gran Sacerdote
*del Tempio di Giove*

Vestale

Magistrato

Littore

Soldato

cornices, and his cellars and crypts with their expansive, suggestively illuminated vaults."

He not only used space as a kind of "objective correlative" or illustrative image for the operas of the period but also as an interpretative link that brought together the action presented on the stage and the audience listening to it. All the pre-Verdian operas can be recognized by this, for they offer room for audience participation through these always imaginative yet orderly, sometimes solemn yet never overwhelming sets. And the costumes, too — for the men by Rossetti and for the women by Majoli — were distinguished by this note of coordinated, imaginative composure. After Sanquirico left La Scala in 1832, the season which opened with one of his finest masterpieces, the sets for Bellini's *Norma,* a long time elapsed before a comparable level of coherence and inventiveness was attained — certainly more than a hundred years. During the initial period, the sets were presented unsigned, as the product of artisan teamwork. Shortly after, they were signed by Menozzi and Cavallotti, and after August, 1843, a distinction began to be drawn between the "architectural" sets by Merlo and Fontana and the "landscape" sets by Boccaccio. Gone probably also from the public's taste though certainly from the spectacles on the stage were the prodigious feats of lighting and machinery, startling and of naive magnificence, that were an integral feature of the scenery for the famous grand ballets for which Sanquirico and his assistants were summoned to collaborate with the illustrious choreographer Viganò.

And indeed Salvatore Viganò (1769-1821) was the third great personage at La Scala during the years between the Austrian restoration and the Risorgimento. The choreographer's art is even more ephemeral than that of the actor and singer, who are well aware that their creative life is "written on water", as has been said since time immemorial. Choreography is even more likely to vanish from memory, entrusted as it is to the play of movements in the air, an enchantment of presences that give it life and communicate it through the unrepeatable encounter produced by each particular occasion. Viganò tried to establish certain firm criteria so that the exact invention of his ballets could be repeated with other dancers; but these remain inert descriptions and a limited alphabet of movements. A choreography cannot be repeated. It exists through the relationships among actual persons, their physical qualities, their style, which is made up of both willed and spontaneous movements that represent the gesture's participation in the language of their time, of their country at that specific historic moment, of the school which hands down a special way of moving and being, and the taste of an audience which accepts it and, even before that, understands it in its own way as the years go by.

Viganò's choreography, which attempted to organize all the elements of the performance, coordinating the music (often supplemented by compositions of his own), the steps, spaces, sets, stage action and effects of light and shadow (based upon a concept and use of light so different from ours and strictly determined by the then available technical means), in order to create an appropriate, true, often allegorical action, has been definitely lost. What we have retained are a few memories, the enthusiastic admiration of his contemporaries, and the

*57. The perspective which tried to reconcile the Classic with the Romantic, nature with architecture, gave a special colorfulness to La Scala, even in Spontini's opera* La Vestale *(1827), or Donizetti's* L'esule di Roma *(1828), two operas which were born in other theaters. The artistic event which put the seal on*

*this approach to opera was Bellini's* Norma, *composed for La Scala in 1831. Here we see the set for the forest of Irminsul, where the feeling for the land and a sense of mystery are presented with a kind of classical harmony.* Norma *is the opera in which La Scala most fully defines its style and ideal sentiments. So,* *after having in some sense adjusted to Rossini (with his vitality held in check by Sanquirico's composed, sedate sets) La Scala went on to assist in the birth of Bellini's masterpiece.*

58. *Salvatore Viganò (here in a contemporary portrait), the great choreographer of the period of Rossini and Sanquirico, modified the gestures used in acting and invented scenes of fabulous effectiveness, in which the pantomine produced a greatly suggestive movement.*

59-60. *Two of Sanquirico's sets for* Norma *(Act III) and for* L'ultimo giorno di Pompei *show how, compared to ten years before* (Gazza ladra, La gioventù di Cesare), *this lesson of imagination and movement had been accepted.*

58

59

60

fleeting allusions of witnesses and historians. So it may seem all the more strange that we should be able to call great an artist of whom nothing remains but a memory and who lived in a society with concerns and interests so remote from our lives and culture.

Nevertheless, in his own time, Salvatore Viganò represented not only the esthetic master-image achieved by La Scala in this art, too, and therefore the definitive consecration of the theater's originality, but also La Scala's answer to the passion for ballet. This had grown during the 18th century thanks to Noverre's greatness but was now excitedly manifesting itself, adding the pleasure of the image to the joy of almost physical participation in the sublimated being of the dancer, who throws off the shackles of everyday gestures, the typical aspirations of the 19th century, and is born again to harmony, elegance, absolute beauty, a life which proceeds to the measure of music. Actually, during the first years of the century, La Scala had formed an important institution, the ballet school, which later was to supply ballet teachers to and become a model for academies all over the world. Of course, the need which inspired this initiative was that of having well-trained professionals, since private schools no longer seemed to offer sufficient guarantees in this regard; but, above all, it was the need for a permanent and continuous breeding ground that would insure the harmonious technical and stylistic training demanded by the grand ballets for which La Scala was now famous. The official inauguration of this school, the Imperial and Royal Dance Academy, occurred as early as 1813, under Napoleon. And this period had already seen the major creations of Viganò, who came to La Scala at the peak of his artistic maturity. His career as a dancer, when he had usually danced together with his stupendous Spanish wife, Maria, had come to an end, and he had already given proof of his remarkable abilities as a choreographer in several minor theaters. For him, as well as Rossini, his La Scala debut took place during that extraordinary and fortunate 1811-1812 season, with the ballet entitled *Gli Strelitzi;* in 1812, in fact, he had his first important success, much debated yet finally resounding, with the ballet *Noce di Benevento,* which in the April of that year clearly demonstrated the extent of his originality. The ballet had been composed ten years earlier in Vienna, where Viganò had been active; the music was by Süssmayr (Mozart's pupil, who had finished the Requiem), and it was presented in Milan with a score rearranged by Viganò himself. The sets were by Sanquiroco and Petroni.

The theme was fascinating and already showed, with its fairy-tale echoes, the trend to Romanticism. A walnut tree is populated by witches and demons who descend into the woodland and bewitch Dorilla, the wife of the good Roberto, until eventually the spell is lifted, the wood is transformed into the good fairy's garden, and the dancing becomes gay and festive. The elegance of these enchantments can be brought back to us not only by the original music, which is in the Viennese manner, but also if we think of Niccolò Paganini's variations, *Le Streghe,* which were inspired by this score. But the ballet that really became a landmark for his name and fame, though actually the whole style of the epoch could be summed up by other ballets, was *Prometheus,* produced in 1813 with La Scala's lavishly rich and numerous com-

*61. A scene from the ballet* Gli Strelitzi, *scenery by Sanquirico, choreography by Viganò. The attitudes of the mime remind one of a kind of pantomime of colors more than a ballet as we understand it today, but a pantomime with an exact and harmonious taste and feeling.*

62. *Antonia Pallerini, in Viganò's ballet* Giovanna d'Arco, *dancing the leading part. La Pallerini was the student of the other great choreographer of the period, Gaetano Gioia, the specialist in heroic ballets.*

63. *A typical image of the delightful classicism of Viganò's ballets, in which an unbridled imagination somehow joins with a precious figurative harmony of an 18th century kind, perfectly matched by Sanquirico's sets (here a detail from the ballet* I Titani*).*

62

pany, the sets by Canna in April and by Landriani in October (the latter, La Scala's official scene designer, while Sanquirico, who was younger, collaborated with these men before taking complete control of the theater's scene designing section). The costumes were by Pregliasco and the music was by Haydn, Mozart and Beethoven. At first, in Vienna, where it was created in 1801, this ballet relied only on Beethoven's music. It was succinct and peremptory. It had not been thought necessary to add other music, albeit by such eminent colleagues (from Haydn a passage of *The Creation* to emphasize the coming of light to the universe). Luigi Rossi, who has written a history of ballet at La Scala, while recounting the Milanese plot, shows us how the very fact of staging the ballet at La Scala brought about a change in its proportions, and his terse comparison is quite illuminating:[13]

"Also the text was apparently somewhat inflated and, at least on paper, it is remarkably more ponderous when compared to the first version. In Vienna the beginning of the action was very quick. Prometheus approaches two statues that he himself has prepared and infuses life into them with the aid of fire. But the two creatures show neither intelligence nor gratitude toward their creator, all the more because he is thinking of destroying his handiwork. High up on the mountain, the Virtues, Arts and Muses... are gathered around Prometheus in 'erudite symposium'. Prometheus tries to awaken mankind to reason and for didactic purposes he offers a fruit, with the painful result of unleashing a savage fight for possession of this modest gift. Discouraged, Prometheus appeals to Minerva, who descends in her chariot, 'crossing the stage diagonally' with a spectacular flight to which was later added a series of atmospheric effects, such as a starry sky, the setting of the moon, and the coming of dawn. All marvels that the stage 'mechanics' of the time, despite the lack of electrical equipment, re-created so well as to elicit boundless stupefaction from the audience.

"The theft of the fire from the gods, enacted in the 'small Prometheus' with directness and simplicity, turned out to be extremely awkward and cumbersome in La Scala's 'colossal' edition. The fire descends on a terrified mankind huddling in the forest, and then spreads to the various trees. Out of each tree issues a genie bearing a torch and approaches a man to instill him with the light of reason (this scene was inspired by Albani's famous painting *La danza degli Amori* at the Brera Museum). While Jupiter, angered and irritated, orders Vulcan to bind Prometheus in chains, men 'with torches held high' follow their benefactor to the temples of Virtue. Here occurs the typical 'apotheosis' of 'grand ballet', as it will be revived several decades later in Mazotti's elephantine allegories in his various *Excelsiors* and *Amors*. Inside the temple, man worships the 'social faculties — the Muses, Graces, Sciences and Arts', personified, naturally, by mimes and

64

female dancers with towering headdresses.

"Prometheus is chained to a rock in the Caucasus. The Cyclops hammer into his chest 'a mythical diamond nail'. Jupiter's voracious buzzard... plummets down to rip open his heart. But Hercules arrives, kills the predator, and liberates Prometheus, who is crowned by Immortality. Another, final apotheosis: in the upper section of the stage, on a pillow of clouds, the council of the gods appears.

"A libretto which, at a simple reading, seems rather comical, if it were not for the great number of witnesses, all of whom were anything but unqualified, who affirmed the exact contrary."

And here he quotes Ritorni,[14] Viganò's official biographer and commentator, who claims to be summing up the general judgment expressed by many qualified spectators: "I consider myself fortunate to have seen *Prometheus* with my own eyes, a ballet about which the populace and those who were not present have formed an erroneous conception: namely, that it was a spectacle based on stage mechanics and an illustrious new world. On the contrary, whatever in it was material representation had the effect, as it should, of imperfect imitation; while whatever was, shall I say, moral representation, the sublime and astonishing expression of poetic ideas and dramatic situations, truly shone forth as the value of the work."

As always happens in such cases, Viganò aroused feelings of competition and rivalry. Francesco Clerico (at La Scala from 1779 to 1811), who had gained a reputation in pantomime ballet, a kind of mime in which dialogue was the basis for the action, tried to enter into an ideal competition with him as the true proponent of classicism; but all that the confrontation demonstrated was that in Viganò the action was projected into the pictorial beauty of the scenic movements and the harmony of authentic ballet, producing a precise dramatic coordination of all the components of the performance and an agile, tremendously attractive rhythm. On the other hand, considerable prominence was achieved by Gaetano Gioia (at La Scala from 1794 to 1824), who was able to carry forward in his own manner developments of the "choreodrama", as Viganò's concept was called. After so many years, cultures and images, it is difficult to pinpoint exactly the difference that existed between the two great choreographers, who, among other things, had adopted the same working methods. In fact, both added their own music to that of other composers so as to render suitable for the ballet a score composed for them or, often, adapted by them from pre-existing compositions, either in their entirety or as a kind of collage. They were also friends and co-workers. *Gabriella di Vergy,* a great success, with music by Brambilla and Romani and staged at La Scala in August, 1822, was first created at Reggio in 1815, when Viganò had taken to dance in it his pupil Pallerini, who was also the featured ballerina at La Scala.

According to Ritorni's description, she was an example of striking realism rarely encountered in a ballerina, particularly in those days: "A physician assured me that only a member of his profession could appreciate how close the imitation of that anguished death approached the truth, so much so that she was advised to be less energetic and forceful onstage." But Gioia, who always existed in Viganò's orbit, gained recognition with his heroic ballets, and it was in fact at La Scala in 1809 that he triumphed with his famous *Cesare in Egitto,* presenting some extraordinary scenes which even amazed Viganò. Prince Eugène ordered paintings made of the ballet's most striking moments, and after one of the performances Napoleon personally sent for Gioia and presented him with a diamond ring and a gold snuff-box. Needless to say, Napoleon felt that he himself was being celebrated, the close colleague of the great and clement Julius Caesar, who was extolled in the ballet. And, in view of Napoleon's position, the gifts made quite an impression. Meanwhile, the art of ballet developed and thrived, in all directions. Not only in the footsteps of such great interpreters as Luigi Costa (at La Scala from 1808 to 1828) of *Prometheus* fame, or the erotic Nicola Molinari (at La Scala from 1811 to 1836), the comic character dancer Celeste Viganò (at La Scala from 1811 to 1828) who was Salvatore's sister, but also because of the teaching at the Conservatory of two particular dancers, Jean and Teresa Coralli, husband and wife, who themselves had been fine performers and one of whom, Jean (called Giovanni on La Scala posters), was destined to become one of history's foremost choreographers.

This new La Scala master-image, which filled it with new creative energy during the years of the restoration in Europe, was also a unique cultural event. Was it Classical or Romantic? So the question was posed, and it is still being asked in that form. Those were the years when one enjoyed speaking in such terms, and discussions were endless at the back of the boxes at La Scala, because of the 18th century's classical heritage, the presence of neoclassical taste as defined in the literature, and the exultant, irresistible onslaught of the Romanticism that swept down from beyond the Alps. What exactly was intended by either term, Classicism or Romanticism, was not very clear. The politicians were the most uncertain and contradictory in their evaluation, though Austria realized quite soon and with lucid insight that it was preferable to encourage Classicism as Napoleon understood it, since it was demagogic, sterile, quietist, self-congratulatory and pleasure-loving (in music the imperial predilection for heroic ballet went hand in hand with a taste for comic opera in a pathetic vein *à la* Paisiello) rather than perturbing Romanticism, which, though it originated in German-speaking lands, led by its excitation of the emotions and imagination to the discovery of the significance and destiny of one's own country and somehow helped to reveal man's inner life, his unity, dignity and history as an integral part of a people. It is easy to discern the components in Viganò: the themes, the Romantic protagonists, the plastic forms, the classical ideality, the synthesis which brought together Mozart and Beethoven, that touch of truth which is simply itself, defying classification not only because it represents a personal manner or process of thought but also because it imparts a sense of harmony to a tumult of contemporary

66. *A whole world predominated on La Scala's stage during the years of Sanquirico and Viganò (whose ballet for* La Vestale *is shown below): the world of antiquity, mostly Roman, through which noble contrasts and the passions of every age were experienced.*

67. *Two worlds lived side by side in La Scala's audience. The folk or people's world which jammed the top balcony whose realistic, dramatic and comic bard was the dialect poet Carlo Porta and which also saw itself reflected in the heroes populating the ballets of the choreographer Gaetano Gioia.*

68. *Stendhal was the intelligent bourgeois with a strong aristocratic tendency. He described himself arriving "dead tired" in Milan after a journey but rushing off immediately to La Scala. When he saw the marvels there, he thought: "My journey has been repaid."*

67

68

realities, arresting them for an instant on the crest of the changing times. And it was precisely as a fusion of these two versions of *Prometheus,* the Viennese and the Milanese, that Foscolo joined together the recourse to mythology and the lightning-like power of the myth of fire, which was destined for Romantic greatness. As he writes in his poem *I Sepolcri* (1807):

A spark friends robbed from the sun
To illumine the subterranean night.

Sanquirico was known for many years as a neoclassicist because his work was juxtaposed to the most irrational type of fantasy or the most concrete realism, that is to say, the varied illusions of subsequent scene designers. But from a kind of proto-Romantic naturalism, his development picked up along the way the late archaic and complex classical stimuli of his time, taking him back to that original ambiance which, as one would say today, he was "revisiting". And certainly both in his images and his forging of a relationship with the audience, his artistic discourse was more complex and personal; and the most clearcut, recent explanation of this, on the occasion of the 1968 exhibit, the essay in the catalogue by Mario Monteverdi, is quite incisive: "To speak of (him) as an exponent of neoclassicism (...) rigid, theoretical, cold (...) is the greatest injustice that one can do this artist."[15] But especially for Rossini it is understood that the discussion is more than a debate upon the various polemics, upon form versus emotion or conservatism versus novelty, but rather concerns a profound and complex originality, as, à propos the revival of *La gazza ladra,* Fedele d'Amico wisely pointed out:[16]

"One must not forget that at its roots Rossini's music exists before 'expression', that is, before any specific emotional orientation; it is valuable essentially as pure vitality, of a kind unknown to the music of earlier centuries, and so is intoxicated by itself, by its irruption into the world. That does not prevent it from incarnating, when it wishes, this or that word in the lyrics; in some of Rossini's works, especially his comic operas, with *Il Barbiere* in the lead, there is in fact not a nuance of the text which the music does not capture. Yet the affirmation of that vitality in its undifferentiated state can also be glimpsed in the background, and it is the most profound reason for our emotion; for when it came to 18th century psychological rationalism — from Rousseau to Diderot, from Gluck to Cimarosa — Rossini played with it as a cat with a mouse, and always at a certain point in his finales, and not only in these, he strikes it with lightning by sending all his characters into the gulf of the same vortex.

"The ductility and receptivity of so much of Rossini's music in relation to the aims of the text, or the interpreter, originates here. But to say 'so much' does not mean to say everything; several pages one comes across in his serious operas could not exist in his comic ones, and at his peak in *William Tell,* there is not a trace of an openly comic style. Yet *Tell* is as far from the 'drama' of a Gluck or a Mozart as it is from that of Verdi, and it demonstrates how the serious and comic — the Pan-like churchyard choruses of *Tell*, the Dionysiac deliriums of *L'Italiana in Algeri* and *Il Barbiere* — were for Rossini only two guises of the same reality."

So this is how La Scala's master-image of those years appears in most present-day criticisms, that master-image with its capacity to gather together the totality of the available elements and mold them into a unified whole, but even more to lift them to a kind of expressive and culturally pristine reality, responsive to the society of the time as well as that later on of Rossini's, and also to the audiences of the time through the two interpreters who then did their work, Sanquirico (and his collaborators) and Viganò (and his imitators). And the public of the time lived in a society which was becoming more and more unified, like its theater, where the boxes gradually assumed a common decoration which gave more and more the idea of a theater and a place and not just a space to contain orchestra, balconies, and the many diverse, marvelous sights of the individual boxes, and would soon (in 1821) also install a huge central chandelier that cast a very bright light. Yet the auditorium was still darkened during the performances, thus favoring a common concentration, which was not custom elsewhere. It was a moral unification which, in a certain sense, was learning at the same time how to achieve political unification. From this point of view, the return of Austria in 1814 and its attitude after the Congress of Vienna had a positive effect. We can see this from the diagnosis of the man who experienced the Milanese Risorgimento most fully and wrote about it most profoundly, Carlo Cattaneo, in his essay *The Insurrection of Milan in 1848,* an insurrection which he led and whose antecedents he saw very clearly:

"To preserve its rule, Austria had only to leave to the retrograde the illusion that its soldiers were nothing but armed servants. However, it was good for us that Austria itself acted as the subverter of its Italian subjects. Forgetting that the imperial name descends from an ancient cosmopolitan authority, which permitted each people to live according to the customs of its majority, and flouting in its subjects that sense of national honor which political partisanship does not completely extinguish, Austria did not want to be anything else in Italy but a German power. It adopted harsh and arrogant methods; it harassed and humiliated its own followers. And so the marvelous event took place — they finally realized for the first time that they were Italians."[17]

So little by little La Scala began to be something more than a place to meet, an auxiliary office for business affairs, a pleasant setting for chance or obligatory encounters, and something more than an occasion to discuss everyday realities while listening to music, as though opera were a species of sonic backdrop. By Rossini's time, opera had reached out to the audience, not only playing a part in its encounters and re-evaluations but also forming an inseparable aspect of life, the touchstone of truth.[18] And in fact it was a prime promoter of the feeling for unity; even though its architectonic forms reflected the profound differences of a society which was seeking something as a unit but existed in sharply defined and separated social strata. Indeed, among the many

sources for marvelous statements that can be quoted about our theater during those years there can be found those of Stendhal and Carlo Porta, the Milanese dialect poet, and we like the idea of uniting these two authors in a single aura of literary splendor. Stendhal, in his *Life of Rossini,* written in 1823, when Rossini was thirty, and in his novel *The Charterhouse of Parma* (1839), reveals the very aroma of the epoch, evoking it in a way that short quotations cannot capture, since it is not a matter of ideas but rather of a way of experiencing La Scala, responding to it with acute sensibility and intuitive feeling, an almost physical joy at being there, an emotion of participation without problems, intense and intoxicated, making us sense the mysterious, somewhat confused harmony that was exuded by an auditorium resounding with voices and instruments and refulgent with beautiful, elegant women. And in 1816, in his travel notes *Rome, Naples and Florence,* Stendhal tells us with great emotion: "I have just left La Scala. The truth is, my admiration has not lessened in the slightest. La Scala is for me the best theater in the world, because it is the theater that gives one the great musical pleasure.... As for its architecture, it is impossible even to imagine anything grander, more magnificent, more imposing, more new." He is enchanted by the audience and the atmosphere; but he is also curious and very attentive, observing acutely in Milanese society a characteristic tone of easy-going sobriety. "At the onset of winter a Milanese lady may have made for her four or five dresses, costing about thirty francs. The silk dresses in her wardrobe, which date from the period of her marriage, are preciously preserved for eight or ten years and are brought out for premières at La Scala and the festival balls. These people all know each other very well, so why should they be overly concerned with elaborate apparel?"

On the other hand, Carlo Porta, plebeian and dialect poet, shows us a completely different way of participating in La Scala's life, as seen from the top balcony, where sits his poor hero Giovannin Bongee, doomed to defeat — indeed, as they say in Milanese dialect, one of *i desgrazzi* or "hardluck cases". He goes to see the great ballet *Prometheus,* "when all of Milan rushed to La Scala, and the foreigners came down in waves from here, there and everywhere, from thousands of miles away", and when the balcony-bird who wanted to get a seat had to be there "with his supper half in his throat and half in his hand". While reading this little poem, one smiles continually at the innate Milanese talent (the year is 1813) for scaling down all exultant marvels. Jove's eagle which gnaws at Prometheus's liver, first pointed out as the dancer Giovannin's wife wants to see, since she — the dancer — lived close to her grandmother, is later described as a turkey that pecks at the leading male dancer:

That's the one dressed like some cock
Who pecks at the star dancer's buttock.

Standing on line all afternoon in the piazza in front of La Scala, then suddenly running up the stairs to struggle for a seat, and then *zonfeta* — or, literally translated, kerplunk, to give the auditory mimesis of a grateful behind hitting the long-yearned-for seat; and then the laughter and chattering during the two farces which are sung by "that goose of a singer" and precede the ballet. And then the signs of the zodiac and the chariot of sun which remind Giovannin — "at the most beautiful moment

69. *La Scala reflected the city and stood at its center. As the proclamation issued before the inauguration declared, all carriages must line up in an orderly fashion from Piazza del Duomo. The other people arrived on foot and in small groups.*

69

of the ballet" — of being "me too up in the air with the clouds, and seeing lounging about paradise all the saints in their reliquaries with little lamps lit all around the cornice". And the sharp little shriek his wife, Barborin, lets out when the lamp-lighter pinches her behind, while all the others pretend that nothing has happened, and a soldier threatens to toss Giovannin over the balcony when he becomes furious. One smiles; but in the meantime one gets a vivid picture of the rough, crude people's Milan, the people who live at the edge of the enchanted circle, who are ready to join in the fun, but are still so far outside of it. And certainly, even if the beautiful is beautiful, and the reawakening of consciousness is always a contagious reality in which one participates and which helps people to see each other, the joy and quiet of the boxes is quite a different thing from the situation of those "hard-luck cases" who pack the balcony:

And so (my dear sir) the ballet, though beautiful —
And if you see Viganò, please, not a word —
Neither I nor Barborin liked it.

These were, however, years of concord that Milan lived through between the disillusionment with the Napoleonic Republic and the period of uprisings and excitements of the Risorgimento. They were also undoubtedly anxious, restless years, since noble ideas can often lead to cruel deeds; indeed, the idea of independence soon became a source of violence, and many Austrian officers living in Milanese homes were killed as conspirators. They were naive years, too, considering the faith in economic growth, when Austria certainly would not permit the Italian economy to pass from a phase of highly specialized handicraft and limited commerce to an industrial and international phase, and in fact in the next few years many large stock-holding companies suffered severe reverses. And years of subjugation, too; the censorship was alert in the theater and outside of it; a newspaper with strong patriotic feelings and an inspiring historical viewpoint, *Il Conciliatore,* was quickly suppressed; operas presented at La Scala were subjected to the examination of an expert who changed verses in the librettos when he caught a whiff of possible political allusions; and, on top of everything else, taxes were high and burdensome. These were also years of social injustice; there had not been established a situation honestly conscious of the workers' human dignity in their relations with the aristocracy and bourgeoisie, which during these years was just beginning to flourish. The letters of composers and singers to the aristocratic impresarios — or whoever happened to be in charge of La Scala — still bore above their signatures such obsequious formulas as "your very humble and devoted servant" (though this was a formula inherited from the Baroque age, and so wasn't given much weight). Yet these were also great, intense, fertile years; and years of concord, too. A forward thrust, not only of the bourgeoisie and the privileged intellectuals, but also a broad popular feeling, propelled the entire city into a search for autonomy and independence, giving birth to a unified discussion which sparkled in all the magazines and conversations and was motivated by common exigencies and the conviction that the problem was a general one involving both art and thought, politics and historical diagnosis, all of which pointed to new prospects for freedom. This extraordinary moment of daring yet meditative history saw perhaps for the first time an uncontrollable confusion of international events bear down heavily on specific citizens; yet the awareness of being in some way part of these great and intricate international events still proved to be fertile, even if analysis was difficult and the men of the period were untrained and unprepared to carry such analysis through to the end. In an essay on 19th century Italian culture, which also touched on these years in Lombardy, Mario Apollonio sketches a stimulating synthesis:[19] "The mobility of the innumerable forces which were at work in this geopolitical picture, the contradictory character of all too many situations (Napoleon's tyranny is col-

ored, as soon as it has fallen, by liberalism and it is considered the liberator of the peoples; the German people, the victor, finds itself in conflict with federated Austria, which, with its imperial tradition, had succeeded in leading the Danubian peoples in the struggle against the new French centralism; and Europe had grown economically, due to the expansion of a colonial domain which the first of the world revolutions, the American, contradicted; yet, on the other hand, the economic potential of the United States had grown due to the forced labor of imported Negro slaves), and, finally, that touch of the adventurous which political actions still had in the 19th century, and which they inherited from the romantic Napoleonic exploits, induces us to think that never as in the new Europe of the 19th century has the participation in universal history of the small group or individual been so fervid and so alert. The poets speak to each other from rural solitudes that are boundlessly distant: the American farmer Walt Whitman and the feudal lord Tolstoy at Yasnaya Polyana, Count Leopardi in a small town in the Marches and Count Manzoni in the suburban countryside of Brusuglio. And though Parini's old patrician society continued its insouciant existence, the new groups, together with the intellectual bourgeoisie of half of Europe, were rallying around certain embattled ideas."

So, during these years of concord, restlessness and generous impulses, the Milanese who attended La Scala felt as though he stood at the center of the world. And La Scala was indeed a daring arena of talents and showed an unusual openness to ideas, or at least reflected a straightforward, good-natured Milanese feeling of pride and affectation. In fact, La Scala satisfied many needs and many levels of expectation, welcoming and reflecting the new ideas, ferments and passions of the historic moment, yet continuing to be concerned with its international prestige as the purveyor of the best theatrics, incomparable stage sets, and singers chosen from among the best in Europe and therefore the world. In short it was the sort of theater which today we would call a "consumer's" theater, that is, dependent on the immediate, changing tastes of the society which financed it, in those years a loose collection of the old nobility and the new bourgeoisie which had been born from the upheavals attendant on the Napoleonic victory and the Austrian restoration and was molded by the ancient game of keeping in good odor with the authorities and managing somehow to remain afloat through the political storms. The singers still remained at the center of attention, as was natural; and running all through La Scala's history, as in all of musical history, one can easily see how decisive a part their physical presence, their style of singing, their voices and their psychology played in the birth of the various operas; indeed, their names are inextricably linked with those of the composers in the story of the operas' creation. At this time, that is from Rossini

70-75. *But during the restless, generous years of the restoration, La Scala began more and more to feel at the center of the world, taking up those key ideas that were changing it. Onstage the characters of the newly conceived Romantic opera began to gain attention and success. Thus the tenor Donzelli and the tenor Rubini (above in* I Puritani, *below twice in* Il pirata) *seem to take over the space of the new ideals. And the beautiful peasant girl Adina (sung here by Tadolini) displays her pretty face, mistress of the secrets of love.*

70

72

74

71

73

75

down to and including a good deal of Verdi, their style of singing was still tied to the school of *Bel Canto,* with its agility, fluid lights and shadows, and those *fioriture* of melody which are so essential a part of the "coloratura"; in fact, as this style developed, it became expressive also in a lyrical and dramatic direction. For example, a tenor like Giovanni David (at La Scala from 1814 to 1827) had a clear, plangent tone and sang the high notes in falsetto; and the same falsetto technique was also employed by Giovanni Donzelli (at La Scala from 1816 to 1838), who, however, had a dark, almost baritonal timbre and was Norma's first Pollione, which he sang with a vivid awareness of the role's dramatic possibilities, whereas Giovanni Battista Rubini (at La Scala from 1827 to 1830) managed to conceal in the highest notes these "head" or falsetto tones by a tender, extremely suggestive emotional coloring which gave him an extraordinary expressiveness, so much so that people thought of him as a romantic character who could arouse feelings of intense rapture. Within the careers of the individual singers one noticed a fascinating interpretative progress and an attunement to the new music. Thus, among the sopranos, the Frenchwoman Henriette Méric-Lalande (at La Scala from 1833 to 1844) represented the polished elegance of the brilliant style, full of trills and *fioriture,* yet, engaged to play the leading roles in Bellini's operas *Il pirata* and *La straniera,* her voice suddenly proved capable of rich, passionate, impetuous flights; while Eugenia Tadolini (at La Scala from 1833 to 1844) turned out to be a romantic creature of angelic suavity. In sum, there was being created that vocal enrichment which, among the baritones was best exemplified by Antonio Tamburini (at La Scala from 1825 to 1830, but very active outside La Scala until 1840), whose chief characteristics have been described by Rodolfo Celletti:[20] a "clearly virtuosic bass: lightness, agility, flexibility" with "a fullness and limpidity of sound," "cleanness in vocalizing and ornamentation" and "gay élan," on all of which were grafted the qualities dictated by Romantic taste — "pathetic effusions," "the moving accents of a sorrowing father," and "the heartbroken tone of an unhappy love." And meanwhile the interest in the roles to be interpreted, the desire to possess a broad repertoire led to that uncertainty of choice between soprano and contralto which characterized Giuseppina Ronzi (1835) or Caroline Ungher (at La Scala from 1828 to 1830), and which found its greatest artists in the ardent, extremely beautiful and moving Giuditta Pasta (at La Scala from 1831 to 1835) and the explosive, alluring Maria Malibran (at La Scala from 1834 to 1835), who so astounded people that they called her a genius, as is testified to by a scholar and music critic of the caliber of Fétis after he heard her in London. These two great interpreters marked the turning point in singing techniques; they forced the connoisseurs into debate and were adored by the public, for they represented a new vocal expressiveness which by now was freed both of the virtuosic technique in the Rossini style and what was usually meant by beauty of timbre, that is, smoothness, fullness of tone and equality of register. But Bellini used to say that Pasta was an angel (and he was utterly conquered by her), while the great French actor Talma claimed that by some sort of intuitive response to the role she could improvise what someone else could only acquire after a year of study. And Malibran made Bellini

*76-78. Giuditta Pasta, Romantic interpreter. A star and a fascinating woman, full of the usual whims, such as the substitution, as Malibran had done, for the last act of Bellini's* Romeo e Giulietta *of an act of Vaccai's which was more facilely effective.*

*Yet she was also capable of bringing to life the myth of Romeo and Juliet in all its passionate sadness. No longer is beauty of voice and appearance incompatible with hope and pain.*

completely forget that he was in an English theater and began shouting furiously and applauding his own opera *Sonnambula,* while from Verdi she elicited such adjectives as "sublime" and "great, very great." And yet, so much skill and importance, such a vivid devotion to the cause of the new opera should not lead us to think that the singers then approached opera with the values of the singer-professionals of our day. Apart from the scant general preoccupation with clear pronunciation of the libretto's words, which were known by the audience because they had read them in advance and remembered and recognized them after so many repetitions, above all in the serious genre where the melodic line was more crucial and the recitative was sustained by the orchestra instead of the harpsichord, all the singers, even the greatest, were vain, capricious, and made claims that today would be absolutely intolerable. But, to mitigate this, we must remember the atmosphere of permanent emergency in which these singers lived. For example, there was the habit of replacing the original arias with others more striking or more congenial to their voices, often written by some other composer. At La Scala, too, the singers would arrive with arias they wanted to execute during the course of the opera, arias that began to be called, with witty resignation, "trunk" arias. And Maria Malibran herself, so modern in her conception of opera, tended to put the credibility of her roles above everything else, to such a point that in October, 1834, in Bellini's *I Capuleti e i Montecchi* she replaced the third act with an act from Vaccai's *Giulietta e Romeo,* where the character of Romeo, which she interpreted, stood out more eloquently and the expressive immediacy of the score seemed to her greater.

The characteristic traits of a "consumer's" theater are also in evidence when one reads the scores of the minor composers, since they were not very attentive to the unity of the work and left the various "set pieces" to the mercy of momentary musical and theatrical exigencies, not demanding a continuity of interest from an audience which was already quite distracted. Moreover what is meant by a "consumer's" theater can be seen even more strikingly by reading the long lists of operas which were put on, a great number, even so many as forty new operas during the decade that ran from 1830 to 1840. Of all these, very few have remained in the repertoire, and a few more, though without ever becoming a staple part of the repertoire, have had the honor of an occasional performance in the 20th century. And among all these composers few are still famous and still performed: aside from the case of Giacomo Meyerbeer (1791-1864; at La Scala from 1820), who in 1820 and 1822 presented *Margherita d'Angiò* and *L'esule di Granata,* two operas now shrouded in the profoundest oblivion, and later in Paris became the reigning glory of so-called Grand Opera. Among the composers who were famous at the time only Mercadante and Pacini are still being listened to,

78

though rarely and with a bit of an effort, and only Donizetti and Bellini are habitual presences in the repertoire. And yet Saverio Mercadante (1795-1870; at La Scala from 1821) was an excellent musician, skillful in his orchestration, moving and dramatic in his songs, who received thirty performances of his first work, *Elisa e Claudio,* fifty performances of *Adele ed Emerico* (1822), thirty-six performances of *Il giuramento* in 1838 and forty performances of *La vestale* in 1841. And Giovanni Pacini (1796-1867; at La Scala from 1818), who was a great success from his debut in 1818 with his opera *Il Barone di Dolsheim* (forty-seven performances) down to his *Saffo,* which was staged in 1841, the year after its success in Naples, receiving twenty-three performances, was a greatly beloved composer, chiefly among the most brilliant society, and overflowed with melodic inspiration presented in the sort of solid musical framework possible only to a man of great talent. Yet these composers and their operas seem now to answer only the common exigencies of the taste of the period, forming and elaborating certain formulas that were regarded as sure-fire and that permitted the frequent recurrence of the same dramatic themes, the same allusions in the titles, without venturing into an area of personal originality or being able to attain the highest forms of musical synthesis. At bottom one feels in them the success syndrome that the impresarios indefatigably embodied and pursued; and it is not without significance that from 1826 to 1832, after La Scala's management had passed from Balocchino and Crivelli to the directorial group of the Royal Imperial Theaters and then to Cavaliere Glossop, it was finally put in the hands of an association in which the impresario Domenico Barbaja was both a member and the moving spirit, the same man who owned the gambling concession at the theater from 1808 to 1814, that is, as long as gambling was permitted at La Scala, and who in 1816 in Naples had presented Rossini with a significant recipe for a particular opera.

"Here is what I want," he told Rossini. "At the very beginning of the opera I need a cavatina. I'm not giving you three thousand ducats a year so that, with your hands crossed on your belly, you can spin out the sort of tale you would for a dramatic actor. Then I need a big aria for Colbran. She is the sort of woman who'll tear my eyes out if she doesn't get her special aria; then some nice flights for David, and a curse for Benedetti, who curses very, very well..."

And yet it was just this theatrical climate, catering to the public's emotions and tastes, which led in all of Italy and at La Scala to the successful appearance of those composers and scores which still today, in the light of a critical scrutiny, are obviously the most valid contributions to the art. Besides Rossini, who continued to be presented, the most beloved and most performed composers soon were Donizetti and Bellini. Between 1830 and 1840, that is, in eleven seasons, sixteen of Donizetti's

Gius. Gerzini lit.

Gio. Salucci lit. 1004

**GIOVANNI PACINI**

80

operas were performed, and they were given in all four hundred and thirty performances; and seven of Bellini's operas were performed, and they were given in all two hundred and fifteen performances. Now, since there were no changes in the subscribers, nor a big turnover in the people who held seats in the boxes, it is clear that each opera was heard several times and that people sought greater comprehension precisely where matters of greater artistic interest were involved because of the work's high quality. And if one reads the scores today, it is easy to see that the operas of Donizetti and Bellini offer many different levels to the listener. To begin with, they satisfy the most immediate needs of those who looked for unfailing, obvious emotion; but also, if examined more deeply, they reveal an extraordinary richness and coherence in their creative structure and plan. For example, Gaetano Donizetti's (1796-1848; at La Scala from 1822) *Lucrezia Borgia,* which was composed for La Scala in 1833 and in which today we can feel the force of that coherent climate, that sinister brilliance which depicts events, dialogues and confessions as a kind of grotesque dance of death, and its instrumentation, which uses the strings to underline the sarcastic speeches or the characters' emotional tumult, while the woodwinds swell in volume and register to provide a setting and atmosphere for the beautiful, treacherous streets that wind among Ferrara's tall palaces, or to summon up distant, heartbreaking memories. But at that time the opera was a success because of those traits which Edwart[21] summed up about thirty years later, when he introduced this work in the score published by Ricordi: "The lyrics of this opera are by Felice Romani and constitute one of his best librettos. The music is in a popular vein and bears the imprint of a certain gloom demanded by the extremely grim subject. And it was just these two qualities which were difficult to bring together: popular music imposed on a grim, dark theme! This is a very varied musical picture in extremely vivid colors; in it alternate the shouts of the exalted, the loves of the heedless, the plots of a vendetta and the agonies of death."

Also *La Straniera,* composed for La Scala in 1829 by Vincenzo Bellini (1801-1835; at La Scala from 1827) was enjoyed, indeed evoked enormous enthusiasm from La Scala's audience and was given twenty-six performances, probably for the reasons explained in an article that appeared the very next week in the *Gazzetta Privilegiata di Milano:*

"In *La Straniera* Bellini aimed at expressing and constantly distinguishing between many emotions — the sorrow of a terribly unhappy woman, the candid attentions of a brother, and the impassioned transports of a lover blinded by affection and anger. He presented the woman's sorrow through pathetic melodies spun out by almost hushed, whispering voices enlivened here and there by harsh tints or, to put it more accurately, by intentional dissonances. The brother's attentions were expressed by ample mod-

81

ulations preferably resting on the middle chords and always of an extremely chaste purity, while the lover's transports were conveyed by impetuous, vehement sounds, now softened by delicate half-tones, now erupting with the plangency of unchecked emotion. He entrusted to the chorus that place in the opera which in painter's language is called 'the final linear plane.' If, while singing, the chorus discovers the tranquil surface of a lake, or, gathered in a temple, lifts up its voices in votive prayer, he does not use a heavily accented melody but rather an indecisive and nuanced *cantilena;* and that enchanting effect of hundreds of far-off voices was painted, if one may put it this way, without outlines, in the style of the airy distances of certain landscapes. If the chorus announces to a wretched man some suspected sinister events, or piles scorn upon scorn, trouble upon trouble, one expects a rather forceful treatment, though not overwhelming or deafening. In short, an esthetic concept which always made it possible for the composer of *La Straniera* to keep the melody close to the truth of emotions, independent of all pre-established forms, and to make use of the wholly modern prestige of melody solely to reinforce the dramatic situations."[22]

Today this score seems to us to have an elusive mobility, and its fascination rests in its 19th century "singularity," the peculiar way it has of unfolding a story without rules and equilibriums, pushing the characters seemingly beyond their very story into a kind of rapt bewilderment that tinges the lyrics and dramatic situations, and in which song is the only reason for being and traverses the theatrical time and space with arcane suggestive power, almost as though romantically seeing itself. Behind the technical and artistic motives in the specific scores lay two civilizations which were strongly felt and expressed: in Donizetti it was Lombard moralism, and in Bellini the Sicilian sense of rapture at the conquest of an ancient, deep-rooted motif. Two fundamental realities which, more than defined or delineated, were felt and experienced in a pure emotional state; and which, whatever the varied fortunes awaiting these operas, always marked the presence of these two great opera composers in La Scala's seasons.

Direct testimony, starting with the evidence of many letters, shows us that the experience of Bellini and Donizetti at La Scala was dominated by the conditions of work familiar to other composers. So we know that when he composed *Lucrezia Borgia* Donizetti labored mightily to write and orchestrate the opera in two months, collaborating with the librettist Felice Romani, who had prepared the work for Mercadante and hesitated for quite a while before giving it to Donizetti, trying to get better terms, and when it was being written had trouble with the censorship which in the long run forced the opera to travel about Italy in seven different versions and with seven different titles,[23] and all this meant so many changes, cuts and modifications that Romani refused to sign it. In Lombardy, as all over Italy, the censorship had begun to see in opera not only a spectacle that would soothe rambunctious spirits but something which in fact would provide an opportunity for the discovery of and reflection on the great political and human themes of freedom. In any event, Donizetti received the libretto at the end of November, set it to music in a few days and soon had the opera in rehearsal. Not only that; he

also had to yield to the whims of the star, Méric-Lalande, who after the opera's finale wanted the addition of a bravura piece so as to be sure of the final round of applause — a piece which actually remained in the score although it was hateful to the composer, who firmly advised against it.[24] As for his experience with the opera *Maria Padilla,* two letters reveal to us, through the audience's reaction, the conditions that led to the success of an opera which ended by being given twenty-four performances — certainly not a smash hit but a more than fair success. For the first performance Donizetti writes a short, rapid note: "December 27th: called out twice, six pieces applauded; other applause here and there." For the second performance a schematic but detailed chronicle is set forth in the letter to Antonio Vasselli on December 28, 1841:

"Historic drama of the second performance of *Maria Padilla* at the I. R. Teatro della Scala, Milan. December 28, 1841:

"Maestro on the stage.

"Cavatina of Ines — the Maestro called out once.

"Cavatina of Maria — the Maestro called out once.

"Entrance of Don Pedro — applause; the Maestro called out once.

"Duet of Don Pedro and Maria — great applause. The singers called out, not the Maestro.

"Second Act

"Chorus — applause.

"Cavatina of Ruiz — (Domenico) Donzelli called out.

"Duet of Maria and Inez — the Maestro called out twice.

"Final *stretta* — little applause.

"Third Act

"Trio of the two ladies and the second tenor — applauded.

"Duet of Ruiz and Maria — the Maestro called after the adagio, everyone afterwards.

"Chorus — nothing.

"The romance of (Giorgio) Ronconi, or Don Pedro — the Maestro called out once.

"Finale — the Maestro called out for the adagio. Everyone out at the end. The Maestro twice alone and twice with the singers."

And on Bellini's account we know the troubles, disagreements and conflicts which accompanied *Norma* and how much its lack of success upset him after its first performance. It suffices to know that the very famous aria "*Casta Diva*" was rewritten any number of times because the singer Giuditta Pasta considered it unsuited to her particular voice, so that, as Scherillo, Bellini's biographer, declares: "The Maestro had to use all his skill to convince her, but he never succeeded fully"; that, finally, they came to an agreement concerning the definitive version: La Pasta would "keep it for a week, singing it every morning, and if at the end of seven days it was still repugnant to her, Bellini promised to change it,"[25] and that Pasta was finally convinced and on the day of the performance she sent the Maestro a gift of a lamp and a bouquet of cloth flowers, which had been her companions day and night while she had rehearsed in her studio; that the singers rehearsed right up to the morning of the first performance and that the welcome was not hostile but cold — despite a first-class company which, among its singers, had also engaged Donzelli and Giulia Grisi — so cold that the composer expressed his

84

85

84-85. *Romantic portraits of two of La Scala's stars. Giulia Grisi, a famous Norma (but at the first night she sang the part of Adalgisa) and Ignazio Marini, who became famous in Verdi's time singing parts from the Romantic Italian and French repertoire.*

disappointment in a famous letter to his friend Florimo that very night:

"I've just come from La Scala, first performance of *Norma*. Would you believe it? A fiasco! A terrible fiasco!!!... But don't be upset, my good Florimo. I am young and feel in my soul the strength to get my own back after this terrible collapse."

There is, however, a profound difference between the experiences and destinies of Bellini and Donizetti at La Scala. Donizetti, out of the more than seventy operas he composed, had many staged at La Scala, but was rarely asked to write any expressly for it, indeed only five: *Chiara e Serafina,* when he was twenty-seven (1824), and then, in succession, *Ugo conte di Parigi* (1832), *Lucrezia Borgia* (1833), *Gemma di Vergy* (1834) and *Maria Padilla* (1841), none of which can be counted among his masterpieces, though all are significant and interesting because of certain efforts at dramatic and instrumental enrichment, such as that pre-Verdian scene in his opera *Ugo*, which reminds us of *Trovatore*—Emma praying inside as onstage Bianca explodes in sorrow; or those formulas from Bellini's *Il Pirata* used in *Padilla's* tauter and orchestrally more complex drama: the sign, in fact, of a lively, alert desire to present in Italy's most solemnly official theater the proof of his cultural awareness and professional skill. Donizetti's relations with La Scala were touchy and ill-at-ease, and we find him giving vent to such feelings in an affectionate letter in June 1842 from Vienna to the Milanese lady Peppina Appiani, in which he describes requests to compose operas he has received from the most prestigious theaters in Europe and ends up distorting the facts out of bitterness, but with a light ironic touch: "But what about my Milan? Oh, I'd leave everything for that ungrateful Milan, which pulls a nasty face at the birth of *Anna, Elisir, Lucrezia, Gemma* and *Padilla*... and yet, if I have worked with gusto, it has all been for Milan.... And yet, I still long for Milan.... And yet, Milan does not want me!"

However, Bellini, out of ten operas, had three of them staged by La Scala and was supported, helped and acclaimed. Even the difficulties over *Norma* were not due to his having to hurry the composition, nor even to the singers' feelings about him, but rather to the difficulties which arose out of the encounter of the interpreters with an unusual interpretative problem, and in fact when the singers felt less anxious about it they carried the opera triumphantly through another thirty-three performances. Such things happen in all theaters, where all productions are plucked out of a tangle of professional, artistic and human problems, and chance plays a great part, too. Yet a certain basic orientation can be seen to emerge clearly in the final result. Donizetti was not only a great, highly individual composer, he also represented an epoch, a whole way of life, and did so in a full, very felicitous fashion. He was the harbinger of a frank, passionate, and free Romantic mentality, displaying quite strikingly

86-88. *The Romantic style began in a clear-cut fashion with Rossini's* Otello. *La Malibran, impassioned and imploring, La Pasta more languid, but two great Desdemonas. Controlled in his wrath, the famous Donzelli in the part of Otello.*

89. *So, while Sanquirico's sets were being loaded with elements that contrasted with their dignified linear purity, there was born — as shown here in Pacini's opera* Gli arabi nelle Gallie *(1827) — the theme of the handmaidens, inherited from 16th century painting.*

86

87

88

90-101. *In order to imagine La Scala's life in the years between Rossini and Verdi (the 20's and 30's of the 19th century) one must think of these poses, where an ample Baroque eloquence is animated by feverish agitation or sculptural solidity.*

*The inspired and excited attitudes struck by the Grisi sisters (91); Méric-Lalande's impassioned outstretching of her arms (92); Giuditta Pasta's statuary pride (94-95); the costumes*

that sudden new aspect of things which 19th century creativity was stamping on all of culture. Indeed, as Franca Cella has said:[26]

"The cultural perspective is not provincial but European; from the beginning of the century... opera has approached the various romantic themes; after passing through the period when Romanticism was argued about and then finally accepted, the librettists began to respond to the great names and themes from the other side of the Alps (Shakespeare, Hugo, Dumas, Byron and Schiller), popularizing them in acceptable forms, though to translate means to transmit, not to diminish."

And this new feeling appeared more and more in the Italian theaters, even before there had been attained a highly intelligent dramatic and musical synthesis, a suggestive and daring manner of understanding life, imagination and the theater which was quite different from the inheritance of the past. This was the theater described by Gianandrea Gavazzeni in a well-known youthful page in his book on Donizetti:

"The musical opera was accompanied by a trunk from whose insides were taken swords and daggers, plumes and cloaks of fine ermine, clothes and instruments of war that were to be employed on the most varied occasions.

"So there descended on the stage lit by smoky lamps views of regal halls, castles and shadowy, mysterious convents. Dense, dark forests were animated by the painters of backdrops with an arcane rural life which, from time to time, was disturbed by the summons of hunting horns.

"Beneath the motionless shelter of oaks the men-at-arms or hunters would sing in those choruses of conspiring against the tyrants, whispering or barely moving their lips in rapid rhythms which would suddenly swell in sonority and then would fade away in staccato sounds until they were no longer heard. At that point, members of the chorus would converge cautiously from every side of the stage, sliding their slippers over the boards, hiding behind the flats and backdrops to infuse their faces again with the flush of wine-soaked tipplers....

"At night, from behind the laurels rose a dirty yellow moon, while two lovers were caught in the dreadful conflict between noble emotion and personal affection. Knightly heroisms now had to be sustained by the tenor, while the majestic woman grew tender and let the orchestra's pleasant arpeggios soothe both her heart and her song.

"The bass and baritone were always given lonely, thundering romances. And when these were not crude and irate, the betrayed man would intone them with a certain sadness not untouched by a clumsiness so sincere as to rise swiftly into caricature."[27]

In these scenes and from these characters the most fluent melodies would pour, conflicts would surge, the singing was no longer caressing as in the past, or at least it no longer resolved its function in pure melody but rather

*E figlio mio.......pietà*

Imogene nel Duetto dell' Atto I. dell'Opera il Pirata.

90

91

92

and appearance of the Marchisio sisters (96); Tamburini's enchanted wonder (97); Marini's costume with its plumed cap (98); Lablache's imposing bulk (99); the sketches for La Favorita (100-101), drawn near the end of the century and evoking the gestures and styles of the period in which the opera was composed.

93

96

99

94

97

100

95

98

101

in a melody closely tied to the dramatic action, the circumstances, the orchestra, the spaces of the action and the dialectic of inner thoughts; and at the same time opera grew more robust and rested more than ever on the lyrics, expressing both their strong, perennial meaning and the new weight of history. This whole way of understanding opera was so opposed to La Scala's history until that moment as to demand a drastic act of innovation. And La Scala met the challenge. After so many years of success with comic opera it realized that the abstract light or heavy comicality of the Neapolitan school could no longer hold the stage; but it did not see that the comic sense of comedy itself was changing, and that a more down-to-earth humanity now typified the characters. As a result, *Il Barbiere di Siviglia* was first produced in Rome in 1816, Donizetti's *L'elisir d'amore* (1832) had its first performance a few steps down the street at the Canobbiana, and *Don Pasquale,* where the comic quite clearly shows its tragic underside in both the protagonist and his environment, was actually first staged in Vienna in 1843. Also those themes in the French Opéra-Comique style, half serious and half sentimentally tearful, which then evolved from the merely theatrical into intense poetic events, had their career completely outside La Scala. Donizetti's *Alina o la regina di Golconda* (1828) was first heard in Genoa, and Bellini's *La Sonnambula* was presented in 1831 at the Teatro Carcano in Milan. Then, too, a whole new historical interest, which began to scrutinize the old royal courts in order to discover deceits, cruelties and the expiations of innocents, on whom descended the pity of the orchestra and chorus, and whose inspiration came directly from the character of Ermengarda in Manzoni's tragedy *Adelchi,* enjoyed its heyday far from La Scala: *Anna Bolena* at the Teatro Carcano in 1830, *Maria Stuarda* at Naples in 1934, and the very next year *Lucia di Lammermoor,* just to mention three of Donizetti's operas. La Scala was something different: it was the scenery of Sanquiroco; it was Classicism veined with an elegantly controlled Romanticism as expressed in the librettos of Felice Romani, the poet of the Royal and Imperial theaterst it was the myth of the noble and beautiful, as at firs; the 18th century, later Napoleon and Austria, and finally both Viganò and Rossini had taught it. If La Scala had been only a "consumer's" theater, it would have initiated either a vehement promotion of tradition or a speedy adjustment to the new fashion and the new discoveries. But La Scala was much more than tradition or "consumption," it was a theater; and it made its choice: to reconcile the Classic tradition with the Romantic. But not by having recourse to a mixture of the neoclassic and the pre-romantic, such as the composed, vibrant, tragic emotion to be found in the Empire contours of Spontini's *Vestale,* composed in Paris in 1807 and reaching La Scala only fleetingly in 1823; and not by reviving ancient myths in a tone of greater emotional intensity, as in Cherubini's *Médée,* which was composed in 1797 for Paris

*Fernando*

102

to music), and sorrowful mediation (as in Lalande). The gesture serves to express the movement of the spirit and the nature of the involvement with the music; but also to explain what the lyrics say, accentuating in this manner concepts, emotions, and the meaning of the action.

103

*Ines di Castro.*

*Atto terzo*

ALUNNA
DELLE GRAZIE
NELLA MIMICA
INIMITABILE

104

105

97

Hr Cornet                                    Dlle Schröder.

MASANIELLO.  FENELLA.

*Es ist meine Schwester!*

(Stumme von Portici)

107

and had to wait until 1909 before it arrived at La Scala. Its purpose was to reconcile so as not to exclude, and to let the new life find breathing room in the old space and style. In this connection, Bellini was the most suitable composer, not only because of his pure song which seemed to recapitulate the old Classicism but also because of his thrust beyond Romantic passions, which are not avoided but rather seen in a glancing light. To remain loyal to an artist has always meant for La Scala having little to do with others, and if Barbaja's protégé, whom he had brought to Milan in 1828 for the première of *Il Pirata,* was not completely congenial to the new director of the Imperial theaters, Duke Visconti di Modrone, this did not mean that other composers were being favored. *Norma* remained La Scala's ideal opera in its Romantic phase, just at the beginning of the Risorgimento: forests and temples, love and death purified in the melodic line, that lexicon which exalts literary dignity and moves us deeply, and those awesome scenes which through Sanquirico's sets have handed down to us a definitive historic image. To reconcile: even *Il Conciliatore,* the famous blue sheet edited by Porro Lambertenghi, who ideally "headed" the Romantics from his box at La Scala, was born with this intention: "*rerum concordia discorsa,*" to reconcile Classicists and Romantics. A perhaps limiting yet awesome and generous effort during those concordant, restless, anxious years — to feel all of one's history in harmony with the history of tomorrow, which had already stepped boldly across the threshold.

Verdi came and overturned everything. Political caution, traditional refinements, music with blue-blooded credentials, the theater that purveys enchantments, moments of relaxation or utter abandon. He arrived in 1839, a young rustic Maestro from Busseto, toward whom the soprano Strepponi and the impresario Merelli displayed an immediate faith by producing a fair opera of his, *Oberto, conte di san Bonifacio,* which had a pleasing success; and when he left the theater in 1893 after his last opera, the world had changed: Italy was the nation which had been born from the Risorgimento and was now unified, Romanticism had transformed people's minds and spirits, and La Scala had in turn become Romantic, a prominent factor in the Risorgimento, boldly innovative, gathering around Verdi, a national glory and a European musical divinity. That is how they tell the story of Giuseppe Verdi (1813-1901; at La Scala from 1839), and for once the myth happens to agree with the actual story.

This time history is telling the truth, for it looks at the results, from all these efforts it shows us the consequences and from all the struggles the victor, and out of all the contradictions and difficulties comes a well-rounded over-all attitude; and so one cannot help but see how great and definitive Verdi's presence was in La Scala's history, even if the theater in reality was never so closely identified with him as it had been with Rossini and Bellini. Besides, the myth summed up the events in a more exemplary and useful manner; and it does not matter that at certain points the events have to be stretched a bit to fit the myth. In fact the Verdi myth began to develop from the very first day. In 1881,[28] a life of Verdi which gained a large audience included an auto-biographical story he told to his publisher and friend Giulio Ricordi. It was full of mistakes, yet perfectly in tune with the expectations and enthusiasms of the readers, who saw everything humanly possible in the extraordinary beginnings of Verdi's career — early success, tragedy, half-failure, inspiration, and then the come-back, together with the farsighted intelligence of La Scala, which had recognized his genius and had supported him. The episode goes back to the time when, after the success of *Oberto* (fourteen applauded performances), the impresario Merelli commissioned Verdi to write his second opera *Il finto Stanislao o Un giorno di regno.*[29]

"I was living," Verdi tells us, "at that time in a small, modest section of town near Porta Ticinese and had my small family with me, my young wife Margherita Barezzi and my two small children. As soon as I started working I was struck by a serious angina which kept me in bed for many days. When my convalescence began I realized that within three days the rent would fall due, for which I needed fifty *scudi.* At that period, though this sum of money was no small matter for me, it could hardly be said to be terribly serious. But the painful illness had prevented me from making provisions for this in time, nor did my communications with Busseto (the post left

twice a week) give me the chance of writing to my excellent brother-in-law Barezzi to obtain the needed sum immediately. I wanted to pay the rent at all costs on the right day so, though I disliked having recourse to the help of others, I decided to ask Engineer Pasetti to approach Merelli and request the needed fifty *scudi,* either as an advance on my contract, or as a loan for eight or ten days, that is, the time necessary to write to Busetto and receive the money.

"There is no point in telling here the particular circumstances due to which Merelli, through no fault of his, could not advance me the fifty *scudi.* I was particularly concerned not to let the rent day pass without paying it, even if it were for only a few days, and my wife, seeing my preoccupation, gathered together her few gold jewels, left the house and managed somehow to collect the sum needed and gave it to me. I was deeply moved by this loving act, promising myself to give it all back to my wife, which I could do soon because of the contract I had.

"But here the great misfortunes began. My baby boy fell sick at the beginning of April; the doctors could not understand what his illness was and the poor child got weaker and weaker, finally dying in the arms of his desperate mother. But that wasn't all: a few days later the baby girl also fell sick!... and the illness also had a lethal end!... But that wasn't enough either: at the beginning of June my young wife was struck by a violent form of encephalitis and on June 19, 1840, a third coffin left my house!... I was alone... alone!... In less than two months, three persons whom I loved had disappeared forever: my family was destroyed!... In the midst of this terrible anguish, so as not to go back on my word, I had to compose and finish a comic opera!... *Un giorno di regno* was not liked: the music bore part of the blame, certainly, but another part could be laid to the execution. With my soul afflicted by my domestic misfortunes, exacerbated by my work's lack of success, I convinced myself that I could never expect consolation from art and I decided never to compose again!... In fact I wrote to Engineer Pasetti (who after the failure of *Un giorno di regno* had no longer come to see me), asking him to get Merelli to release me from my contract.

"Merelli got in touch with me, asked me to come over and treated me like a capricious youngster!... he would not admit that I should be upset by so unpleasant a setback, etc.; but I was firm in my intention, so, releasing me from the contract, Merelli said: 'Now listen Verdi, I cannot force you to compose... my faith in you is not diminished: and who knows, some day you may decide to pick up your pen again!... All you have to do is tell me two months before the season and I promise you that your opera will be put on.' I thanked him, but these words were not enough to change my mind, and I left... I settled in Milan in La Corsia de' Servi; I had lost my confidence and no longer thought about music, when

108. *Verdi arrived as a young man from the Parma countryside. A success* (Oberto)*, a fiasco* (Un giorno di regno)*, and then a triumph with* Nabucco*, helped by the libretto by the crude but useful Solera. The enchanting Giuseppina Strepponi supported and helped him.*

108

one evening in the winter as I came out of the Galleria De Cristoforis, I bumped into Merelli who was on his way to the theater. It was snowing heavily and Merelli grabbed my arm and invited me to accompany him to La Scala's rooms. As we walked along we gossiped, and he started talking and told me that he was rather embarrassed about a new opera he had to present; he had signed up Nicolai, but he didn't like the libretto.

"'Imagine,' Merelli said, 'a libretto by Solera, stupendous, magnificent!... dramatically effective, grandiose attitudes; beautiful verses!... But that stubborn Maestro refuses to consider it and says that it's an impossible libretto!... And I don't know where the deuce I can find another composer right away.'

"'I'll get you out of this difficulty', I told him. 'Didn't you have a libretto written for me called *Il Proscritto*? And I never wrote a note of it. You can do with it what you wish.'

"'Now that's a fine idea!... It's really a stroke of luck.'

"While talking in this way we reached the theater; Merelli called Bassi, poet, stage manager, bouncer, librarian, etc., etc., and told him to look immediately in their archives and see if he could find a copy of *Il Proscritto*. He found it. But at the same time Merelli picked up another manuscript and, showing it to me, exclaimed:

"'You see, here's Solera's libretto! Such a fine subject, and he turned it down!... Here, take it... read it.'

"'What the devil am I supposed to do with it?... — No, no, I have no desire to read any libretto.'

"'Oh, now... what harm can it do you!... Read it and then bring it back to me.' And he handed me the manuscript; it was a large manuscript with large characters, as was the custom then. I rolled it up and saying goodbye to Merelli set out for my house.'

"As I walked along I felt a kind of indefinable malaise descend on me, in short a feeling of sadness, a preoccupation which made my heart heavy!... I got home and with an almost violent gesture threw the manuscript on my table, while standing there in front of it. The manuscript book as it fell on the table had opened; without realizing it my eyes stared at the page which was there before me and I caught sight of this verse:

*Va, pensiero, sull'ali dorate.*

"I ran through the following verses and was enormously impressed, all the more since they were a paraphrase of the Bible, which I had always loved to read.

"I read a section, then I read two more; then, still firm in my intention not to compose, I made an effort, closed the manuscript and went to bed!... But not on your life... *Nabucco* was running through my head!... Sleep didn't come: I got up and read the libretto, not once but twice, three times, so many times that by morning one might say that I knew Solera's entire libretto by heart.

"Despite all that I did not feel that I could change my mind and so the next day I returned to the theater and gave the manuscript back to Merelli.

"'It's fine, isn't it?' he said to me.

"'Oh, very beautiful.'

"'Well, then. Set it to music!'

"'Don't even dream of it... I don't want any part of it.'

"'Set it to music! Set it to music!'

"And as he said this he took the libretto and stuffed it into the pocket of my overcoat, seized me by the shoulders and with a sudden forceful push shoved me out of the backstage office; but not only that — he locked the door with a key.

"What was I to do?

"I went back home with *Nabucco* in my pocket: one day one verse, the next day another, one day a note, another day a phrase... little by little the opera was composed.

"We were in the autumn of 1841 and remembering Merelli's promise I went to see him and told him that *Nabucco* was composed and that therefore he could stage it in the coming Carnival-Lent season.

"Merelli declared that he was ready to keep his promise but at the same time he told me that it was impossible to present the opera that coming season, because all the performances were already decided upon and they already had three new operas by famous composers; putting on an opera by an almost new composer was dangerous for everyone but especially for me. It was more convenient therefore to wait for the spring, a period when he didn't have any commitments, and he assured me that he would sign up some good singers. But I refused; either at carnival time or not at all... and I had my good reasons, since it was not possible to find two other singers so suited to my opera as Strepponi and Ronconi, who I knew were under contract, and on whom I counted a lot.

"Though Merelli was quite disposed to meet my request, he was not so wrong as an impresario: four new operas in one season was a great risk!... But I too had good artistic reasons to counterpose to his. In short, after all a lot of yes's, no's, embarrassment, half-promises, La Scala's coming program was published but *Nabucco* was not announced.

"I was young, I had hot blood!... I wrote a nasty letter to Merelli, in which I gave free rein to all my feelings of resentment. I confess that as soon as I sent it I felt rather remorseful... and I was afraid that everything would be ruined by this.

"Merelli sent for me and when he saw me he exclaimed in a gruff voice: 'Now is this the way one writes to a friend?... Now come, you're right: we'll put on this *Nabucco*. You must remember though that I'll have heavy expenses for the other new operas. I can't have scenes and costumes made purposely for *Nabucco* and I'll have to make do with what we find in our warehouse that is best suited to it.'

"I agreed to everything because what I wanted most of all was that the opera be put on. A new program came out on which I finally read: *Nabucco*!... I remember a comic scene I had with Solera a short while before this. In the third act he had written a love duet for Fenena and Ismaele; I didn't like it because it slowed up the action and it seemed to me to take something away from the Biblical grandeur that characterized the drama. One morning when Solera was at my house I told him this; but he did not think it right, not so much perhaps because he didn't agree with it but because he was annoyed about having to go back and rewrite something already written. We argued back and forth; he wouldn't relent and neither would I. He asked me what I wanted in place of the duet and I then suggested writing a prophecy of the Prophet Zaccaria. He did not think the idea a bad one and after hemming and hawing a lot, he said that he would think it over and then he would write it. That wasn't what I wanted because I knew many, many days could go by before Solera would finally decide to

109

110

*suddenly. He will return an old and very famous man, and in 1888 he will stroll across La Scala's piazza, to be photographed in a very changed world.*

111

write a verse. I locked the door, put the key in my pocket and half seriously, half jokingly said to Solera: 'You don't get out of here until you write the prophecy. Here's the Bible, you already have all the words put down for you.' Solera, who had a furious nature, didn't take kindly to this action of mine: a glitter of rage flashed in his eyes. I spent a bad few moments because the poet was a hulk of a man who could have easily overwhelmed the obstinate Maestro. But suddenly he sat down at the table and a quarter of an hour later the prophecy was written!...

"Finally, in the last days of February 1842, the rehearsals started; and eleven days after the first rehearsal at the harpsichord we had the first performance, which took place on March 9th, with a cast composed of the women Strepponi and Bellinzaghi and the men Ronconi, Miraglia and Derivis.

"And it was with this opera that one can truly say that my artistic career began; and if I had to fight against so many opposing forces, it is certain, however, that *Nabucco* was born under a favorable star, since everything that might have had a bad effect instead contributed in a favorable sense. The fact is, I did write a furious letter to Merelli, so it was quite probable that the impresario would send this young Maestro to the devil; yet the exact opposite occurred. The costumes which were made over for the show proved to be marvelous! And old stage sets, which had been refurbished by the painter Perroni, made an extraordinary effect; especially the first scene in the temple, which had so great an effect that the audience's applause lasted for more than ten minutes!...

"At the dress rehearsal we didn't even know how and when to bring the band on stage; Maestro Tutscht was embarrassed; I pointed out a beat; and at the first performance the band came on stage so perfectly in time with the crescendo that the audience burst into applause!"

There, suggestively conjured up in a distant memory we have the atmosphere surrounding Verdi's first great hit and the peculiar fate that led him to triumph with *Nabucco,* which was given eight performances in March and fifty-seven in August of the same year.

But reading letters and documents of another, less idyllic and sharper tone can perhaps give us a better notion of the actual relations between Verdi and La Scala, which indeed, for almost his entire career, were ones of struggle and tension. To begin with, there was Verdi's peasant tenacity in his relations with all those who, in the world of impresarios, publishers, or business in general, neglected to respect his economic and artistic rights. But even more important was Verdi's absolute insistence on obtaining the maximum results from any performance of his work, together with conditions of maximum concentration in the audience that came to hear it. After *Nabucco,* he set out to repeat the success, using a libretto also written by Solera which again had a Biblical, patriotic subject and created that tumult of ideas and situations, of theatrical music on every level and language which is entitled *I Lombardi alla prima crociata* (1843). During the rehearsals, Verdi excited the company of singers, chorus and orchestra in the manner that the singer Emanuele Munzio (1825-1890) has described:

"He shouted so much that he seemed absolutely out of his mind. He pounded his feet so loudly that you'd think

103

he was playing a pedal organ and sweated so much that big drops splashed on the score... And just a glance from him or a gesture and the singers, chorus and orchestra seemed to have been hit by a current of electricity..."

And he aroused so much devotion in the prima donna Erminia Frezzolini that she swore that either the opera would be a success or she would die right there on the stage. In fact, the company's feelings proved to be right, and the public was so enthusiastic that the opera was given twenty-seven performances. But the operas he wrote after this, most of which were more important and required much greater artistic commitment, such as *Ernani* (1844) and *I due Foscari* (1844), were given to other theaters in Venice and Rome. When he returned to La Scala in February 1845 with *Giovanna d'Arco,* which after seventeen performances became a popular favorite and was played by barrel-organs throughout the city (in fact it appears that one barrel-organ, the largest ever seen in Milan, executed a version of the entire opera), he was so indignant over the way it was staged that he broke off all relations with the theater, and for twenty-five years refused to let La Scala do the first performances of his works.

Thus the whole great phase of the "popular trilogy," *Rigoletto* (1851), *Il Trovatore* (1853) and *La Traviata* (1853), was staged far from Milan. And also the new exploration of spaces, themes and relationships, from *I Vespri Siciliani* (1855) and *Un ballo in maschera* (1859) to the new versions of *Macbeth* (1865) and *Don Carlos* (1867) were all born far from Milan in Rome, Venice, Paris, and even as far away as St. Petersburg, which was the case with *La forza del destino* (1862). La Scala continued systematically to take Verdi's operas from the other theaters, and with great success. But this was because the people loved opera and Verdi was the greatest living Italian opera composer. So this was the tie between them, and in the midst of operas by such ephemeral composers as Carlo Coccia (1782-1873; at La Scala from 1815), or operas from the repertoire by composers such as Otto Nicolai (1810-1849) who in 1841 began his connection with La Scala with the revival of *Il Templario,* which had forty-six performances, and of course revivals of the great names, Rossini, Bellini and Donizetti, Verdi remained a constant and unfailing presence on its programs. But as for the rest, the relationship between Verdi and La Scala seemed to have gone up in smoke. A basic reason for this was Verdi's mistrust of La Scala's methods in staging his operas. Of course, he knew that they had great singers, even singers endowed with fiery temperaments, like the soprano Luigia Abbadia (at La Scala from 1841), or with great musicianship and extraordinary emotional expressiveness like the contralto Marietta Brambilla (at La Scala from 1833), or of exceptional vigor like the baritone Achille De Bassini (at La Scala from 1845), who had in fact triumphed in his opera *I due Foscari*. But he mistrusted the performance as a whole, the seriousness of its minute and coherent preparation. Moreover, La Scala's artistic organization never succeeded in solving the overall problems, even when its management passed from Merelli to Alessandro Corti, then from Cattaneo and Pirola to Augusto Boracchi and, finally, to Alberto Mazzucato, who represented the artists' group in the theater, and gradually, through a number of other names, returned to Merelli from 1861 to the middle of 1863. We know, for example, that Angelo Boracchi was involved in what he called "a high reformatory mission", and that this boiled down to hiring a real dramatist as the "theater's poet", and the mission entrusted to the "poet" was at least "to let the famous singers know to some degree... the subject, action, characters and emotions of the lyrical drama, and impart life and motion to the scenes."[30]

Boracchi was not very competent; what he achieved was an untrammeled luxury in the *mise en scène* rather than an intelligent coordination of the various elements, since he believed in the solemn legend that La Scala had to be pre-eminent at all costs and soon ended by forcing it into bankruptcy without reforming anything. But it should be said that the situation was beyond any simple remedy, since Leone Fortis, the Triestine playwright and journalist who was chosen to be the "theater's poet" under Boracchi, could speak of the singers' absolute indifference to the opera's action, singing the words with no attention to the actual libretto, looking on them only as a peculiar material amalgamated with the notes which their throats had to emit. In the so-called rehearsals many of their performances, Fortis declares, "were reduced to knowing how many times and when in their pieces they had to walk from right to left, or vice versa." But this preoccupation was reserved only for the cabaletta — how many strides they had to take and when "so as to rush from the back of the stage to the front center in order *to attack it* with the most sensational effect." Most often their acting simply amounted to displaying their open palms to the audience, their arms spread wide apart or their right hand resting on their heart, as though it had just been pierced by an arrow. And through all this the singers "not only did not feel the emotions they expressed but had such vague ideas about them as barely to permit a very generalized and superficial distinction between these emotions and those which were diametrically opposed to them". During those years Verdi's *Ernani* was a very popular opera, the manifesto of French Romanticism converted into music and an intense drama by the most powerful Romantic in the Italian theater; in the years that ran from 1844 to 1850 it was performed at La Scala ninety-nine times. Nevertheless, when it was revived on January 19, 1857, Fortis thought quite significant this amusing episode which had the tenor Miraglia (at La Scala from 1843) as its protagonist:

"We were following a rehearsal of *Ernani* and I heard the tenor, who in fact was a featured artist, sing in the recitative which precedes the duet and trio of the last act: 'Does not Elvira hear an infernal snicker? / Which amid the slipshod shadows laughs at me,' so I had to hear him repeat the same absurd word before I could believe my own ears.

"'Pardon me,' I said, 'You are singing: "slipshod shadows laughs at me."'

"'Perhaps.' And then to be sure he hummed the two verses. 'Oh, yes, you're right.'

"'Well, then,' I told him, 'what you should say is "coruscating laughs at me."'

"The tenor stared at me in utter amazement; then, with a gentle smile and a movement of courteous deference, he said: 'As you wish.'

"'I'm not the one who wishes it; it's the meaning which is clear because...'

"The tenor seemed frightened by my threatened explanation and cut me short, saying: 'It's all the same to me; but you can take my word for it, these words change depending on what theater you're singing in. In some places they want them as I sing them, in others as you say.' "After such an argument, I threw up my hands. 'Well,' I said, 'here in the theater of Milan we insist on my version.'

"Generally these were the conditions at La Scala, as they were in fact in nearly all Italian opera houses; and it was very hard to change them, for, as Fortis also has testified: 'Whenever I tried to introduce in the operas the stage movement, liveliness and veracity of prose drama — changing the ridiculous conventionalism which ruled in these matters — I found myself confronted by the same old statement: "But that's the way we've always done it."'" Verdi's separation from La Scala probably also has its roots in psychology and memories. A letter to Tito Ricordi about the lukewarm success of *Simone Boccanegra,* which had been staged at La Scala a few days before, with the intelligent but weak Sebastiano Ronconi (from 1858 to 1859) in the main part, is the occasion for him to express his anger, and his low opinion of it and lack of faith: "The fiasco of *Boccanegra* at Milan had to occur, and it has. A *Boccanegra* without Boccanegra! Cut the head off a man and then try to recognize him if you can! You are surprised at the *discomfort of the public?* I'm not at all surprised. It is always happy when it has a chance to make an uproar! When I was twenty-five I still nourished some illusions and believed in its courtesy; a year later the blinders fell off and I saw with whom I had to deal. Certain people make me laugh when with a tone of reproach they seem to imply that I owe a great deal to this or that public! It's true; at La Scala they applauded *Nabucco,* and *I Lombardi* was done a second time, either because of the music, the singers, the orchestra, chorus, the *mise en scène,* but the fact remains that all these things together made such a fine spectacle as not to dishonor those who applauded. However, a little more than a year before, this same public maltreated the opera of a poor sick young man, who had been short on time and had a broken heart because of a horrible misfortune! All this was quite well known but it didn't help to restrain their discourtesy. Since that time I have no longer seen *Un giorno di regno* and it may well be a bad opera, yet who knows how many other, not much better operas have been tolerated and perhaps even applauded. Ah, if at that time the audience might not have applauded but at least managed to listen to it in silence, I would not have had enough words to thank them! But since it has looked kindly at other operas of mine which have gone all over the world, our accounts are squared. I do not mean to condemn it; I admit the severity, I accept the hisses, on the condition that nobody brings up this matter of applause."

To begin at the Scala, stay there long enough to fight and win a few battles and then leave was a frequent practice for artists in the opera—above all, for the singers, because of the great size of the auditorium and the demands of a rather merciless public as regards execution; but also the composers preferred the working and artistic conditions in other theaters, which were less rich in history and a backlog of great names and were more inclined to welcome the work with warmth and sympathy. The extraordinary fact is that twenty-five years after having left it, and after having composed and staged twenty-four operas, Verdi returned to La Scala to produce two important revisions of *La forza del destino,* 1869, and *Simone Boccanegra,* 1881, the European première of *Aida,* 1872, which in fact was a more important than the première in Cairo, and two new works, *Otello* in 1887 and *Falstaff* in 1893, which concluded his long career. He returned, be it understood, with many demands and determined to dictate all the conditions. And La Scala of those years, first under the management of Brunello and Zamperoni and later of Giuseppe Bonola and others, but above all under the new artistic discipline which gave birth to the orchestra conductor's official responsibility and a new technical and artistic coherence in staging the operas, was able to achieve an unquestionable excellence that met all of Verdi's strictest requirements. Verdi's great concern when he came to La Scala, where the music was handled with firm professional dignity and even brilliance under the guidance of Franco Faccio, was that of the performance as a whole, as a spectacle. In those years, from 1859 to 1899, the permanent scene designer at La Scala was Carlo Ferrario, the creator of La Scala's visual style during the second half of the 19th century. He too was a reconciler, distant from what the Romantics had inherited from the Baroque by dramatizing it, that is, from the suggestive contrasts between the delightful and the grim, but Romantic in his imaginative sensitivity to the relations between colors and, above all, between constructions and nature: a decisive advance in a theater where for many years there were scene designers who specialized either in landscapes or buildings and interiors. Ferrario, who was also a talented painter, understood especially the Verdian conception which insisted on a strict connection between the stage settings and the work, not only through the precise reproduction of the milieu which, if possible, was historically accurate and convincing, but also as a precise concordance between the logic of the score and the logic of the visual suggestions. Other scene designers had worked well with Verdi, even though they might not have been able to give such complete pictorial expression to his ideas; and moreover Verdi was chiefly concerned that the opera's dramatic aspects stand out vividly. Thus his "premières" were shared out between Ferrario (the revival of *Don Carlos, La forza del destino,* and *Otello*) and Zuccarelli (*Simone Boccanegra* and *Falstaff*), and his favorite Gerolamo Magnani, who did *Aida,* came from his native region Emilia and taught at Parma.

As for the execution of the music, which the composer naturally supervised, animating and directing the rehearsals, the impressions which are reported in the histories, memoirs, and newspaper reviews always reflect flattering judgments. Verdi himself was absolutely enthusiastic on March 1, 1869 when he wrote to Piroli: "I have just come back from Milan at midnight. *La forza del destino,* as you must know by now, had a real success. Excellent execution. Stoltz and Tiberini were superb, the other singers good. Orchestra and chorus were divine. How much fire, how much enthusiasm in those crowd scenes!" The execution of *Aida* with Teresa Stoltz (the soprano who later would have an intense and affectionate relationship with him), Waldmann, Fancelli and Pandolfini was, he felt, "most likely incomparable." And yet his

faith in La Scala had not grown very much; and, again in 1877, he mocked at Giulio Ricordi over the mentality of the Milanese audience, which during those days had finally acclaimed Adelina Patti: "You wanted her to have your baptism; as if all the audiences of Europe which have gone crazy over her did not understand anything! Milan... the first theater in the world!... Don't you think that all this looks a bit too much like the Frenchmen's detestable saying *chez nous?*... Then, just between us, come, admit it, six years ago what a mediocre orchestra and what a miserable chorus! Very bad machinery and sets, a horrible lighting system, impossible equipment, in those days the *mise en scène* was UNKNOWN... Ah, well! Today things have improved a bit but not very much, indeed very little!"

Yet what he had faith in was his own presence, at La Scala as elsewhere; and his mind which coherently ordered every aspect of the spectacle, overlooking nothing, as is shown in his letter of August 29, 1872 about the success of *Aida* at Padua, which was written to Arrivabene, a knowledgeable friend, though slightly suprised at the Maestro's great efforts over the *mise en scène* of his operas: "Yes, it matters to me, for it is the proof that the spectacle in itself is interesting, and so they will learn to do it properly in the future. You know that at Milan and Parma I was personally present, and at Padua I wasn't, but I sent them the same chorus which sang at Parma, the same set designer and stage manager, and the same equipment and costumes which had been used at Parma. I sent Faccio, who had conducted the opera at Milan. I was in constant communication with them by letter every day so I knew what was happening — and the opera went well. The theater was packed and they made money."

This coherence in the scenery and stage action was a much different category from the bedazzling spectacular performance so prized by many prestigious opera houses. In an essay of elegant good sense on the problems of scene designing in the 19th century, the authoritative critic Andrea della Corte recalls that Verdi was quite hesitant about an invitation to come to Paris for the production of an opera of his, because of the diverse conceptions, even from those of his own librettist Du Locle, as regards *Don Carlos:*

"Already in 1865 he had deplored the ostentatious magnificence of the *mise en scène,* the 'frame' of the Grand Opera, as a result of which 'the picture was destroyed,' to quote a fiery Verdian image; now he hesitated to accept the invitation of that *'grande boutique.'* When *Don Carlos* was performed there on March 11, 1867, it had, as they say, a *succès d'estime.* He attributed the tepidity to the scant emotion of the singing and the vain attention to scenic ornamentation. 'Up till now all sorts of visual effects and acrobatics; and then metaphysics; later perhaps astronomy — everything, everything, except music.' He wisely concluded: 'Du Locle at Milan will most likely

116-119. L'Italia musicale — here are reproduced the 23rd, 24th, 22nd and 21st numbers of its first year of publication — and the collection of Ricordi character sketches offer us two precious documents which show how Verdi's world is already so different, even in its scenic images, from the previous one. Thus in I masnadieri *the sketches seem to be taken from an edition of Manzoni's novel* The Betrothed, *the clothes evince the great care spent on costumes in this period, and the gestures and scenic elements prove a whole new interest, even though simplified, in pyschology.*

116

118

117

119

120-122. *This same attention, at least to the specific nature of the character, can be seen in the costumes for* Rigoletto, *which were gathered by the Ricordi publishing house. They are drawn to catch the characters, to show what they must express. During the chief years of his creativity, Verdi did not find at La Scala and in its presumptuous, magnificent but dispersive organization the conditions conducive to realizing theatrical credibility; so he preferred to stay away from it.*

# FIGURINI dell' Opera RIGOLETTO del Maestro G. VERDI

120

Rigoletto.  Rigoletto  Cᵗᵉ di Monterone.  Giovanna.  Cᵗᵉ di Ceprano, Marullo, Borsa.  Cᵗᵉ di Ceprano  Paggio

121

Alabardieri. Usciere.  Cᵗᵉ di Ceprano, Marullo, Borsa,  Maddalena.  Sparafucile.  Paggi delle Dame  Segni di Corte.  Paggi del Duca.

122

Al suo venerato ed ottimo amico, l'egregio Avvocato

**ANTONIO VASSELLI**

L'EDITORE

**TITO DI GIO. RICORDI**

# IL TROVATORE

Dramma in quattro parti di Salvadore Cammarano

POSTO IN MUSICA DAL MAESTRO

# GIUSEPPE VERDI

Cavaliere della Legion d'Onore

Riduzione per CANTO e PIANO
di L. Truzzi

Proprietà dell'Editore che si riserva il diritto della stampa di tutte le riduzioni, traduzioni e composizioni sopra quest'Opera. — Reg. all'Arch. dell'Un.

## MILANO

DALL'I. R. STABILIMENTO NAZIONALE PRIVILEGIATO DI

## TITO DI GIO. RICORDI

Contrada degli Omenoni N. 1720 e sotto il portico a fianco dell'I. R. Teatro alla Scala.
FIRENZE. Ricordi e Jouhaud. — MENDRISIO, C. Pozzi, che ne ha fatto regolar deposito al Consiglio di Stato. — PARIGI, Blanchet. —

124-126. *At La Scala the sets and especially the acting in the years from* Nabucco *to* Otello *were, however, different from the imaginations of the designers of the scores, frontispieces fixed gestures, as in the costume sketches for Violetta and Flora in* Traviata. *In short, there is a contrast between the stereotype on the stage, which repeated the typical attitudes of male and female singers even off the stage (as here the famous Teresa Stolz) and the powerful imaginative freedom of Verdian truth.*

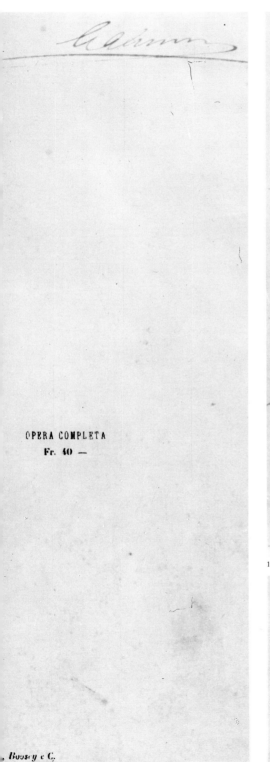

OPERA COMPLETA
Fr. 40 —

Boosey e C.

124

123    125

126

laugh at the *mise en scène*... But let's get things clear — if one thinks that the drama and the music are a pretext for a great display of decorations and costumes, then he is right. But if the decorations and the costumes must serve (as they should) the drama..."[31]

This reforming, extraordinarily exemplary purpose of his was not at all felt in the theaters as a help or a great precedent to be welcomed — a lesson, an opportunity. A letter of 1879 to his friend Countess Clarina Mawei, clarifies his thought on the subject à propos an article which had been sent to him on Massenet's coming to La Scala for the fortunate opera *Le roi de Lahore*:

"Genoa, February 21, 1879

"Dear Clarina:

"Thank you for the small book of poetry by Professor Rizzi which I will read and which I will write to you about later on. Thanks also for the newspaper clippings you sent me, newspapers which I knew because they had been sent to me directly, I don't know by whom. Among these newspapers there was one which said many harsh things... spoke of intrigues, *camarilla,* cliques, etc. If there is something true in all this I don't know or wish to know, but I do know that all this uproar over an opera, all this praise and adulation remind me of the past (it is well known that the old always praise their youth) when, without any *reclame,* without knowing almost anyone, we would present our muse to the public, and if they applauded we would say or we wouldn't say, 'thank you,' and if they hissed, we'd say: 'We bid you goodbye till the next time.' I don't know whether this was good but it was certainly more dignified. Out of all these newspapers, Corticelli had me read one which gave me a lot to laugh about. That newspaper proposed to carve a plaque which would be put up on La Scala: 'In the year 1879 there arrived a foreign Maestro who was welcomed festively and given a banquet which was attended by the Prefect and Mayor. In 1870, a certain Verdi personally came to stage *Aida* and he wasn't even offered a glass of water.'

"At that time I said, what are you talking about, a glass of water, I was lucky not to be beaten with clubs! Now don't take this sentence literally, for it simply means: over *Aida* I had quarrels with everyone, and everyone looked at me askance, as if I were a ferocious beast. And I hasten to tell you that the fault was mine, all mine, because, to tell the truth, I am not very gracious in the theater, and even outside of it. It is because I have the misfortune never to understand what the others understand; and precisely because I don't understand I can never manage to offer one of those mild sweet words, those sentences which send everyone into ecstasies. No; I shall never be able to say, for example, to a singer: 'What talent! What expression! It couldn't be better said! What a paradisial voice! What a baritone! One would have to go back fifty years to find a voice like that... What a chorus! What an orchestra! This is the first theater in the world!...' Oh, but here I'm getting mixed up a bit... Many, many times I have heard people in Milan tell me (even when they were staging *La forza del destino,* which should tell you everything, and one must remember that): 'La Scala is the first theater in the world.' And at Naples: 'The San Carlo, the first theater in the world.' And in the past they used to say in Venice — 'La Fenice, the first theater on the world.' And

129

130

at St. Petersburg — 'first theater in the world.' And at Vienna: 'first theater in the world.' (And as for this, I would go along with them.) And then, in Paris, the Opéra is the first theater in two or three worlds. So here I am left with a deafened head, with staring eyes and open mouth, exclaiming: 'And I, such a stubborn mule, don't understand anything,' and I conclude by saying that among so many firsts perhaps it would be better to have a second. But let's forget the jokes, which, by the way, are really jokes that would make me laugh if I too didn't happen to be an artist...''

In all of Verdi's new activity at La Scala, side by side with the success and the veneration he aroused there is also a certain rebellious wind that has risen out of the new Milanese culture. It is the moment of discontent, of picturesque protest against an official life which in theory should be that of the new Italy dreamed of by the patriots and among whose prophets Verdi could be numbered, but in practice was the bourgeois arrangement acquiesced in by an Italy hastily united through a compromise with Piedmontese hegemony. As is well known, this rebellion had none of the traits typical of profound thought and took its name from the external aspect of the rebels: the "*scapigliatura,*" or, literally translated, "the disheveled ones," which referred more to their hair styles than their thoughts. Yet once the reliquaries of the Risorgimento's revolution had been tucked away in their glass cases, people were comforted by the news of economic improvements caused by the efforts to set up new industries and the building of a new national railway system, and felt equally remote from the ideologies of Romanticism, which had become a spectacle of battlemented towers and battles, betrayals and baritones, handmaidens and big-bosomed, heavily sighing sopranos, while the "disheveled" took Alessandro Manzoni as their easy target in art and in music that other great figure, Verdi. So, amid a thousand contradictions, men of letters like Carlo Dossi, painters like Tranquillo Cremona and composers like Ponchielli dreamed of a pure art and, together with this, the union of all the arts. They enjoyed mocking laughter; they sought out contradictions; they brandished again the names of the first German Romantics, Heine, Jean-Paul, even Goethe. In 1872 Weber's *Der Freischütz* (1821) finally arrived at La Scala. German symphonic music began to be listened to and understood, and German chamber music, too. On June 29, 1864, at two o'clock, the first concert took place of the Quartet Society,[32] which was founded to discover the chamber music repertoire and performed Mozart, Mendelssohn and Beethoven, among which particular prominence was accorded Beethoven's celebrated *Septet*. In opera the name of Wagner began to be venerated, indeed was counterposed to Verdi's, and even in La Scala some people in the top balcony began to mock the *um-pah-pah* in Verdi's accompaniments, that is, the simplicity of that triple time which rhythmically and harmonically supports the blazing

117

131-140. *Verdi's great return to La Scala with his new operas. These pictures are taken from special issues of the prestigious magazine* Illustrazione Italiana, *showing us the main characters in* Otello *and two scenes from* Falstaff, *freely imagined.* *The characters are drawn by Edel, the scene from Falstaff with Dame Quickly is painted in Hohenstein's watercolors, while Amato's cover carries us into a splendid, fluid vision that brings us to the threshold of Art Nouveau.*

131 133 135 137

132 134 136 138

139

140

jet of melody in many of his masterpieces; and people even accused him of having copied Wagner a little because he had begun enlarging the horizon of his instrumentation and was definitively leaving behind the "set pieces" in his operas. It was a matter of bringing themselves up to date, a bit provincial, somewhat exciting, and quite predictable. Among Verdi's harshest critics the most cultivated intelligence and the sharpest mind was that of Arrigo Boito (1842-1918), poet and composer, who in an outspoken toast celebrated the première at La Scala of the opera *I profughi fiamminghi* by the young composer Franco Faccio (which had only four performances):

> To the health of Italian art
> Because it has escaped for the nonce
> From the circle of the aged and the dunce.

And in which he looked forward to the advent of a new music:

> Perhaps he has already been born
> The man who will lift art, truthful and pure,
> On that altar smeared like the walls
> Of a brothel.

And Verdi caught the allusion, reacting quite calmly to it in a letter to his publisher Ricordi: "If I, too, among others have dirtied the altar, let him clean it and I shall be the first to come and light a candle on it."

Now, Verdi's enormous culture, extensive and above all very intense, and decisive in its independence and tastes (above everything, he loved the Bible, Shakespeare and Manzoni, knew and loved Ariosto more than Tasso, had a great deal of the German chamber music in his library, indeed a lot of music he pretended not to know) would have probably been able to give a more intellectual reply to this attack. On the contrary, barricaded in his Emilian countryside or solitary in his room at the Hotel Milan, Verdi never descended into the fray except when forced to by the pressure of friends, and not in order to polemicize but rather to continue imperturbably with his own work. So, during his last years, by now quite old, he expressed his devotion to Alessandro Manzoni, composing in his honor the vastly impressive *Requiem Mass,* first performed in the church of San Marco and then conducted by him at La Scala in a memorable performance in May, 1874, and later on he devoted himself to Shakespeare. But meanwhile the rebels of the past gradually began coming over to his side. Arrigo Boito had already revised the libretto for *Simone Boccanegra.* The Milanese "*scapigliatura*" had already had its brief hour, and the tumults had died down. And Verdi came back to do battle at La Scala. By now the fame and importance of the composer had received so much attention that the newspapers not only highlighted the arguments and hostilities among his adversaries but also clustered around him, as though to protect him, with an emotion bordering on stupefaction. The magazine *L'Illustrazione italiana,* which was published by Treves, devoted splendid monographical issues to his last two operas. Relations with Boito were lively and friendly; when they did *Otello,* the composer had a great deal to say about the libretto, but he was pleased to accept *Falstaff* practically as written. By this time, Boito had made his name as a librettist and poet; La Scala had made a fiasco of his first work as a composer, *Mefistofele,* presented on March 5, 1868, and then rehabilitated it somewhat by ten performances thirteen years later. However, it gave a warm and immediate welcome and fourteen performances to another libretto entitled *La Gioconda* that Boito had written under the pseudonym Tobia Gorrio, which was set to music by the naive and brilliantly gifted melodist, the Maestro from Cremona, Amilcare Ponchielli (1834-1886; at La Scala from 1873) and presented in 1876. This opera set to music all the most incredible, wild Romantic intrigues.

The collaboration and discussions between Verdi and Boito were common gossip, everyone was intensely interested, the nicknames they used for their operas became popular terms, going from the newspapers straight into the people's conversation: *Otello* became "Chocolate" and *Falstaff* "Big Belly." Verdi continued his war on the improvised and the commonplace. When they rehearsed *Otello,* a company of famous singers with such names as Romilda Pantaleoni (at La Scala from 1883 to 1891), the great singer and actor Victor Maurel (from 1870 to 1889), the legendary tenor Francesco Tamagno (from 1878 to 1901) and the conductor Faccio were put through the tense and arduous labors demanded by the never fully satisfied Verdi, as Giorgio Graziosi[33] recounts: "In 1886, Faccio had reassured Verdi: 'Don't worry, Maestro, I will relay to Pantaleoni all the suggestions you gave me in the precious letter I received yesterday concerning the scene in Act II... As soon as Tamagno arrives I will make him study and will pay particular attention, as you wish, to his musical *precision*...' Verdi presided over the interminable and exhausting rehearsals and the implacable old man never ceased inculcating his phobia against any slowness in tempo. 'Faccio,' he would shout, 'don't fall asleep!'"

As for *Falstaff,* here too it was first the affectionate and repeated proposals of friends, later the scrupulous, loyal collaboration with Boito, who was then busy composing the long-awaited *Nerone* (which was a resounding flop on May 1, 1924, when it was staged posthumously.)

"Montecatini, July 7, 1889.

"Dear Boito:

"I told you yesterday that I would write today and I am keeping my promise even at the cost of annoying you.

"So long as one roams freely about the world of ideas everything seems to smile upon one, but as soon as one puts one's foot on the ground, at that very moment of practical action, doubts and discomforts are born.

"When you drew your picture of *Falstaff,* did you ever think of the enormous number of my years? I know very well that you will answer by exaggerating my health — good, excellent, robust.... And it may even be as you say; yet, despite that, I would deserve being accused of great temerity if I took on such a task. And what if I can't stand up under the work? If I don't manage to finish the music? Then you would have wasted time and trouble for nothing! I would not have it so for all the money in the world. The idea is intolerable to me; all the more intolerable if your work on *Falstaff* should lead you, I do not say to abandon your *Nerone,* but to distract your mind from it or to delay the date of its production. I shall be held responsible for this delay, and the lightning bolts of public malevolence will fall on me!

"Now, how can we overcome these obstacles? Have you got some good arguments to oppose to mine? I would like that, but I'm not so ready to believe them. Now let's think of all this (and be careful not to do anything

*141-142. Verdi was a serious, awesome dramatic genius. These caricatures show him bringing up skeletons from the other world in his* Requiem. *On the other hand, Boito was a rebellious, bohemian intellectual — a* Scapigliato — *intent on overturning the world and its pieties.*

*Dies irae !!!*

141

142

*And yet even these pictures make us feel that Verdi was much more cultivated and much more untrammeled in his emotional response than this citified intellectual. The great composer was able to make great art from the small anxieties and disquietudes of culture.*

*143. So Otello and Falstaff were born: "Chocolate" and "Big Belly" as Boito and Verdi used to call them between themselves. Maurel, the first interpreter of Iago and Falstaff, was the first to give life to these characters who, born from the collaboration of Shakespeare, Boito and Verdi at La Scala, will never die.*

to harm your own career), and if you can't find someone to do it and I can find some way of lifting about ten years off my shoulders, well then... How marvelous. We can actually say to the public: 'Here we are again!' To us.
Farewell, farewell"

And finally, the rehearsals: and once again the old Verdi, just like the ebullient young man described by Emanuele Muzio, coherent and very determined, whose spirit and art may have changed but certainly not his constant war against slipshod work, lack of concentration, and also the attitude summed up in the sentence: "We have always done it that way" — which, in fact, during his absence, had often resounded at La Scala during rehearsals, as is described by Giulio Ricordi:

"Verdi's scores are very precise and clear. The clarity of conception which the Maestro had while composing is also true during the period of rehearsals, which have been worked out in advance by him and unfold perfectly according to a carefully thought-out plan, and so the opera is ready long before the time set for its production. It is not true that Verdi is grouchy and displays excessive severity, as is generally believed; in fact he is precisely the opposite. With a kind of military precision he arrives at the theater on the dot, at the time set; but he expects, and quite rightly, that all the artists will be just as punctual, and so he won't brook the slightest waste of time. As soon as he sets foot in the rehearsal hall and has greeted the people there, he immediately gets to work. Verdi is extremely patient, he knows how far the vocal means and intelligence of each artist can go, and he is able to use them to the most advantage. Above all, he demands a clear, precise pronunciation because, as he says, it is necessary that the audience understand and become interested in what the characters wish to express; in a particular verse he marks out the specific word which should catch the listeners' attention, but not simply that — sometimes the syllable which must be pronounced more emphatically. He does not want them to alter the phrase or rhythm with useless grace notes and pauses; he pays attention to every beat, every note. To attain elegant diction he makes the singers repeat a line ten, twenty, thirty times, and he does the same for the exact pronunciation of a word, which not a few times has been altered by the so-called famous singing methods...

"When the musical part is perfectly understood and mastered, Verdi begins to *give color* to the various characters. He shows each singer the type of person he wants them to represent, and so what the vocal and facial expression should be. All the singers then gather around the piano and follow the Maestro's instructions attentively, and try to act them out, while he in a low voice indicates the proper vocal inflections. This is the real point of departure for the *mise en scène*: the singers, surer of their parts, become more lively, and the most intelligent among them even begin to gesture a bit. Verdi observes them attentively, admonishes them, encourages them, praises

143

Al Signor Angelo d'Eisner Eisenhof
ricordo del Falstaff
milano 9 febbrayo 1893
V.<sup>re</sup> Maurel

them, helping them to become even livelier. The parts which had served in the early phase of study have gradually, almost unconsciously, been left on the piano stand; the artist has gained distance from them and is beginning to dress, as the Maestro put it, in the costume of the character. Verdi's eye becomes piercing and never leaves the singer for a moment; then two or three gather about him and Verdi shows them the proper steps, motions, gestures, suggesting and correcting. If a movement or a gesture does not satisfy him, he then takes the place of the character and, declaiming or singing, indicates quite forcefully how it should be interpreted. "From the rehearsal hall they then pass onto the stage; the first sketch of the *mise en scène* then assumes its full development: the voices are joined to the movements, and nothing of what happens on the stage and in the orchestra escapes him. The minute attention he has given to the instruction of the singers, and which he had already lavished on the scenery and costumes, now becomes clear and evident: he is the true creator of his opera, he impresses on it his powerful vitality and so, in a relatively short time, when one considers all the meticulous study of details that has been accomplished, the new work is ready to confront the artistic trial of the first performance.

"Last October Verdi completed his seventy-ninth year, that is, he has now entered his eightieth year, preserving intact a youthful imagination, an iron memory, miraculous energy and vigor: his tall, robust figure, his fiery, piercing look, his long, sure step excite a wonder-struck respect in all who work with him.

"Do you want proof of Verdi's active life?... It will suffice to say what his work schedule was during the rehearsals of *Falstaff*. From nine to ten-thirty in the morning revision of the score, the parts and various transpositions; from twelve-thirty to four-thirty in the afternoon rehearsal at the theater — and many times from five to six o'clock a partial rehearsal with some of the singers in the hall at Hotel Milan — and, finally, from eight-thirty to eleven-thirty in the evening another rehearsal in the theater."[34]

In all the memoirs and histories of the Risorgimento and the fight for Italian independence, writers have always mentioned Verdi and La Scala as though these two names were linked in a sacred and symbolic manner; and, actually, the history of music in the theater experienced, particularly at La Scala and with Verdi, a series of events of proud and prepotent patriotism. It could not have been any different; in the Milan which sought its revenge and found it, La Scala, even independently of Verdi, expressed clear and recurrent manifestations of political will: the theater completely deserted in 1823 for three consecutive nights because of sentences against Confalonieri and other patriots; the Austrian dancer Fanny Elssler forced to dance alone when her dancing company left the stage after hanging effigies of Pius IX around their necks after the Pope had authorized hopes of national unification, which he had blessed; the boxes left empty for the holidays in 1857 in honor of the Austrian Emperor Franz Joseph; the eve of the new war in 1859, with the entire audience rising to its feet during the performance of *Norma* to sing along with the chorus "War! War!" And even outside La Scala, Verdi had gathered about him patriotic hopes, expectations, enthusiasms and furors:

*Ernani,* with its chorus, "If the lion of Castille reawakens," and the *gloria* to Charlemagne changed by the most politically ardent members of the audience into a *gloria* to Carlo Alberto, then the king of Italy; *Attila* and Ezio's sentence, "You can have the entire universe, if you leave Italy to me," which prompted the audience to shout, "If you leave Italy to us," completely overlooking the fact that with that sentence Ezio is preparing a dirty betrayal; *La battaglia di Legnano* and the patriotic delirium it provoked in Rome in January, 1849; Verdi's behavior which was always aware of and actively sympathetic to Italy's cause; and his very name, which with a naive and vivid play on words lent itself to being shouted as a patriotic slogan — "Viva Verdi" being an acronym for "*Viva Vittorio Emanuele Re d'Italia*" or "Long live Victor Emanuel, King of Italy." In truth, Verdi was not very conscious of politics; or, to put it more accurately, if he was skillful in his actions, he was less than skillful in his analyses. He was in fact a fervent Mazzinian and a moderate liberal, a senator of the Italian Kingdom in 1860 who retired to the quiet of his home after having been elected. Certainly he was a man at whom the censorship had looked many times with suspicion; at La Scala he was the man who had composed music to "*Va, pensiero,*" "Go, Thought," and "*O Signore, dal tetto natio,*" "Oh Lord, from my native hearth," the two choruses of *Nabucco* and *Lombardi* which had stirred the hearts and consciences of Milan's citizens. And yet, in the Lombard profile of Verdi the patriot, these operas revealed a thought, indeed a political intuition that meant much more than the decision to make war (in which, as he explained, he did not participate actively for reasons of health), or to attempt to gain control of Piedmont— in fact an attitude somewhat similar to that of Manzoni, the novelist and poet. These two choruses are the prayers of oppressed peoples who have known a united country and harmonious nation and now distantly lament it, or feel a distant nostalgia for it. One of these choruses has a Biblical setting and the other chorus occurs during a Crusade in which a young, innocent woman, at the climactic point of the opera, erupts in an overwhelming tirade in favor of peace. That phrase, "Go, Thought," accompanied the entire Risorgimento: a chorus in one voice but all in unison as in a great popular song that celebrates the beautiful but lost country. And when Verdi returned to La Scala it was with *Simone Boccanegra,* an anguished, tragic meditation on power and also on his own weariness; and then in *Aida* it was with a meditation on vacuous, cruel military stupidity and the conflict in an unhappy slave between the nation and love, a conflict resolved only in the grave and with the opening of the heavens; and in *Otello* a meditation on the passion which must submit to the ruling power in Cyprus, which brings about this passion's defeat; and all is finally brought to a conclusion in the great comic fugue of *Falstaff:* "*tutto nel mondo è burla,*" "the whole world is a joke," "*tutti gabbati,*" "everyone tricked," — the gaily sung other side, in a defiant flight of musical bravura, of the tragic theme of nullity, deceit and insanity which he had already tried to set to music in *Macbeth* and had not succeeded in completing in the abandoned *King Lear*. And it seemed that the farewell in *Falstaff* was his, too; yet six years later La Scala, in an extraordinary concert, heard his *Pezzi sacri* for the first time: that orchestral farewell

*144. Verdi left La Scala with a concert at which was played his* Pezzi Sacri. *It was listened to almost distractedly, after all the honors paid to his last operas. But when Verdi died, all of Milan gathered around his coffin and his spirit.*

which opens with such an immense dilation of sound as though to span the abyss, and with a single voice that repeats three times, stubbornly: "*In Te speravi, speravi,*" "In Thee we put our hopes," like an indisputable certainty, the sole remaining hope of the old, anticlerical, peasant composer. Over his grave in the House of Rest, which Verdi had had built for needy musicians, on February 26, 1901, a great crowd of people sang in low voices: "*Va, pensiero.*" At the dawn of a tragic century, a free and peaceful Milan continued to sing of its beautiful but lost country, using the notes of its Maestro.

144

Whether reasonable or not, everything that occurred in Piermarini's auditorium was in general self-consistent. But what about all that didn't occur? The information concerning the chronology of performances is full of surprises. Why in the world should a ballet like *Giselle,* that masterpiece by Jean Coralli, who danced and taught in the Milan of the Rossibi era, have arrived at Milan only on December 31, 1950, more than a century after its birth? How did it happen that Bethoven's *Fidelio* was discovered at La Scala only in 1927, one hundred and thirteen years after the composition of its definitive version? How can one explain the fact that Mozart's *Marriage of Figaro* was absent from its stage from 1815 to 1905? On what did such choices and events depend? Who made the choices and what were the influences that shaped these choices? It is a dense tangle of events and circumstances, ideas and combinations, in which, if one wishes to orient oneself, one must trust to a few, rather feeble rays of light, and without too much hope of getting to the bottom in all instances, or even of attaining any real clarification. Naturally, La Scala's organization had the greatest importance in all this. As we have seen, those most directly responsible were the impresarios, a category which can be easily ranked as the most powerful, the real bosses of the theater, discontented tyrants who were more involved in balancing the books or making a profit than in anything to do with artistic or humanistic matters, even though they were at times able and curious, as Eugenio Gara has observed:[35] "It was a tyranny which was often hard to bear, yet it was undeniably fruitful. For the most part the impresarios were people of humble origins, uncultivated but extremely intelligent, stingy one day and generous the next, people who did not disdain the ribald or even the delicate and refined, easy to anger, if necessary ready to brawl, though their rancor didn't last too long, astute, calculating, greedy, with all the bad qualities one can name, yet nevertheless they had two fine traits: they understood and loved their profession... They were particularly inspired and intuitive about opera, having characteristics which stood midway between the charlatan and the true connoisseur..."

It has already been seen how influential the great impresarios were both in the choice of singers and composers; and even more so since the direction of La Scala, controlled by the box-owners and the municipal committee in charge of the theaters (which was Imperial until 1859), entrusted the management to these professionals; and among them there were finally a few who had power over all the others, since they were the ones who could deal with the agents controlling the most important singers. The determining effect of a Barbaja or a Merelli had an indirect but decisive influence on the entire history of Italian opera; and also that of a Lanari, a man perhaps more sensitive than the others to the need for a stable artistic level (Donizetti, for example, always referred to him for

*145-146. The impresarios were the major influence on La Scala's life. And they were bolstered chiefly by the composers, especially the Italians, at the expense of a knowledge of Mozart or Beethoven; the music publishers also had similar interests.*
*Barbaja and Merelli represented two worlds and two epochs.*

*Barbaja was an imaginative, capricious tyrant who ruled in the lobbies of the theaters (also at La Scala) during Rossini's time; Merelli was an insinuating adviser. But both men dominated their worlds, backed by the power of organization and money.*

the final corrected version of a score — "the score is the one used by Lanari"), from whom even famous singers asked for certificates declaring that "they had sung under his auspices," the person who, while one of the two managers in charge of La Scala for a year, commissioned Bellini to compose *Norma*. This category became a trifle less important during the last twenty years of the century, when Italy was by now unified, the most famous operas were the sort that guaranteed a well-known repertoire, and the news about how performances had fared ran swiftly from theater to theater. For example, in 1833 Donizetti in Rome wrote to Giovanni Ricordi about the performances of his opera *Furioso nell'isola di San Domingo* in these words: "If you have any news of the *Furioso* at Turin, whether it is true or false, good or bad, tell me, since it is still my child, and I will always say: May lightning strike anyone who meddles with the music of others." Yet the old impresario was still very much alive, as can be seen in a man like Vincenzo Jacovacci, who could still in 1872 write to Verdi, who had complained about the women singers in the company of *Un ballo in maschera* at Rome: "What else do you want! The theater is packed every night. Next year I shall find good women singers, so the opera will still be new for the public. This year you get one half, the other half will have to wait."[36] So until the end of the 19th century La Scala's management responded to the oscillations and expediencies of the impresarios, who certainly were not interested in catching up to the rest of Europe, particularly in a cultural sense, and were little inclined during the most passionate years of the Risorgimento to set off a general polemic against Austrian and German composers. However, in the second half of the century, above all after 1860, independent Italy gave a warm welcome to artists who came from Vienna, so La Scala could admire the dark, impetuous voice of Antoniette Frietsche (at La Scala from 1865 to 1877), whose name was prudently Italianized as Antonietta Fricci, the aristocratic delicacy and fiery dramatic temperament of Maria Waldmann (at La Scala from 1871 to 1879), and the vigorous, imposing nobility of Teresa Stolz (at La Scala from 1871 to 1879), friends and great interpreters of Verdi. La Scala also had to meet the competition of the nearby theaters in Milan, three of which, as we have already seen, were quite important: the Teatro del Re, in operation from 1813 to 1872, chiefly devoted to staging plays but which also staged operas; the glorious Teatro Carcano, in operation from 1805 to 1913, which was the first to put on *Anna Bolena* and *Sonnambula* in the space of two and a half months (December-March 1830-31) and which again in 1893 presented the first Italian performance of Massenet's *Manon;* and its twin theater, the Cannobiana, which was in operation from 1779 to 1894, until the Teatro Lirico Internazionale, set up by the music publisher, Sonzogno, was inaugurated in its place. Of course, La Scala had

greater financial resources; and so it could use its money to outdistance its rivals. The whole problem of how people working in opera were paid is one of the most complicated imaginable. It is almost impossible to find references to a constant form of currency in the different Italian states before the unification, though it is true that a standard exists today by which we can measure past values with some sort of consistency. Moreover, the purchasing power of the money varied from moment to moment and from one currency to the next. Generally, the singers got the highest pay and earned salaries which were about as large as those earned today, relatively speaking. The composers were paid less than the singers, though a famous composer, even if forced to work all the time to keep up with the demand for his operas, managed to live rather luxuriously. The music publishers more and more took over the task of guarding the composers' rights and gathering in their royalties, and so also assumed a large organizational responsibility. The birth of an important publishing venture was always looked on everywhere with favor, above all by the composers, for at that time scores were constantly being stolen and haphazardly interpreted in a slipshod manner, leaving out whole passages and even reworking the instrumentation in certain of its aspects. This partly explains the extraordinary growth of the Ricordi publishing house, which soon succeeded in winning the confidence of the theaters and composers due to the enterprise and organizational abilities of its founders and heirs. Giovanni Ricordi (1785-1853), the founder of the house, was an exemplary representative of that Milanese skilled artisanship which transformed itself into an industrious upper middle class. The son of a glazier, he left his father's not too prosperous business for music. After playing first violin at the Teatro Fiando, he set up a copying office where he prepared the manuscript scores needed for the performances in the opera houses; and then he became, according to the then existing custom, prompter and keeper of the score at the Lentasio and Carcano theaters. In 1807 he went to Germany to study the steel engraving method of printing at Leipzig, with the Breitkopf and Härtel company. He brought back valuable experience and a steel engraving press, with which a year later he founded the "Music Press" in Milan. In 1814 he became copyist and prompter at La Scala with the right to publish all of its scores, and in 1825 he bought its entire archives. After making a number of shrewd contracts with the impresarios, he established good relations with the theaters in Venice and Naples and absorbed such small competitors as the print-shops of Artaria (1837) and Longo (1840).
His company grew very rapidly. In 1842, perhaps on a suggestion from his son Tito, he founded *La Gazzetta musicale di Milano*, a weekly newspaper which carried news and criticism, was modeled on the German and French periodicals and, in the uncertain and contradictory

situation affecting Milanese newspapers and magazines, soon became the most prominent and fundamental, both in its first period from 1842 to 1848 and its second from 1850 to 1859, when Mazzuccato was its chief editor. Yet it exerted a slightly diminished influence during the years when the news media grew because of the development on a national level of reviews, magazines and journalism in general, but it became important again in 1906 under the new name of *Ars et labor,* when its readership was interested and excited by the continuous appearance of critical articles of high quality and the documentation of certain operatic roles (see the sketches it published), which gave it an attractive format. Throughout the 18th century Ricordi's printing plant in Milan, at the start Omenoni, later on the avenue of Porta Vittoria, at the start under the control of the founder, after 1853 under that of his son Tito and, finally, the famous Giulio, Tito's son, a former army officer and a composer of refined taste who wrote under the pseudonym of G. Burgmein, was the center of Italian musical ferment: the proprietors' auditions, discoveries and friendships were on everyone's lips and became proverbial. In 1888, the company under Tito could count 100,000 different publications; they had by now also absorbed the rival publishing house Lucca, which had been launched in 1825 by a former employee of the Ricordi press and folded after many happy experiences and a few bad setbacks (after *Il corsaro* Verdi had left Lucca for Ricordi) leaving a glorious history behind it (particularly the periodical *L'Italia musicale* which in 1848 became *L'Italia libera*). All this was put in the hands of the delightful, competent but rather weary Signora Giovannina, also a figure in musical Milan and therefore important in La Scala's life. The periodicals and newspapers had a consistent effect on the life of the theaters; and some effect on the public, who were not as deeply moved by the polemics about fundamentals as by the reportage that helped to form embattled cliques around the composer and, of course, the singers, too. Critical reviews in the newspapers throughout the life of La Scala and right down to the present day have had an influence chiefly on the decisions of the theater's directors; they really don't affect the public so much as to fill or empty the theater, nor do they decree a success or failure. Moreover, during the 19th century they did not perform a real role in educating the public's taste, remaining either in the area of detailed but competent reporting or in that of polite literature. In Milan music criticism in its most mature form and with a coherent aim was born perhaps with Giuseppe Rovani (1818-1874), a man who was profoundly involved in the political, Risorgimental, artistic and literary life of Milan, and was also capable of grasping certain esthetic truths in a fascinating and concrete manner.[37]

So then, this chain of organizational circumstances determined the choices. It was not a good idea to give performances of foreign works but rather to promote their imitation or re-elaboration, when the promoters were sure that they would not depart from the taste which protected the sacrosanct ascent and affirmation of Italian composers. That all this took place to the detriment and loss of cultural possibilities and of moral exigencies which could have been aroused in the public hardly worried the impresarios, the publishers, or the periodicals tied to the various economic groups; nor did it alarm anyone, so long as the national production of operas remained at a fervent rhythm and a good level. On the other hand, Beethoven and Mozart were not great names in Italy because musical culture was completely oriented towards singing, and above all singing in the "Italian style." The conception that animated the symphonic and chamber music of the great Austrian school was quite remote, as can be seen from the programs of the concerts of symphonic and chamber music, when the practice of holding them had spread.

Culture also had its influence. But culture around La Scala was not so much the culture of academies with an 18th century flavor, by now extinct or reduced to an amusing folklorish survival, nor did it involve debates over the ideas published in the reviews, but it was much more a culture of encounters, of immediate human contact, of the places where people met, discussed and refined their ideas. In this milieu the salons assume a decisive role: these meeting places which were maintained in the houses of refined or lively ladies, with the purpose of welcoming persons and discussions whose echo would spread immediately through the city. Particularly sympathetic to the composers was the salon of Giuseppina Appiani or "Peppina," the friend of Donizetti and Verdi and the patron of young talents, who was a trifle more inclined to vigorous help and frivolous conversation than cultural meditation; also Countess Samoyloff was a close friend of the musicians or, more accurately, close to those who had opted for the Austrian tradition even at the cost of being hissed such as the composer Giovanni Pacini, or the tenor Poggi, who in 1845 was maltreated at La Scala as an Austrian sympathizer during a strange evening in which the last two acts of *Ernani* and *Giovanna d'Arco* were staged and, at the end of his romance, the audience threw sheets of paper at him which looked like laudatory sonnets but turned out to be invective-filled poems in the Milanese folk tradition. In truth the countess, surrounded as she was by a refined and extravagant entourage of carriages, monkeys and parrots, hated and imitated in her tastes, was much more known for her free, voracious habits than for any fruitful discussion of the great developments in opera. But the salon of Clarina Maffei was really a cultural meeting place of the socially alert and the politically deeply involved — her venerated friend was Manzoni, frequent guests were Carlo Cattaneo and Giulio Carcano, the translator of Shakespeare, and a painter like Hayez could meet and talk with poets and composers. Countess Maffei, a very pleasant and gracious woman whose style of life was quiet and subdued, was loved by all of her friends, male and female, was married to Andrea Maffei, the poet and librettist of Verdi's *Masnadieri;* but later on they separated, though still remaining friends, and she then lived with Carlo Tenca, another important figure in 19th century Milanese culture.

All these meetings and discussions in the Milan in which already at the start of the century a profound unification of ideas and actions, economy and art, culture and custom had been attempted under the banner of independence and freedom, helped to impell the world of La Scala, that is, the responsible councillors of the Artistic Commission, to solicit a continual invention and experimentation, though without straying too far from the purpose La Scala had always pursued: to encourage the composing

147

148

147-148. *The culture around La Scala could be found in the salons—bourgeois meeting grounds for amiable, fertile conversation. Clarina Maffei had the most prestigious salon. The ideas which circulated in them also influenced opera's simpler, cruder professionals, like the librettist Piave.*

of new operas; and also, under the political conditions in which Italy then found itself, the unification which had been achieved so differently from the initial Lombard expectations, to welcome Italian operas which had already been presented in other cities. The break with Austria, carried through economically with some reservations, politically with few regrets, was neither labored nor difficult in the field of opera and so was complete for many years. But little came from other countries that was worth accepting. As for ballet, apart from the complex reasons which we will examine later, the notion that it could continue on its own and do it better than all others was never doubted for a moment by La Scala's ballet masters. Thus the culture that surrounded the theater helped to raise its level, or at least to excite new concerns, chiefly among those who had the task of favoring the birth of new works, that is, the librettists. The most cultivated among them, Felice Romani (1778-1865; at La Scala from 1813) developed Romantic themes in a style of trim literary charm and performed the role of the great conciliator, the creator in his librettos of that Scala hallmark which, as we have seen, in *Norma* achieved its loftiest celebration. The hubbub of Romantic excitement around him led him to infuse psychological truth in his characters and to see the chorus as a witness to historic events, and also gave him a feeling for his land and country and the ideal value of loyalty. But even librettists who were less culturally involved proved to be useful to the composers, actually as conduits that helped them take immediate possession of other peoples' discoveries and recreate them, as versifiers of ideas that would become theatrical music: from Callisto Bassi (1800-1860; at La Scala from 1829), Temistocle Solera (1815-1878; at La Scala from 1839) and Francesco Maria Piave (1810-1876; at La Scala from 1848), all librettists of great professional skill who assumed the role of the "theater's poet," taking responsibility for the staging and for maintaining a high artistic level in everything about the performance save the music.

In sum, through all the intricacies of artistic and civil history two concerns and influences are clearly present, conditioning all choices and tastes, activities and productions: an organization which wanted to stage many operas, the best possible, and in such a way that some elements would predominate, generally the singing; and a culture which urged it to experiment with the usual theatrical forms so as to frame the great themes of Romanticism and which also tried to participate as intimately as possible in these adventures. Both — the organization and the culture — were not interested in taking either characters or models from the world, above all the German world. Yet both were stimulating in a creative sense, and this is in fact a constant factor in Lombard history.

*149-150. The dance, which preserves a debonair elegance in the traditional images of popular dance, was transformed in La Scala's ballet into something aerial and astounding through the art of the great ballet stars.*

149

So La Scala in its first century of existence had recognized itself in Rossini: in his vital, overwhelming rhythm which reorganized spaces and thoughts and released the marvels of song. It had welcomed Donizetti, the fervent Romantic who, traveling about Italy and the world, had created characters, recreated history, relying upon the unpredictable circumstances of a changing theater and the force of impassioned melodies. And it had recognized itself once again in Bellini, who with melodious songs in an older manner but with a new understanding, had formed a dramatic reality which transported the audience into a world beyond the everyday, merging Romantic themes and classical composure in a unique lyrical tragedy. It had let itself be conquered by Verdi, the prepotent genius who, out of ancient and contemporary history, voices, choruses and orchestra, had fashioned an infallibly peremptory dramaturgy, a powerful musical and human reality which, for both the audiences and the people, became the song of freedom, the drama of the new age. The world of Rossini and Bellini had been lived out in the spaces and forms conjured up by Sanquirico's stage sets; Verdi's world had achieved resplendent, coherent life on the stage when Verdi himself began to take over completely the preparation of his operas for performance, and when around himself, especially through Ferrario's scenery, he had gathered history, nature and imagination, all set forth with simplicity. The world of Rossini and Bellini, that ample space of soaring inspiration, was matched fully in the dance by the great theatrical art of the choreographer Viganò and his imitators and followers: mythological, historical, fabulous figures set amid a thousand marvels who by dancing symbolized man and his fate, his struggles and his grandeurs. The world of Donizetti and Verdi could have been matched and accompanied by the new Romantic ballet, yet this did not happen. For, curiously but not unpredictably, the ballet, when faced by the great creativity of opera, had many fine opportunities to develop at La Scala, but limited itself to a few great events and a few important figures. The basic reason for this may probably be traced to the pre-eminence of the libretto and its words in Romantic Italian civilization: opera which was at once words and music had conquered the opera theaters (and even when the singers' pronunciation in the intricate passages often made it very difficult to hear the words distinctly, the habit of reading and rereading the librettos made up for this). The lexicon used in the librettos with its marked imaginative and robust suggestivity, gave birth to many forms of folk mythology: the "attacks" of certain romances became proverbial and spawned an infinite number of parodies. But the two components of organization and culture also had a decisive influence in the areas clustered around La Scala. The publishing interests made big profits from the entire operatic spectacle, from all the parts played and sung and from their contracts with the composers, so that they actually made their fortunes from

the opera composers; and, for analogous reasons, the interests of the impresarios were also served by all this. Meanwhile the cultural discourse tended towards the concrete in human problems and a revival of the great European authors — Walter Scott and Byron, Shakespeare, Schiller and Victor Hugo — whom opera made more widely known and displayed in a more congenial light. Then too, ballet, with its shorter time-span and the special physical effort it demanded of the dancers, was less suited to summing up in music the long, complicated narratives which were favored by the 19th century.

Besides, ballet was often by tradition inserted between acts in the opera, and so it was taken as an occasion for a *divertissement* of no great ambition; and so the audience's pre-determined or prejudiced attitude led it to underestimate ballet's expressive function and its possible broader significance. In short, the great passion for ballet inherited from the age of Viganò and his followers no longer centered upon a particular interpreter or dancer and a particular story: namely, upon those elements which by themselves epitomized ballet's fascination and, in a certain sense, the entire life of the time and of society: to epitomize and create, since the summation of the living reality always appears when there is at once something new and prophetic in which to recognize oneself. As a result, the stories in the ballets were more and more reflections, interpretations, or new discoveries in the setting of that Romantic European taste which engaged in discourses on nature, the earth and the village, and transported the unearthly from an atmosphere of simple fable to that of legend, as had been taught in northern lands by the German Romanticism of the beginning of the century, with its Witch-Dancers and its Undines, its confused but suggestive religiosity. When it dealt with earthly creatures, the ballet provided a fascinating occasion that was attractive in itself; and into it flowed the tradition of comic opera, in which the folk dance, even though reinterpreted in academic language, had its place; but there also had its place the free acceptance of folk life presented as the protagonist, counterposed perhaps to the formalistic composure of high society, wearing a military cloak and an expression of impassivity (which is a good setting for striking theatrical effects: the vivacity of the folk contrasted to the patrician immobility of the princes). Yet unearthly creatures also lent themselves to splendid inventions: the body that expresses itself, no longer through conventional symbols as in the sacred Baroque representations but with its own mimetic language, all contained in an aspiration to the heights, the separation from earth, the ineffable free life of the spirit. And in a society which proposed a type of emphatic virility as the heroic model for man to follow, distant from the refined elegance and ductility of classical ballet, the most beloved and representative figure was the ballerina herself.

The great fame of the ballet at La Scala in the middle of the century was therefore due to the presence of three great dancers: Cerrito, Elssler and Taglioni, who, besides being three great artists, with their peculiar technical and expressive development, represented three different concepts of the dance. And the public divided up accordingly, forming into rival factions, to some degree because an artist in a ballet often became an absolute ideal for the enthralled admirer; and, furthermore, because

these three dancers embodied three distinct historic moments, or, rather, three ways of interpreting what history contained or suggested.

Fanny Cerrito (at La Scala from 1838) was a blue-eyed blonde with an attractively curved body. Born in Naples, she was naturally endowed with a roguish sensuality which was as innocent and native to her as anything truly vital and was almost rowdily boyish. That was perhaps why a delicate poet like De Musset was enchanted by this woman, who for him made "Milan less boring than Florence",[38] and also why the academic supporters of absolute composure in the dance saw red when her name was mentioned. (Luigi Rossi, in his already quoted book on ballet at La Scala, reports a typical epigram of her naive enemies: "If a butterfly can leap and prance /Then Fanny Cerrito can dance.") And, finally, this was why she was certainly the dancer of the period whose likeness was most often drawn by painters and etchers. She began her career at La Scala when she was about twenty-one, dancing with Monticini, Galzerani and Vestris, and she was then in her initial phase, that is, she had not yet learned, following in the footsteps of Fanny Elssler, the secrets of a dramatic dance that portrays character. But she already showed not only a strong, very communicative personality but also that special trait which the critic Fedele d'Amico describes, in regard to its historical position, as "standing at the junction between the pure ideal of Romantic ballet and the virtuosic affirmation of free dance."

In 1841 La Scala signed up Marie Taglioni; and so the Milanese public could finally see the *ballet blanc*, *La Sylphide*, which had caused a furor in Paris and was created by Filippo Taglioni, with a rather poor musical score. She was a resplendent sight: the long white tutu, the face masklike, whether radiating joy or soft and sweet in sorrow, the arms sinewy and supple, the body spiritualized and the technique of "elevation," springing straight up onto the tips of the ballet slippers, not only revealed an unearthly creature, the Sylph, born from the dreaming Romantic spirit, but also the new image, the new task of the Romantic ballet dancer who, vibrating in the air and rising up purely, symbolized the purity of the soul and the ideal.

On May 29th Taglioni made her first appearance at La Scala; on June 8th La Scala's orchestra played a serenade in her honor beneath the windows of the Hotel Marino. The balletomanes who followed Cerrito were reduced to a minority; but, of course, they were still vocal; and one evening there was a confrontation at La Scala. After a new performance of Verdi's *Lombardi* in which Frezzolini sang, Cerrito performed three solos from the ballet *Viaggiatori all'isola d'Amore*, Taglioni replied with variations from the *Caccia di Diana* and a "*pas de deux*" from *The Sylph*; Cerrito then replied with a "figure" from the comic ballet *Gli Inglesi nelle Indie ossia La scimmia riconoscente*, and in *La Gazzetta* there was a report of the event:

The Celebrated

PAS DE QUATRE

COMPOSED BY JULES PERROT

As danced at Her Majesty's Theatre, July 12th 1845.

BY THE FOUR EMINENT DANSEUSES.

Carlotta Grisi Marie Taglioni Lucile Grahn & Fanny Cerrito

152. The ballet of the mid-19th century begins in the world of grand ballet and yet separates from it with Sanquirico's scenery, as shown here in the scene of the Palace of Venus in the ballet Pellia e Mileto *by Salvatore Taglioni, developing feminine gestures and roles.*

153. Marie Taglioni, the initiator of toe dancing at its loftiest, most transfiguring expressiveness.

153

133

154. Fanny Elssler, a great ballerina of the most earthy inspiration, ostracized at one point only because she was Austrian.

155. The artificer of the new dance at La Scala was the ballet Maestro, Carlo Blasis. Surrounding him in this print are the pupils and gestures which show us the new ballet language based on elevation from the toes.

154

"A rivalry of curtain calls, a fury of applause, such a storm of shouts and uproars in the audience that a deaf man would have been given a headache. Verdi was acclaimed; Frezzolini, Taglioni and Cerrito were acclaimed. The fanaticism of the audience was incredible, but even more incredible was the patience of those who had first set foot in the theater at three in the afternoon on Monday to procure a good seat and were still there at two-thirty on Tuesday morning, watching the last leaps of the 'grateful monkey'."

Cerrito and Taglioni left; Taglioni returned in 1842 with the ballet *L'ombra*, about the ghost of a dead creature who returns to search for her beloved, the perfect role for her, since the dancer was indeed the ghost of herself; in short, if not a decline, the feeling was that of a farewell. Then Fanny Elssler arrived. Thirty-four years old, she was already fully experienced and greatly skilled. Eight years before, in 1838, she had made an appearance at La Scala, but without leaving the slightest trace. Elssler had then gone to Paris to contest Taglioni's success; and there, too, created two factions. The violence of her interpretative tensions, the physical attractiveness of her body, which was less soft and sinuous than Cerrito's, the wild, virtuoso dancing abetted by a temperament which made immediate contact with the audience, was welcomed and applauded. But she was an Austrian and after that one famous night in 1848, though nothing in her had changed, nobody at La Scala wanted her again. However, La Scala's immense international prestige was based on something else, less popular but every important within theatrical life itself: the ballet school of Carlo Blasis who, together with his wife Annunciata Ramaccini, taught from 1838. This great Maestro intervened in all the disputes about dramatic themes and ballet theory; but above all he strove to achieve what Levinson, in his book on the famous ballet masters, defined as trying "to pilot the bark of classical ballet to the shores of Romantic ballet."[39] During the period in which he had a stable contract with La Scala, that is, until 1850, and even after that in his sojourns in Milan and his trips throughout Europe, Blasis exhibited the interpretative skills of a whole series of marvelous students of his: among whom can be numbered Fanny Cerrito and Carolina Rosati (at La Scala from 1846 to 1847); Amalia Ferraris (at La Scala from 1841 to 1868) who had dazzling successes in Paris and whose body, which was matched by a beautiful face, was described by the critic of *Théâtre* as "formed of air and dew"; Sofia Fuoco (at La Scala from 1844 to 1853) with a stormy temperament and absolute security on her toes, and such other great stars as Carolina Pochini and Caterina Beretta, who will later connect the period of the grand Romantic ballet to that of the great fashion for Romantic ballet. But in Vienna, St. Petersburg and Paris the tradition of ballet was older, more festive, grander; and many of Blasis's students, successful ballerinas at La Scala, were destined to leave

156-158. *Carlo Blasis taught from 1837; for twelve years he was associated with La Scala, then for a number of years he would return every now and then. The taste for ballet in Milan underwent a change, becoming less mythicized, more ordinary and less popular. Carolina Pochini, highly acclaimed star,*

156

I. R. TEATRO ALLA SCALA

Le Rappresentazioni dei più aggraditi Spettacoli d'Opera e Balli in corso, (a scelta e distribuzione dell'appalto) verranno continuate per altre quattro sere consecutive, in tre delle quali ballerà la signora

# FANNY ELSSLER

Verrà anche nella prima di dette quattro sere posto in iscena un nuovo *DIVERTISSEMENT* di Ballo in due parti intitolato

# VENERE ED ADONE

in cui la signora ELSSLER, ed il signor MERANTE saranno i protagonisti.

Si apre per queste un'ABBONAMENTO di L. SEI Austriache per tutti indistintamente, e da pagarsi in via anticipata.

Milano, dal Camerino del Teatro suddetto il 21 Marzo 1845.　　　　Tip. Troßi.

I. R. TEATRO ALLA SCALA

Dovendosi per le necessarie prove ritardare l'andata in iscena del Nuovo Ballo fino a Giovedì 19 corrente, l'Appalto interessò la signora MARIA TAGLIONI ad anticipare la prima delle otto rappresentazioni, ed essa si produrrà Sabbato 14 corr. Marzo in un *DIVERTISSEMENT* espressamente allestito dal sig. FILIPPO TAGLIONI.

Il *DIVERTISSEMENT* sarà composto del celebre passo a quattro inventato a Londra sulla musica del Maestro PUGNI da M.r PERROT per le signore TAGLIONI, CERRITO, GRISI e GRAHN, ed ora eseguito dalla signora TAGLIONI suddetta, GALLETTI-ROSATI, VENTE e FUOCO, eseguito da un ballabile finale in cui avranno parte, oltre le suddette Artiste, la signora WUTHIER, e le allieve della I. R. Scuola di Ballo.

Milano, il 12 Marzo 1846.　　　Tip. Valentini e C., Cont. de Borromei, N. 2838.

# AVVISO

L'Impresa deve portare a notizia del personale addetto al servizio di questi II. RR. Teatri la formale ingiunzione abbassata dall'Onorevole I. R. Direzione dei detti Teatri con riverita nota 8 corrente N. 510-2, che, cioè, *resta assolutamente inibito ai signori Virtuosi ed Artisti primarj, secondarj, o di basso servizio, si di canto che di ballo, il prodursi sulle scene con barba o mustacchi, quando ciò non sia portato dai rispettivi figurini, e questo sotto comminatoria delle misure di rigore, a sensi del vigente Regolamento per la polizia del Palco scenico.*

Milano, l'11 dicembre 1852.

*L'Impresa degli II. RR. Teatri*

# PIROLA e CATTANEO.

157

*introduced the second half of the 19th century; while the world welcomed Blasis's students, such as Sofia Fuoco, not knowing or caring that the name on her birth certificate was the very Milanese name of Marietta Brambilla.*

SOFIA FUOCO
nella
Tarantella

the theater for greater triumphs abroad. A student of Blasis, at least privately, was the magnificent Carlotta Grisi, who in 1841 with the splendid *Giselle* by Coralli and Perrot, synthesized the two worlds of Romantic ballet in a story which brings a young girl enamored with dancing to the center of a village's life. She then dies of love and is transformed into a wili, a dancing spirit in a white tutu, still able, though dead, to lovingly communicate with the prince who deceived her, when he appears at night at her grave, and who would have died at the hands of the other wilis if Giselle had not saved him by prolonging his dancing until dawn. But Grisi did not dance at La Scala; and *Giselle,* whose story was interesting in itself, arrived at La Scala two years after its birth, but with the new name of *Gisella* and the choreography by Cortesi and the score by Adam completely refashioned and patched up by Bajetti; and it should be said that the definitive, authentic version arrived only a century later. Far from Milan, dance experienced its most glorious hour, and actually the very kind of ballet which had been born in Milan. Marie Taglioni was the daughter of the choreographer Filippo, who had been Viganò's leading male dancer; and the theaters of Europe acclaimed, under the adventurous name of Sofia Fuoco, a dancer who in reality was born with the indelibly Milanese name of Marietta Brambilla.

158

The history of La Scala should now be thought of by keeping ideally before you not a stage set but one of those transparent curtains which hang from the proscenium and behind which the melodies and gestures of the music drama, the history of politics and culture, of taste and art, of science and technical advance seem to take on space, solidity and life — in brief, a view of all of history. This is a period which is one of the most decisive and dramatic for Italy. Unification had been achieved under the House of Savoy, and at the end of the century Italy found itself free and independent, as they put it in those days. The life of the factories began to spread an awareness of the problems that go hand in hand with the development of classes and the first wealth gained by the others from an industrialized existence. The South's development was neglected and it continued in its position of hardship and passive economic inferiority. Literature had left behind the phase of intense, wide-ranging European dialogues and had bent down to take a closer look at regional life in its own country. The figurative arts had begun to struggle out of the sentimental, decorative backwater in which they had taken their ease. The great patriotic tensions had somewhat relaxed and the satisfaction over the victories won was gradually changing into a consideration of how far the ideal was distant from reality in the everyday life organized under a stable, by now entrenched bureaucracy. The experience of a true communal life began to grow with the development of common work; the newly built railroads shortened distances and brought people together. Elementary education began on a large scale in schools set up by the government...

From 1857 on, La Scala was given its own large square, which in fact disrupted the beautiful play of proportions that Piermarini had invented: that portico projecting as on a roadway, not so that it might look like a monument but in order to welcome and invite Milan's citizens to enter the theater's splendor. Since the 1851-52 season that wonder and splendor had increased because of the dazzling use of gas lamps, which actually on the inaugural evening, when Verdi's *Luisa Miller* was presented for the first time at La Scala, made the stage look dark, since it was still lit up by oil lamps. But not many more changes were made in the great Milanese theater. In 1879, the vault was painted in a monochrome and artificial panels and rose windows were added; and this was the greatest change. Everything was left in its original state because La Scala wanted to represent tradition, the attained goal, no longer the theater of its own time but Milan's theater for all and every time, untouchable, born from the great beauty of the 18th century and now become the symbol of the victorious Risorgimento: the theater of Rossini, Bellini and Verdi. So, in the second half of the 19th century, in this beloved and imposing hall which reminded one of certainties at the very moment that certainties were beginning to crumble, and of an im-

159

160

memorial life at the very moment that life was inexorably changing, La Scala once again tried to "reconcile." This time it meant being hospitable to international taste, in fact the French and German experiences, adapting them to its own dimension and in its own spirit, and in accordance with certain affinities or differences. This led to immediate cultural advantages and obvious mystifications. On the organizational plane it gave rise to fervid, generous initiatives which were to have long-range results; and on the creative plane it stimulated a completely new sort of opera season, the period of *Verismo,* whose intentions and many of its esthetic effects could be debated, yet it undoubtedly was original, a style in which the unified Italy in the long run saw itself mirrored. Thus while the creative parabola of Giuseppe Verdi was still in progress, coming to its grand conclusion in the rediscovery of Shakespeare through the operas *Otello* and *Falstaff,* there took place a number of complex, extremely intricate developments which, though differing profoundly in their origins, intentions, and the paths they intended to blaze, were nevertheless part of the same atmosphere, the same taste and social customs.

The first development, the most subterranean but also, eventually, the most evident, was the growth of the orchestra's importance. In La Scala's history the orchestra, until the middle of the 19th century, was hardly at the center of attention. For the performance of operas there was no real conductor; the rehearsals for singers were entrusted to the composer himself or to the "*maestro al cembalo,*" that is, the harpsichordist, while the orchestra followed the lead of the first violin. There is, however, a prestigious tradition surrounding the harpsichordists that was carried on by Giacomo Panizza and Giovanni Bajetti from 1833 to 1852; and another excellent musician, Alessandro Rolla, was "first violinist and leader of the orchestra" from 1803 to 1837. A January, 1834, letter of Donizetti's to Duke Visconti, who was then in charge of the Imperial Theaters, pointed not only to an uncertainty in the conducting of the orchestra, but also showed that La Scala, when it came to the efficient arrangement of the instruments, was behind the times as compared to other important theaters. "I hear from friends who have written to me, that you are upset by the new arrangement of the orchestra in the Royal Theater of La Scala... I, more philosophically, would not be upset but would simply reply that in all the leading theaters the orchestra is arranged in this way, and this way of dividing (a little more, a little less) the instruments is not without its reason; if a true advantage did not result from it, we would then have seen a return to the first arrangement. The principal quartet of the orchestra,[40] being gathered together at the center, can in turn lead the rest of the instruments, and the composer who finds himself in its midst and next to the first violin,[41] has (whenever he wishes) the advantage of giving the principal, both with his voice and his gestures, the indication of the tempos

161

he desires, a very advantageous thing in terms of the present taste."

The composition of the orchestra was practically the same throughout the first half of the 19th century and, except for some increase in its members due to specific circumstances (the number of tubas playing Wagner; an increase in percussion instruments; and the addition of such instruments as the saxophone, xylphone, and so on), it remained the same in its overall composition until the 20th century. The orchestra that Verdi considered "normal" was composed of fourteen first violins, fourteen second violins, twelve violas, twelve cellos, twelve contrabasses, one piccolo, two flutes, two oboes, two clarinets, two bassoons, two trumpets, four French horns, four trombones, two harps, kettledrums, bass drum and cymbals. After 1854, the task of leading it was in the hands of a "concert master," Alberto Mazzucato, who in the course of the successive seasons was flanked by Giacomo Panizza and Francesco Pollini; from 1858 to 1859 these names went on the placards and programs, and from 1867 on, the title of "Concert Master and Conductor" was bestowed. But the first person to carry out a real reorganization of the orchestral situation was Franco Faccio (1840-1891), who supervised the rehearsals and the conducting of the operas from 1871 to 1888. He was a fine conductor and had succeeded Eugenio Terziani (at La Scala from 1868 to 1871) on Verdi's recommendation. He was also the unlucky composer of *Profughi fiamminghi* (1863) and of *Amleto,* which flopped in 1871 after having had a fair success in Genoa, and who then dedicated his musical knowledge to this interpretative task. He immediately proved his mettle in two events: the European première of *Aida,* which had a fantastic success with the public and the critics, and the première at La Scala of Weber's *Der Freischütz.* The next year it was under his baton that Wagner began, with *Lohengrin,* his long, inevitable and generally fortunate career at La Scala, despite the difficulties of the first encounter. Franco Faccio also had an important insight, feeling that the moment had arrived to institute a regular series of symphonic concerts. Until then, La Scala had welcomed concerts only as occasional events, either to celebrate some extra-artistic event in a solemn manner or to salute the art of some extraordinary interpreter: for example, Niccolò Paganini (at La Scala from 1813 to 1827) or Angelica Catalani (1816 and 1823), and the violinists Rolla, Bazzini, Bignami and Remeny; or the cellist Alfredo Piatti (1841), Johann Strauss's orchestra in 1871 and La Scala's orchestra in 1875, with Franco Faccio conducting. There had been glorious moments, too: Rossini's *Stabat Mater* in 1842, right after it had been played in Paris; and in 1864 Verdi's *Hymn of the Nations* with lyrics by Boito in 1864; while Verdi himself had conducted Rossini's *Messa Solenne* in 1869 in memory of the composer's recent death, and his own *Requiem* immediately after its first performance in the cathedral

# PARSIFAL
## DRAMMA·MISTICO·IN·TRE·ATTI
## DI
## RICCARDO WAGNER

of San Marco at Venice. And there had also been curious moments, with a touch of amiable originality: in 1861 a concert of *glasspiel*, or musical glasses, played by the Neapolitan virtuoso Comigio Gagliano; and in 1874 a concert of the orchestra of Viennese Ladies conducted by Madame Amann Vienlich. But these shows were not too different, as exceptional offerings, from the prose plays on the program — memorable in November, 1860 were the performances of Adelaide Ristori in Giacometti's *Giuditta* and Metastasio's *Didone abbandonata;* or from the festivals, for example, on April 10, 1864 there was actually held an "Italian and Savoyan Tournament" presided over by Prince Umberto and for which Maestro Faccio composed a fanfare played by trumpeters on horseback, who gave the signal for the start of the events, which included running with javelins at targets, jumping over hedges, and various other feats on horseback. The organization for a permanent presentation of concerts was completely lacking; and lacking, too, was the will or need to explore symphonic music. It was Faccio who set up the organization, and so after 1879, for the first twenty years under the auspices of "La Scala's Orchestral Society," later under the "New Society of Symphonic Concerts," and finally as a simple emanation of the *Ente Autonomo,* the name for La Scala's incorporated directing body, the organization of the performance of symphonic music was granted an independent life. It was difficult to ascertain what the cultural contribution of the series was at the beginning, since the programs were as alien to our tastes as it was possible to be and indeed were almost wholly determined by the taste of the period. The first season at La Scala, with four concerts in the spring of 1879 conducted by Luigi Mancinelli, opened with the symphony from *Nabucco* and included Rossini's posthumous *Chinese Polka,* obtained from some mysterious source, Ponchielli's prelude to a romance for baritone, Boccherini's *Minuetto* for a string quartet (announced as the "Famous Minuet") and, as it went on, passages from operas, a symphonic intermezzo by Mancinelli composed for Cossa's play *Cleopatra,* the encore on request of Ponchielli's prelude, and so on. Something closer to symphonic taste as we understand it today was heard a year later, with the concerts conducted by Franco Faccio: two sections from Mendelssohn's stage music for *A Midsummer Night's Dream,* an adagio from a quintet by Mozart, most likely transposed, and at the last concert in 1881 Beethoven's entire *Septet* and in 1882 passages of Beethoven's symphonic music (the *Andante cantabile* and *Scherzo* of the 2nd Symphony), the entire score of Beethoven's Seventh Symphony at the first concert in 1883, a great deal of music by Italian opera composers (such as Rossi and Foroni), Godard, Goldmark and Cowen, an aria by Bach, other minor and major operatic composers, and finally a movement from Mozart's Symphony in G minor in April, 1884. And so on, until there began to appear in 1890 a bit more of Beethoven, a bit of Wagner and other predictable famous names, when the Orchestral Society got a permanent conductor, Giuseppe Martucci, who was succeeded over the years by Charles Lamoureux, Vittorio Vanzo and, in 1896, Arturo Toscanini. And yet this new phase of playing symphonic music had already become a gust of enthusiasm and a commitment, a lesson. Armani and Bascapè[42] recall these beginnings with a pleasant touch of nostalgia:

"Soon after being born, La Scala's Orchestral Society, which was under the direction of Giulio Ricordi and was composed of one hundred and twenty musicians, launched into a fascinating adventure. In 1878, on the invitation of President Gambetta, it went to Paris where the festivities for the World Exposition were under way, and played at the Trocadéro. First amazement, and then a tempest of applause. It is said that the President rose from his seat and embraced Faccio, shouting, '*Voilà les zouaves de l'orchestre.*' After Paris, the orchestra traveled to London and Strasburg, went time and again to Switzerland, and made several tours of Italy. (When patrons for the tours were not to be found, the musicians would foot the bill, taking on the risks themselves; in those days idealistic motives counted for something and people were ready to give up a little money for an 'ideal'.)

All this new attention to the life of the orchestra, which coexisted with the interest in singing, for the first time in Italy focused on the idea that there might be an alternative to opera, in which the dramatic structure consists in the roles, which the voices define. So now listening pleasure shifted more to the orchestra, not as the mediator between the world of the opera's characters and the audience's responsiveness but as a beguiling protagonist in itself. Of course this shift followed and accompanied Richard Wagner's first successes at La Scala. For though it is true that in Wagnerian opera the singing had great importance — and La Scala from the start sought great or good interpreters for these casts — yet it is also clear that an overwhelming sense of novelty and discovery was aroused by Wagner's use of the orchestra, starting with the remarkable prelude to the first opera presented at La Scala, *Lohengrin* (seven performances in March and April, 1873), which must have seemed to an audience accustomed to Italian and French opera a scandal, an incomprehensible game, or a downright marvel. Presented by a cast in which the protagonist was the eclectic Italo Campanini (at La Scala from 1871 to 1873), who had already sung it in the memorable Italian première at Bologna a year and a half before, together with two other firstrate singers, Gabrielle Krauss (at La Scala from 1872 to 1873), a limpid and tragic Elsa, and the famous baritone Victor Maurel (at La Scala from 1870 to 1889), destined to become the first Iago and the first Falstaff due to his refined and intelligent interpretative skill, who sang the part of Telramund, *Lohengrin* nevertheless had a rather disappointing and greatly criticized welcome. Yet these debates quite clearly established from the start, both in the experience of opera-going and the history of La Scala, that Wagner loomed as the absolute alternative to the world of Verdi. Produced again as late as 1888, *Lohengrin* fared a trifle better and was given seven performances; and, finally, in March 1889, it broke through with seventeen performances. From then on Wagner was assiduously present: *Die Meistersinger von Nürnberg* inaugurated the next season with sixteen performances, *Tannhäuser* opened the 1891-92 season and received fourteen performances. Since 1888 the season now ran only from December 27th to May and so repetitions were less numerous than in the past, even in the case of enormous hits. But there were more Wagnerian revelations: in December 1893 *Die Walküre,* in December 1896 *Die Götterdämmerung,* and in December 1898 *Die Meistersinger,* again without any cuts and with Toscanini as the conductor. But one must go right down to 1927 before the entire *Ring* cycle was presented under the baton of one of the theater's most adept collaborators, Maestro Ettore Panizza (at La Scala from 1922 to 1948).

The second obvious development was that of a profound, irresistible change in the mode of singing. This is the period of the most resplendent star-worship; and soon there will be joined to the voices of those who have gone to the theater and the voices of the newspapers which described what happened there the voice of the phonograph record which had just begun its long history. But both technique and interpretation signalize and go to meet a new historic moment in music and custom, which is above all a scaling of the heights of eloquence, vocal power, dazzling bravura. Julian Gayarré (at La Scala from 1876 to 1888) triumphed in *La Favorita, Les Huguenots* and *I Puritani* and prompted the critic of *Perseverance* to say that he was a "genius of singing" and the last of the Romantics, with his well-balanced singing and his naturalness as an actor. Destiny is now on the side of powerful throats capable of peremptory, ringing notes; like the voice of Francesco Tamagno (at La Scala from 1877 to 1901) who had, moreover, a stage presence of imperious, tragic nobility; and those singers who in the past would have tried to mature their voices so as to make its timbre more homogeneous and would have trained their artistic expressiveness by the methods of the traditional school, now tended to force their voices to get startling effects with hugely stentorian, impassioned phrases. Adelina Patti (at La Scala from 1877 to 1878), who was engaged at a fabulous salary to sing in a series of operas from *La Traviata* to *Il Barbiere di Siviglia, Il Trovatore* and Gounod's *Faust,* with her exquisite clarity and the native beauty of a voice of astounding freshness, was the last enthralling interpreter to entrust the whole expression of her soul to the musical lines. But she already marked the passing of an epoch, presenting herself as a "light lyric" soprano, that is, no longer attempting the daring feat of combining coloratura tones and dramatic consistency, and by her example eclipsing definitively, at least for several generations, the figure of the dramatic coloratura soprano. The dramatic was in the process of becoming something else; there had begun the period of Gemma Bellincioni (in 1886), and of singers who fulfilled the expressive task by "cries and sudden flarings," as Eugenio Gara has written, at the price of a kind of pomposity, of effects which, to avoid academic artifice, could easily become sheer melodramatic artifice. Of course this type of singing and this taste in the audience, which was accompanied by the appropriate acting style based on obvious, heavily accentuated, hammy gestures, as though the singers were being swept away by an overwhelming passion, also has an influence on the fate of the operas being presented. Quite singular indeed is the fate of French opera in our theater, for the most magniloquent, melodramatically striking and congenial to vibrant, plangent voices were in fact works in the French "Grand Opera" style, and they were brought with unwavering enthusiasm to La Scala's stage and were fervently applauded. For example, Halévy's *La Juive*, which, with a fair cast, had eleven performances in 1865, and then, with a better cast, inaugurated the following season with twenty performances, and four years later reached a grand total of

twenty-three performances, while Meyerbeer had a middling success with *L'Africaine, Robert le Diable* and, above all, *Les Huguenots,* though the mounting of these operas was not as full of stage machinery and suggestive scenic effects as was the custom in Paris, nor were the mediocre set designers of the period able to imagine the composer's intentions as the great Sanquirico had been able to long ago in 1828 for Meyerbeer's opera, *Il crociato in Egitto,* with the stately, extraordinary image of a ship surging forward on the crest of a wave and appearing to hang right over the audience's head. On the other hand, the other great creation of French opera, the light "Opéra-Comique" style, genial, critically outspoken, with vocality and spoken recitatives, was welcomed when it could be transformed by a somewhat deceptive, expansive interpretation in the Italian style, and recitatives that had often been set to music hurriedly by some third-rate composer. So both the composers Adam and Boïeldieu were never presented; Hérold's *Zampa,* after fifteen performances in 1835, was repeated in 1889 with Maurel as the star and had ten performances; Auber's *La Muette de Portici,* already given in 1839, was staged again in 1868 (four performances), but not for example *Fra Diavolo.* But the revolutionaries of the Opéra-Comique had a special fate: Charles Gounod (1818-1893; at La Scala from 1862), who in 1859 had scandalized and astounded with his opera *Faust,* when he came in 1877 to La Scala to help produce *Cinq mars* was already famous because of forty-six repetitions of his masterpiece in three different versions and twenty-three performances in two different versions of *Roméo et Juliette;* but he found a fourth-rate company and the outcome was not a happy one (six performances, hardly a great success). But when *Faust* was translated into Italian and sung with Italian expansiveness (even by tenors who were not Italian, such as Nicolini and Valero) it became one of the most frequently staged operas in La Scala's entire history. Also Jules Massenet (1842-1912) had received a warm welcome when he came in 1879 to produce his *Le Roi de Lahore* (twenty performances) and *Le Cid* which inaugurated the 1890-91 season was applauded and liked (fourteen performances); but his two most famous operas, *Werther* and *Manon* had a different fate, both being staged by the "régisseur" Band during the 1894-95 season, when he also presented a third, very successful French opera, *Samson et Dalila,* which would have many performances and many different productions (it was approached more from its spectacular side than as the religious oratorio its composer Saint-Saëns had imagined). *Werther* had only six performances and disappeared until 1932; and the disquieting *Manon,* after two performances, was withdrawn and reappeared with some regularity only at the beginning of the 20th century, though still in a much different tone from the voluptuous, subtle nonchalance of its actual score. But the most significant case was that of Georges Bizet (1838-1875). Apart from *Les pêcheurs de perles,* which was always enormously liked, *Carmen,* the opera which in 1875 had marked a violent, striking, and open break with tradition because of the crudity of its recitatave and a singing score that could attain the tragic though arising out of situations and melodies that were usually linked with the light operatic theater, was a completely transformed opera when it arrived at La Scala in 1885, where it had, and has had since, great success, or at

163

164

least has stirred up greater excitement than is reflected in the number of performances. The dialogue had been set to music by Guiraud, with an impassioned, eloquent, expressive accent and the voices were all in a plangent, pompously rhetorical register. A few more years, and then the voices and gestures in this opera would conform to the prevailing tone established by *Verismo,* as expressed by the soprano and tenor team (also husband and wife in real life) of Gemma Bellincioni and Roberto Stagno. Thus in Giorgio Graziosi's extremely significant essay,[43] one finds this opening paragraph:

"In its October 6th, 1890 issue the most important Italian review, *La Nuova antologia,* published an 'Ode for *La Cavalleria Rusticana*' by Guido Mazzoni. There are the 'taut nerves' of the violins, the 'vibrant pipes' of the woodwinds, and 'Lola's eyes flaming with love'; there is Turiddu, 'who in his fatal ruin blindly falls dead'; and finally the peroration:

> José, you too have thought of revenge,
> You welcome this pale Santuzza,
> This Turiddu, transfixed, pierced like you
> Whom Carmen welcomes.

"In this encounter of these four figures in the empyrean of universal art imagined by the inflamed poet one fails to see, Antonio Baldini concluded in an amusing, evocative essay in his book *Lettura* (1943), Lola and Escamillo, linked by fecklessness, who 'stroll off arm and arm through the cactus plants and leave Alfio banging his whip in a fury of spite in the dust...' The fact is that the future historian of literature, the very young Mazzoni, also was quick to associate the main characters of *Cavalleria* with those of *Carmen*. And here in this association, the knots of the *Verismo* theater are immediately entangled in the teeth of the critical comb..."

*Verismo* in the theater and outside of opera is tied to literary *Verismo;* in fact, *Cavalleria rusticana* was born as a short story by Giovanni Verga, and he himself adapted it as "a scene from folk life" for the stage and for Eleanora Duse, the actress of the new reality who was separated by a gulf from the academic style of acting. And generally when one says *Verismo* one evokes a whole movement of the second half of the 19th century which has behind it Auguste Comte's positivistic philosophy, history viewed from Bismark's perspective of political realism, the interest in science and in certainties which can be briefly experienced after so many upheavals suffered in the name of lofty, unverifiable ideals. What appears the decisive attitude in literature is the narrator's renouncing of all commentary on the events narrated, almost as though these events were not merely the dominant but actually the sole objective truth; and even at the cost of heightening the colors and especially the color gray, like Emile Zola, or of submerging oneself lyrically in all of one's characters, like Giovanni Verga. But the experience of *Verismo* opera, which was born in Milan between *Otello* and *Falstaff,* has completely different characteristics and an entire story to itself, except for certain intentions and criteria hastily inserted in the musical productions. An extremely problematic, precarious, naive and original period, *Verismo* should be taken as a whole, as it attempts for the last time to entrust song to effusive, confident emotion in an immediate appeal to the listener, expressing all the anxieties, shadows, illusions and contradictions of a dying century that fleetingly presaged the revolution in attitudes and the world which the 20th century would carry through. At bottom, there is a desire for the truth, even for verisimilitude to a degree that the operatic form, in which all the characters sing, cannot possibly give. Verdi himself had opened a path in *La Traviata*, not followed but still quite significant — the portrait of the persons and classes of contemporary society, deeply examined, perhaps even to redeem it, but beyond all myths and distant allegories. In Verdi, too, there is the preoccupation to present the theatrical spectacle stripped of the usual trappings which disturb the illusion of living in the stage world; and two letters, one to Giulio Ricordi in July, 1871, the other to Edoardo Mascherini in December 1893, proclaim the necessity not only of removing the boxes that protruded upon the stage but also of making the orchestra completely invisible; the latter even at the cost of accepting an idea from his not too well liked colleague, Richard Wagner. And in Verdi, too, there is basically no renunciation of a spontaneous, open faith in his profession, for when Umberto Giordano, while composing *Madame Sans-Gêne,* was worried about how to present the character of Napoleon, the old, wise man calmly replied: "It's simple: just make him sing." But how to make the characters sing, and how to compose music in those years was by now a wholly different problem from the one Verdi had confronted. Alongside French and German operas, the musicians had on their stands chamber music, beginning with Lieder, while, gradually, the region of Russian opera was being explored; Brahms is added to the first discovery of Tchaikovsky, who is now composing; and Chopin is accompanied by Franck, Fauré and Grieg. The young Mascagni writes from Milan to Soffredini, the Maestro at Leghorn, about the prelude to *Guglielmo Ratcliff,* which he has just begun composing: "This is a style of composition which I would almost call Wagnerian. It is the Milanese style; somebody who is not here cannot realize what sort of music is most liked." That is the Milan of this period — Boito is the intellectual who collaborates with a group of recognized journals, writing cultivated and bizarre poems which they publish; but he also collaborates with both Verdi and Ponchielli, an enthusiastic provincial who for the last time made use of heroic, sentimental 19th century myths and at the Conservatory had been the teacher of Mascagni and Puccini. In the theaters, the drawing rooms, everywhere, people discuss the new in Italian art. Italian short stories and novels with regional and folk settings seem to meet and mingle with the books of Zola and of French Naturalism at the print shop of the publisher Treves. Verga lives in Milan, Verdi lives in Milan, and above all the publisher Sonzogno is living through his great vogue there. Edoardo Sonzogno, the heir of a publishing house, began his musical activities in 1874, calling in as his artistic adviser and aide Amintore Galli, the music critic for the newspaper *Il Secolo.* Out of this collaboration came collections of opera transcriptions for the piano, anthologies of favorite operatic pieces and French opera, among which *Carmen* stands out prominently, published from the score of its first Italian production at Naples in 1879. Then the Sonzogno Contests, run by the magazine *Teatro Illustrato,* began; the second contest was won by Mascagni's *Cavalleria Rusticana* and in 1890 the opera triumphed at Rome. From then on, the robust, immediate, violent, and colorfully

*165-166. A composer from the* scapigliatura *group, teacher, at Milan's Conservatory, of both Mascagni and Puccini, Ponchielli launched himself upon the serious adventure of* I Lituani; *he became very popular with his opera* La Gioconda, *which from its première in 1876 to the First World War was given 91 performances, all enormously successful.*

165

166

folkish became esthetic categories, moral exigencies, and recipes for success. In 1894, the Sonzogno publishing house bought the old Cannobiana theater and transformed it into the Teatro Lirico Internazionale, which became La Scala's most important and least inhibited competitor, the theater which represented what could at that moment be regarded as the new spirit of the times. And the imaginary worlds sought each other out, intertwined and pursued each other through the streets of Milan: Puccini in the houses and cafés frequented by the literary men searched for librettists who would create for him the new story of Manon from the old novel by Abbé Prevost; Leoncavallo caught up with him in the De Cristoforis Galleria Café, offended because he had snatched the idea of the stark, colorful world of Murger's Bohemia, and the two bards of the tender Mimì started a furious brawl.

It was still the fashion to feel oneself at the center of the world and to try to respond in one's own way — by creating; and everything in the world was the object of attention. The Universal Expositions throughout Europe suddenly launched the fashion of the Orient; it was an encounter in reality which had slowly ripened; for some time now, the people active in Italian culture had lumped Flaubert's *Salammbô* together with the novels of the French Naturalists. Meanwhile Art Nouveau, reacting against the academicism of mannered painting, burst forth in elegant, tortuous fantasies and luminous, variegated colors which seemed to be connected with the Orient: in short, the so-called "Liberty style" descended upon Italy. And musical *Verismo* in Italy is a style that wanted to encompass and justify everything, experiencing it through its sensibility. Thus, in the new singing styles, the new predominance of the orchestra, music in the manner of *Verismo* and its composite hallmark grows and expands. *Verismo* is the solar, searing climate of *Cavalleria Rusticana,* since the passions of the chief characters are bluntly, unconsciously true. *Verismo* is the below-the-bridge scenes of Puccini's *Tabarro,* with its barge on the Seine. But also *Verismo* is the French revolution in Giordano's *Andrea Chénier,* and even Puccini's *Madama Butterfly* or Mascagni's *Iris,* with their Oriental oleography, since they seem to reproduce faithfully, like the illustrated cover of a magazine, documented milieux and elementary emotions. And everything is aimed at that rather tired, rather lazy bourgeois who has an inclination to passivity and fanciful, escapist entertainments, and regards with a curious eye and listens with a satiated ear to the crack of Alfio's whip and the rattle of Parpignol's little cart.

This whole faithful, naive, sometimes foolishly reckless creative ferment was born and developed chiefly on the fringes of La Scala, having its temples in the Teatro Lirico and Teatro Dal Verme, places which were by their very nature more adventurous. La Scala took its stand with perennial tradition; it accepted the most successful novelties, from *Cavalleria Rusticana* to *Andrea Chénier,* but always with a tardiness, holding back and keeping its own counsel for several years. And when it came to favoring the birth of new works, it followed an even more significant itinerary, not so much as an indication of precise intentions as in terms of the choices actually made. At the very start, La Scala naturally welcomed Amilcare Ponchielli, who had an official position at the Conservatory and collaborated with excellent literary men, from Ghislanzoni and Marco Praga to Boito. In 1874 *I Lituani* had a good reception; in 1876 *La Gioconda* had only four performances but was triumphant, and in 1880 a new version of it refurbished by the author reached fourteen performances. In 1885 *Marion Delorme,* a final attempt to find a new path for a story from Victor Hugo, was well received by the public, but the harsh criticism it evoked gave it little chance of success over the long run. But Ponchielli is still in advance of *Verismo,* which had its concrete manifesto in *Cavalleria Rusticana.* During the initial years of *Verismo,* La Scala had pursued a goal, or, more accurately, ran after a myth, which was that of reviving the themes and atmospheres of the original German Romanticism in a wild, unconventional or serious key. A typical figure of this "*scapigliatura,*" or rebellious climate, is Alfredo Catalani (1854-1893; at La Scala from 1883), the pale-faced son of a headmistress of a girl's school whose patron was Giovannina Lucca. After his operas *Dejanice* (1883), full of castles and madness, and *Edmea* (1886), about a great love in feudal Bohemia, which had a fair success, he conjured up the world of water nymphs on the Rhine in an opera entitled *Loreley,* composed for Turin, and wrote an opera, *La Wally* (1892) from a short story by the Baroness von Hillnern about the myth of snow and ice and the creature who withdraws to that world. But, unfortunately, he died the next year. A figure typical of the serious approach was the Baron Alberto Franchetti (1860-1942; at La Scala from 1888) who put his strong, unshakable knowledge into *Asrael,* composed for Reggio Emilia and presented by La Scala for its inauguration of the 1888-1889 season. Strictly for La Scala and always with a good reception, he refurbished German myths and made a couple of attempts to invest the world of prose drama with his Germanic harmonies and orchestra, using an old subject by Molière and a new tragedy by D'Annunzio: *Fior d'Alpe* (1894), *Il Signor di Pourceaugnac* (1897), *Germania* (1902), *La Figlia di Iorio* (1906), *Notte di leggenda* (1915), all respectable compositions but destined to disappear from the opera stage; and, finally, *Cristoforo Colombo,* written for Genoa but staged at La Scala and accumulating fifty-seven performances in four seasons, whose memory was prolonged thanks only to the puppets of Carlo Colla's company at the Teatro Perolamo. As for Pietro Mascagni (1863-1945; at La Scala from 1891), his experience at La Scala was significant. He was asked to present his first opera *Guglielmo Ratcliff* (1895), full of gloomy, jealously guarded castles and a heavy tinge of the Wagnerian, but he abandoned these phantoms in 1889 to participate in the Sonzogno contest with the extremely diverse folk vitality of *Cavalleria Rusticana,* and on the wave of this notable success (twelve performances) he appeared the next year with *Silvano,* a typical folk sketch in the *Verismo* manner. But the succeeding operas he gave La Scala for first performances were only those distant from this type of realism: *Parisina* (1913), in which he set to music the text of D'Annunzio's tragedy, and *Nerone* (1935). It cannot be said that D'Annunzio had any great esteem for his composers; he considered Mascagni, for example, "a juicy subject for chitchat." However, his presence at La Scala is an indication of one of the cultural orientations which prevailed at the beginning of the 20th century. In 1915 Pizzetti composed *Fedra* from D'Annunzio's play, in 1916

Zandonai's *Francesca da Rimini* was brought from Turin, and already Luigi Mancinelli (1884-1921; conductor at La Scala from 1879) had offered *Paolo e Francesca* again, after its première at Bologna. In any event D'Annunzio is much more prized as a source by the composers of the *Verismo* movement than Verga, who, after Mascagni's success, said that he was interested in further adaptations, though he still felt unready to follow that other path of theatrical innovation and of the popularization of his works which was then coming to birth and was destined to wipe out this particular function of opera almost completely — I refer to the cinema. This position of Verga, which was expressed in two letters in December 1909, preserved in La Scala's Museum, is a significant indication of how rapid by now the rate of change had become in the theatrical world.

It was also a question of environment, presentation and social image. The crude, fat, mustachioed and talented rival of Puccini, the *Verismo* and Wagnerian Ruggero Leoncavallo (1858-1919; at La Scala from 1894), succeeded in getting his *I Medici* (1894) staged, even though the year before it had not been received very well at the Teatro Dal Verme and was in fact an uncertain musical anthology on the Italian Renaissance with a Carduccian flavor. Yet he never had any first performances at La Scala, even though his *Pagliacci* was to become the most frequently presented opera of the 1926-1927 season as soon as it was staged there. But Umberto Giordano (1867-1948), the image of a fine Southern Italian gentleman, who dealt with passions in the language of *Verismo* — now in the French revolution, which devours its own children, now in Russia, which symbolizes the common universal sorrow, and now in the decorative fictions of Sem Beneli and Giovacchino Forzano — was given premières not for *Mala vita* or *Mese Mariano* but for *Andrea Chénier, Siberia, Cena delle beffe,* and *Il re* in 1896, 1903, 1924 and 1929, respectively. Also for the interpreters there came into play this significant choice with a sort of bourgeois tinge, meaning by bourgeois precisely that class and mentality which had narrowed the aims and doused the enthusiasm of the Risorgimento and, at the end of an epoch of fervent hopes which had lasted for almost a century, though not completely satisfied, had defended the privileges which it had gained. La Scala in this period had a very bourgeois way of thinking, almost a category of spirit and custom: "*Scaligero*" or "*Scala-like*" became an adjective to qualify an artistic offering, though with a slight feeling of pity for what this "Scala-like" could not accomplish through a lack of real excellence and that ineffable something which those who worked there knew quite well, even if they were incapable of defining it. Toscanini will propel this bourgeois mentality towards another concept: the concept of excellence in the service of art, of a guide that orients one, a quality that must be consciously sought. But real quality was not wholly lacking. Already in 1900-1901, when Toscanini was just beginning his career, there was an extraordinarily successful and fortunate season which, among other things, was marked by a double debut: the debuts of Enrico Caruso and Fydor Chaliapin.

The first singer came directly from his successes at the Teatro Dal Verme; and he was greeted with great frigidity at the inaugural performance of *Bohème*, as an insignificant little tenor who was trying to bite off more than he

167-168. *A new world, the world of Italian composers straddling the 19th and 20th centuries. The pale Catalani and the bespectacled Pizzetti are shown in these photographs—Catalani seems lost in his dreams of ancient legends, while Pizzetti seems entirely engrossed in his meditations.*

167

168

169-170. *Equally in keeping with their music, Pietro Mascagni and Umberto Giordano in impressionistic portraits which also convey a physical presence and an affable cordiality, a sanguinity only broken by the picture's dimensions.*

171-172. *Yet over all this hovers the secret presence of Gabriele D'Annunzio. The poet launched the fashion of sultry erotic passion, as expressed in* Francesca da Rimini *or in* Parisina *(172), both operas with sensual music.*

169

170

171

PARISINA ◉ DI PIETRO MAS
CASA MVSICALE LORENZO SONZ

173

174

# N Lescaut
## G. Puccini

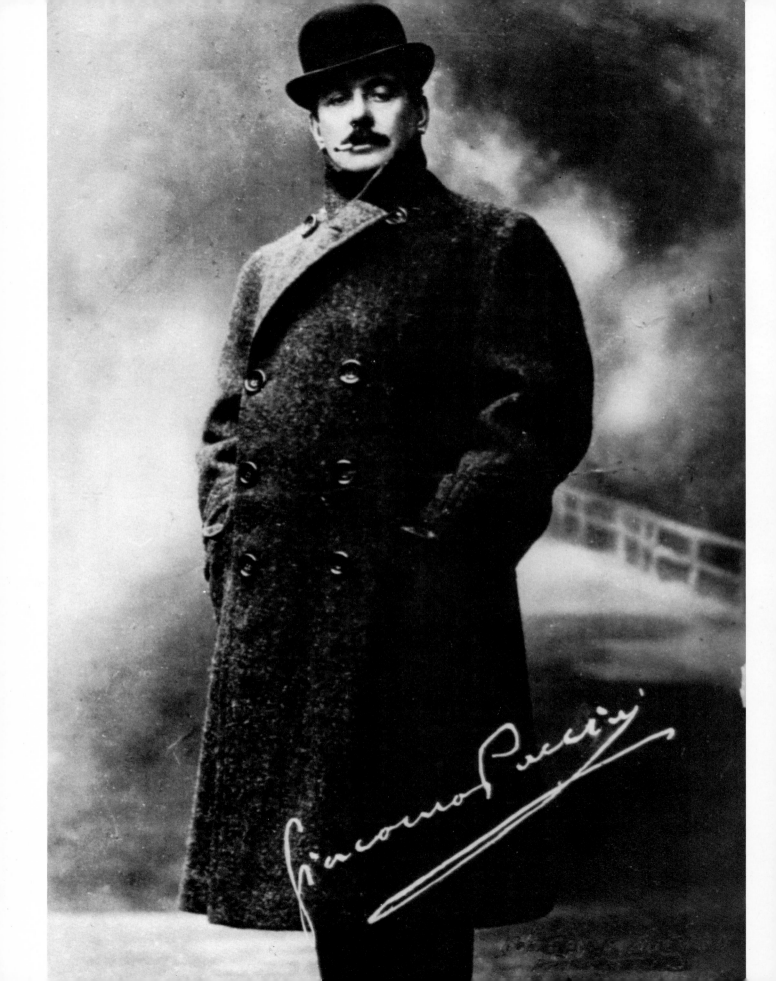

Giacomo Puccini

could chew, and only subsequent performances finally made him attractive to the audience, correcting the adverse judgment of the première. Nevertheless this will be Caruso's only season at La Scala, despite his incredible vocal feats in *L'elisir d'amore,* which are still discussed, in Mascagni's *Le maschere,* at the concert held at the time of Verdi's death and, finally, in Boito's *Mefistofele.* On the contrary, Chaliapin, who was the same age as Caruso and had come from far away, was immediately given a totally different importance and evaluation. His singing in *Mefistofele* set off waves of enthusiasm, and so he returned in 1909, bringing *Boris Godunov* for the first time to La Scala; and after that he often returned to sing, right down to the memorable *Barbiere* conducted by De Sabata in 1933.

This La Scala attitude was not only characteristic of the theater and its directors. For example, criticism, which began to influence opinion due to the fact that people were reading more and culture was reaching a broader group, participated fully in the much debated Milanese première of Mascagni's *Iris,* and it offered many reservations. But usually the critics praised the great musical and artistic "progress" when it came to operas like *Cavalleria Rusticana,* which had had a better fate. And so the audience, the theater and criticism all together had their effect on Puccini's curious and significant treatment at La Scala's hands. For Giacomo Puccini (1850-1924; at La Scala from 1885) seemed to present La Scala with a special case, and it behaved towards him in a rather standoffish and cautious manner, despite the initial success of *Le Villi* (in 1885, the year after its first performance at Dal Verme, with thirteen performances), and despite the very important patronage of Ricordi. In 1889 La Scala presented *Edgar,* taken from a verse play by Alfred De Musset, still less congenial than the story of the *Villi* which, even if it came from France (also the ballet *Giselle* had been written by Gautier; and in France the dancing nocturnal spirits were rather popular in the 19th century), was still a theme from the first phase of German Romanticism: a common point of departure for the followers of *Verismo.* Yet, in the short space of a few years, Puccini made a triumphant stride forward with *Manon Lescaut* (1893) and *Tosca* (1900), which was rehabilitated after its uncertain success in Rome; and then his success grew with crescendo-like speed with the staging of *La Bohème* (at the beginning of the 1900-1901 season). But it was now both natural and necessary to request a totally new work from the Luchese composer; and this was *Madama Butterfly,* presented on February 17, 1904 and one of the most terrible flops in the history of Italian opera. Among the many causes of the disastrous evening, aside from understandable prejudices, ineptness in the staging, and the lack of an intermission after what is now the second act, there occurred a secondary episode that has always been described as an example of "color", of a "misplaced bright idea". This was the use of a few extras hidden in the audience armed with melodious nightingale whistles to render more suggestive the awakening of nature in the prelude to the third act (which followed the nonexistent intermission and was therefore an intermezzo). Soon the entire theater was chirping, the spectators began to imitate other animals, and the situation got completely out of hand. The audience protested against the banal device, either because of its strangeness or because it was really offended, since La Scala often boasted of its touchy, susceptible audience. But if one examines the curious and contradictory history of the musical theater of the period, this awkward, bizarre attempt to put the audience in a real garden, when the feigned Japanese Orient was actually the occasion for precious relations between melody and harmony, and when the elementary plot was taken as a pretext for a delicate and colorful web of impressionistic nuances, it seems to be the pathetic and amusing extreme to which the ingenuity of Puccini and his advisors went in order to reconcile the thousand refractions of the changing times and an art that tried to recreate this time through the precepts of scenic "verisimilitude." The very next day, the opera had already been withdrawn.

La Scala's reconciliation with Puccini took place soon after. In December 1907, there were thirteen performances of *Tosca;* in December 1912, a work new to La Scala was presented, *La fanciulla del West,* and was given fifteen performances, with a company of singers now admirably trained to achieve the *Verismo* tone and at the same time vocal and musical élan: Galeffi, Martinelli, and Poli-Randaccio, conducted by Serafin. Through many repetitions of other Puccini operas we finally reach his last "première", a posthumous one — *Turandot.* The atmosphere surrounding the rehearsals, if one credits Ugo Ojetti's acute little account in his book *Cose viste,* presents us with an entirely different Scala: Toscanini is in charge, passionately intent on obtaining the highest artistic results, Puccini is respected as a great Italian composer who can be ranked with the best, and a mood of intense, nervous expectation has been created before the opening, with the singers playing Turandot and Prince Calaf, Rosa Raisa and Miguel Fleta, respectively, immersing themselves utterly in their parts.

"At the rehearsals of *Turandot,* Michele Fleta, the tenor who sings the part of Cafal, wears a dark maroon overcoat, close-fitting, Spanish-style and rather old-fashioned; Rosa Raisa wears a fox fur coat and a short red dress, in line with fashion and custom. But Fleta standing at the foot of the royal staircase, each time young Clausetti hits the keys of the piano on the left, shakes his shoulders as if he felt a flick from the edge of the silk garment Caramba is sewing for him; and Rosa Raisa, going up and down the stairs, the frigid, very cruel virgin, is already giving little graceful kicks so that you can imagine Turandot's green and interminable train. The rehearsal continues. The female chorus in the sort of tunics worn by plasterers, the male choristers in pajama jackets, all of the same color as a mark of obedience, cluster and break up, kneel and rise at Forzano's command: 'Now be careful, ladies and gentlemen, please be quiet, for God's sake. Run, I said run. Didn't you hear me? Ladies and gentlemen, what are we doing? Oh, good God, let's start all over again. Now, you sopranos, watch your step. Please, be quiet." He is shiny, black, sweating. At every word his hand tugs at his hair; and he makes movements to set his glasses in place. When he comes from the gangway he stands among us in the orchestra and wrings his hands. He looks like a mechanic who, having gotten down from his locomotive, is looking for a water tap to wash his oil-dripping hands and sotty face. He goes back up at a run. Fleta is standing at the head of the gangway and asks him: 'When can I go and eat?'

176

177

"Up there, on the stage, turning their backs to the theater, three gentlemen are seated on three poor church chairs. The man on the right is writing, writing, writing on a scrap of paper stolen from one of the Sybils: this is Carlo Clausetti who took care of the stage direction for the Roman production of *Turandot*. The man at the left, massive and silent, with a conical, towering cranium, is Scandiani. If he stands up he seems able to hold them all back, like an iron curtain. Of the man in the middle we can only see the slim torso wrapped in a shiny jacket of black alpaca, and the part, all the way down to his neck, of his silvery shock of hair. Suddenly he leaps to his feet. This is Toscanini. He takes off his glasses and rushes over to explain to Raisa and Fleta the right way to make their theatrical movements and gestures. When he is Raisa, he stretches out from the top stair over her lover in a gesture of challenge and hatred. When he is Fleta he crouches in a pose of desperation, imploring. He is a perfect actor but he is not satisfied to act, he wants to persuade; it is his miracle to translate art into logic and technique, and from logic and technique create art so that the most carefully studied technique disappears in the melody of the orchestra and the logic dissolves into passion and everything seems natural, born just then, in a sudden burst and sweeping us away. Now the choruses come in and he stands alertly behind Veneziani (the director of the chorus), who beats the time using his arm like the pole of a semaphore without the hinge at the elbow. Now he lifts it rigidly above his head; then down quickly so that it touches his leg. Not Toscanini. It seems that he has before him an invisible music stand, and though his arms are beating the time, they climb, stretch, twirl about. Besides he also sings, and taps out the rhythm with his foot. Maestro Veneziani is not wearing his collar and his pinkish baldness is so placed that we in the orchestra, when he turns his back, think we see the haughty face of a gentleman with a round, black beard; but that face is his back of his skull. "Rest. In the silence we can all hear Fleta asking Veneziani: 'When can I go and eat!'"

At the first performance on April 25th, when they reached the death of Liù, where Puccini had left the score unfinished, Toscanini stopped the orchestra. He turned to the audience and announced that the opera was ended, for at that point Maestro Puccini had died. At that moment people thought with emotion of the death of "poor Puccini," as it was then the custom to say in the period immediately after death; and it was a just tribute of devotion and affection and also a kind of farewell to a measured and alert interpreter of a society which was becoming more and more isolated and unconscious of itself. But the death of Liù was also the death of many other things: the death of a now distant *Verismo,* the death of the time in which new operas were the very basis for La Scala's programs; and the time, too, when the very profession of opera composer was still a viable one.

MADAMA BUTTERFLY

(DA JOHN L. LONG E DAVID BELASCO) — TRAGEDIA GIAPPONESE

DI L. ILLICA E G. GIACOSA • MUSICA DI

GIACOMO PUCCINI

G. RICORDI & C. EDITORI

Two things were striking about the style of acting at this period and they gave a new aspect to La Scala's spectacles. The first was the broad, passionate sweep of the gestures, much more agitated than in the Romantic period and with a more explicit charge of sensuality or truculence. The second is the firm establishment of all the dramatic details of these operas, which seem to be indissolubly tied to the unfolding of the music, the settings, images and gestures, so that even today Verismo operas still retain this dramatic specificity.

179-181. Interesting testimony to the first aspect is contained in the three pictures, opposite, of Eugenia Burzio in Gioconda, so different from Romantic heroines, so tense in the expression of violent emotion, and not, as in Romantic operas, immersed in a dramatic or tragic situation which is summed up in the gestures, or idealized.

179

180

181

182-183. *Also the gestures of the stupendous Salomea Krusceniski and the opulently endowed Maria Labia in Strauss's Salomé exhibit the same mobility, trusting wholly to the music, and give one the feeling of a changing time.*

184. *Even Verdi's Otello (here depicted in a drawing from* Illustrazione Italiana, *which devoted an issue to the opera) though not having dramatic and musical characteristics in common with this epoch, can be seen as reacting favorably to this Verismo atmosphere in its acting style.*

182

183

185. *These pictures of Puccini's operas are quite representative of the second aspect of the acting style and mounting of Verismo operas. Miglioli's set for* Il Tabarro *in 1959 followed the stage directions in the libretto scrupulously and exactly.*

186-190. *Although involved in performances of* Bohème *at such different periods, the Mimìs sung by Maria Labia, Renata Scotto, Rosetta Pampanini, Gabriella Tucci and Mirella Freni wear similar costumes and strike much the same poses.*

185

186

187

189

190

188

191-195. *Since its first production, Mascagni's* Cavalleria Rusticana *has been done with a remarkable constancy as regards the poses and gestures of the singers in the main roles. This atmosphere is expressed by the original interpreters, Bellincioni* and Stagno, *taken here from a poster in La Scala's Museum which was displayed in an exhibition on* Verismo; *an atmosphere which also surrounded the production of* Carmen *(in the photo, Enrico Caruso).*

191

193

192

194

Alfio also makes the same violent, tense gestures in every period. Gian Giacomo Guelfi urged on by director Franco Enriquez (193) will repeat these gestures under the direction of Giorgio Strehler (195). Gino Bechi (194), even in the calm of a meditative moment, one hand on a chair, nevertheless opens his other hand in this same manner. These are all expressive means or technical modules which cannot be departed from when creating the world of Verismo opera.

195

196-207. *La Scala at the end of the 19th century. The building is unchanged, the fascination of the auditorium seems to have increased, with parades of beautiful gowns at the premières, elegance and excitement in the lobby. Operas, now and then a festival ball, once even a tourney with horses.*
*And the work of the people backstage, the stagehands and*

196

199

197

200

198

201

technicians, the splendid display of the carriages. Poor people come in flocks to stare at the rich and privileged. Even those who are not so well-off participate; but they are fewer in number and seated in the top balcony.

202

204

205

203

206

207

*208-211. Invitations to the balls, souvenir calendars, even the pages of the newspapers with the critics' reviews are all gay in tone. La Scala is the temple of art and the refuge of high society,* *a consolation for the impending calamities of a century coming to an end.*

208

210

209

211

212

213

# CHAPTER 9. BALLET'S EPHEMERAL APOTHEOSIS

Thus, during the first years of a unified Italy, opera tried to achieve an ultimate, untrammeled abandonment to the eloquence of song. And if the stardom of the singers, the assurance of the audience, the fertility of the composers, might lead one to think that this was a felicitous period, the truth still is that what one sees is not so much strong certainty as a continual change in objectives and interests, though always with the same assurance in the work and the same methods. Indeed, as we have seen, from the myth of a crude folk *Verismo* to the style of an involuted, tortuous Art Nouveau, Italian opera has had such great facility in adapting itself to the new without substantial changes in its over-all technique or dramatic structure, that it seems to be absent-minded and forgetful rather than intensely alive. It was the instability inherent in Italian history which was reflected in art and which was thus all the more inclined to escape from problems by its art. And there were many, many problems. The bourgeois class which governed without any appreciable differences despite a periodic alternation from Right to Left could no longer keep its cohorts in line. The monetary crisis, the confused international situation, the unjust distribution of wealth, all now weighed on it like brooding anxieties; and meanwhile there was coming into existence, looked at askance, impeded, suspected, a new people's consciousness, and it was organized by the rise of the Socialist party, which particularly involved Milan. And it was precisely in Milan, not far from La Scala, that General Bava Beccaris ignobly ordered his soldiers to shoot at a demonstration protesting the rise in the price of bread as a result of the war between the United States and Spain, and caused about a hundred deaths; a deed for which the general received an even more ignoble decoration from the king as a reward. Two years later, at Monza, a few miles from Milan, the anarchist Bresci would kill the king who gave medals to those who shot down poor people. This was a world in which the freedom bitterly won seemed not to have brought anything but further tyrannies and deaths, and where a war between distant nations could rob bread from the poor; a world marked by weariness with the wars that had disturbed and rent so many generations, a lack of democratic training with which to meet new problems, the attitudes of those who wanted to rest rather than run the serious risk of a premeditated commitment that might lead to other serious duties, as had happened to the Romantics. In short, everything at the close of the century led Milan's bourgeoisie, and also the less well-off classes, culturally a reflection of it, to create a kind of reservoir of certainties that embraced the universe and history by barely touching it, a kind of self-entranced phantasmagoria, a spectacular parade without drama but with the appearance of drama, without grandeur but in the forms of grandeur: an official and sumptuous gangway over which passed the glory of humanity in its apotheosis. And all this was produced at La Scala,

in its grand ballets on history and progress.

However, this activity of re-creating historical characters and making them live on the stage was a quite obvious tendency since the early part of the 19th century: the joy of creating imaginative spectacles and turning historical scenes into a present sight, even if only in a colorful, sumptuous fiction. And the cinema would soon adopt this genre, and exploit it. Now the ballet, which since the 18th century had the tradition of the "costume spectacle," of "historical masquerades" and which offered in the physique and gestures of the dancer the elegance and commanding presence that could adequately represent great figures in a suitable yet idealized fashion, quite naturally possessed itself of this form. Nor was the credibility of the fiction diminished by the fact that these personages had to dance. In fact, throughout the 19th century there had been preserved the distinction between true and proper dance ("French dancers" or "of French rank") and pantomime or mime, even in the course of the ballet itself. And so, alongside ballets which catered to the tenuous, pathos-ridden taste, or the naive 19th century audience's desire for amusement, such as *Le villanelle di Chambery* or *La giuocoliera,* or ballets which repeated the great adventurous Romantic themes, such as *Gabriella di Vergy,* together with the rare ballets which elaborated theatrically subjects which later the opera would make its own (but in quite a different light, such as Henry's *Macbeth* with music by Pugni (1830), Cortesi's *Nabucodonosor* (1838), Galzerani's *Il Corsaro* (1842), Huss's *Gustavo III re di Svezia* — which later became Verdi's *Un ballo in maschera* — (1846) or Casati's *Manon Lescaut* with music by Pio Bellini (1846), all of them successful), there were also ballets with historical subjects which the audiences greatly enjoyed. From 1846 on, the main mover and shaker here was the extraordinary mime Efisio Catte (at La Scala from 1827 to 1870), a student from the school of Blasis, who also in the second half of the 19th century left his mark through his own fine students such as the highly spiritual Caterina Beretta (at La Scala from 1855 to 1877), the gay Carolina Pochini (at La Scala from 1855 to 1866) and the beautiful Claudina Cucchi (at La Scala from 1855 to 1864). He had both the personality and the conviction to interpret the great men of history, so much so that Regli, in his *Essays* devoted to ballet, could early in his career praise his "attitude, nature, love of art, high standards, splendid figure, mobility of physiognomy and expansive heart," and already in 1839, due to all of his successes, hailed him as an "encyclopedic mime." And so La Scala saw Catte in Casati's *Sardanapolo* with music by Pio Bellini (1864, fifty-five performances), and besides impersonating Faust and Des Grieux, he actually played Shakespeare in Casati's ballet *Shakespeare ovvero Il sogno d'una notte d'estate* with music by Giorza (1855, twenty-seven performances and twenty-eight the next year), and was the protagonist in Fusco's *Marco Visconti* with music by Bernardi (1860,

EXCELSIOR
BALLO DI L. MANZOTTI · MUSICA
DI R. MARENCO = PROPRIETÀ
ESCLUSIVA CASA MUSICALE
LORENZO SONZOGNO - MILANO
LUCA
COMERIO

# L'ILLUSTRAZIONE ITALIANA

## AMOR

POEMA COREOGRAFICO

DI

## L. MANZOTTI

Messo in scena

### AL TEATRO ALLA SCALA

nel carnevale del 1886

NUMERO DOPPIO STRAORDINARIO.

MILANO - F.lli TREVES EDITORI - VIA PALERMO. 2.

*(cont.) To stifle this anxiety Manzotti, talented son of a Milanese fruit and vegetable dealer, shrewdly and naively invented the grand ballet in the form of an apotheosis: the triumph of progress — Excelsior and the triumph of love — Amor. Legions of ballet dancers and extras were mobilized for the two ballets, 508 and 614, respectively.*

thirty performances), in Monplaisir's *Benvenuto Cellini* with music by Venzano (1861, fifteen perforances), and played Flik in Paolo Taglioni's (the son of Filippo and brother of Maria) much acclaimed *Flik e Flok,* which ended with the dancers dressed as *Bersaglieri* or crack troops in the Italian army, and in 1862 in Monplaisir's *Nostradamus* with music by Giorza. But the decisive change in perspective, the development of these personages in the direction of an huge celebrative and comforting spectacle took place during the last quarter of the century, the year in which two other significant mimes, Francesco Baratti (at La Scala from 1864 from 1864 to 1876) and Carlo Coppi (at La Scala from 1871 to 1886) transformed themselves, respectively, into Michelangelo Buonarroti and Nero. The inauguration of the 1874-1875 season, together with new mounting of Gounod's *Roméo et Juliette,* was signalized by Monplaisir's ballet, *Giulio Cesare,* with music by a certain Busi; and the Julius Caesar was the son of a Milanese fruit and vegetable dealer, Luigi Manzotti (1845-1905), who made his debut at La Scala in 1872 as the leading mime in Ferdinando Pratesi's *Bianca di Nevers* with music by Marenco, but had already become rather famous as a choreographer in various Italian theaters. In 1876 he was asked to stage his two greatest successes: the ballets *Rolla* and *Pietro Micca* both with music by Chiti, the second having such a startling effect on the audience in Rome that the police were forced to intervene. Actually it was this ballet, produced on January 20, 1875 and dedicated to the Italian folk hero who in 1706 had blown up a tunnel to defend Turin from the French invaders and was killed doing it, which effected the linking of ballet with the history of the 19th century Italian musical theater, a thing that hadn't taken place since the time of Viganò and his followers. Manzotti, almost forty years old, with his romantically curled mustaches and an acting style reminiscent of the idols of his early youth, Ernesto Rossi and Tommaso Salvini, did everything with a flourish — the farewell to his tenderly beloved wife just before sacrificing himself, and then the flash of the bomb, the explosion and the catastrophe. This ballet achieved an elementary and perhaps exterior synthesis, but a conscious one alive with the hopes, certainties and expectations of a century that was fading away; and Manzotti guaranteed its credibility by his skill as an extremely alert actor wholly immersed in his part. He flattered his audience's ideas and practical feelings by this magnificent spectacle which bolstered the certainty that the Italy Pietro Micca had tried to establish was actually there, truly accomplished — in the theater, and what a theater! It was this second aspect, what might be called its spectacular-consolatory aspect, which gradually became the dominant one for Manzotti, who, after returning from a tour which had taken him to the industrious city of Lyons, decided to dedicate his new ballet to the triumph of industry, commerce, science, human inventiveness, and

progress. This was *Excelsior,* which was staged at La Scala on January 11, 1881. It was a great triumph; and in nine and a half months it was given one hundred performances; shortly thereafter, a startling version was done in London, and in Paris a new theater was opened to welcome it. At La Scala the ballet's five hundred and eight dancers awed everyone; people were delighted by the brilliant, pleasantly melodious, functional music composed by Romualdo Marenco (1841-1901); they considered revolutionary the scenery and even more the costumes designed by Alfredo Edel (1856-1912), the "scapigliato" or "Bohemian" painter who, starting with the costumes for *Pietro Micca,* had brought to La Scala the novelty of a painting style separated from realism and quite close to the mentality of Impressionism, but above all a stylistic and craftsman-like conception which would become the definitive example for the new period, since, as Elena Povoledo wrote: "It united daring imagination with very skillful technique. He personally selected the fabrics, studied their reactions under the stage lights and followed the making of the costumes right down to the smallest details. He knew the history of costumes to perfection, but he preferred imaginative solutions, ready to sacrifice documentation, verisimilitude and naturalness to the theatrical effect and the lines of body and costume."

So in a sort of new, lighter, more sketchy *Prometheus* no longer with its roots in the Beethoven's eternal music but with a slight impulsion towards the future in the music of Marenco, the ballet celebrated the victory of the Genius of Light over the Spirit of Obscurantism, which roamed about black and grim and with disturbing intent until it was definitively defeated, while the deeds and aspects of progress were joined to the glorification of all the virtues.

"Just as Viganò's Prometheus opened the 19th century in grandeur, *Excelsior* closed it with an apotheosis; in a colossal choreographic fresco animated by Marenco's orchestral and choral exuberance it celebrated... the victory... above all of perseverance, concord, courage, and work: from Papin to Volta, from Watt to Fulton, from the sailor to the farm steward, the miner and engineer, from cutting the canal across the isthmus of Suez to digging the tunnel through the Moncenisio, from a village on the Weser to the central telegraph office at Washington, from the glorification of humanity in the Temple of the Nations to the apotheosis of Light and universal Peace."

How firmly based this concord and universal peace actually was would be seen forty years later, with the outbreak of World War I. But in the meantime people deceived themselves with a kind of triumphal élan; and once again in February 1886 Manzotti staged *Amor,* a story of love and the world. Two acts and sixteen scenes, 1,600 square meters of painted scenery, 130 flats, 614 performers of whom seventy-two were female dancers, thirty-two male dancers, sixty-four mimes, forty-eight featured dancers, forty-eight understudies, three hundred and fifty extras, three hundred and fifty square meters of negotiable footwalks, together with three hundred stagehands to change the sets, 3,100 costumes, 8,000 props, twelve horses, two oxen, and an elephant whose entrance, as described by the *Illustrazione Italiana* in a special issue devoted to *Amor,* was "announced like the arrival of some great political personage." From the

216

embrace of Adam and Eve and the "torrent of mankind" which poured out on the stage and were in fact small girl dancers who popped out of a hole in the scenery, to the decadent Roman orgies after the Empire's greatness, Christianity with its martyrs dying joyously, Barbarossa, the Lombard League driving out the invading emperor, the allegorical part with Liberty and the personified triumphs of human thought and, finally, the guardian spirits of Art surrounding Love, the whole ballet was the most gratuitous parade of self-glorifying bombast imaginable. But there was a new figurative taste to sustain it. Once again Edel, with a play of images that this time had an Art Nouveau tinge and a daring imaginative flair in the prevailing blue of the costumes, created a setting in which satyrs and gladiators, Egyptian prisoners and Lombard pages all lived in the atmosphere of an unpredictable, tumultuous and elegant carnival.

But this flight from reality, this dancing without a reason at a difficult time of a world that was headed for the tragedy of the whole first part of the 20th century, and which is still the chief fascination of these grand ballets by Manzotti, was then actually mistaken for solid grandeur, true dramatic commitment, even moral substance. When in 1911 Diaghilev's Ballets Russes company brought to La Scala *Cleopatra* and *Schéhérazade* with the music of Arensky and Rimsky-Korsakov and Ida Rubinstein as the prima ballerina, despite the imaginative, inspired setting of this ballet, which at the front of the stage was in full light and at the back showed the dark night barely illuminated by the moon, and the new groupings, steps and gestures of a choreography which had made history in Paris, this new art, which had been welcomed by La Scala (as happened again, with their return in 1926), seemed a distant deviation from the truly Scala-like grandeur of Manzotti and his company; as though Leon Bakst the scene designer and Fokine the choreographer and dancer were simply curious experimenters and not truly revolutionary innovators in the world of the theater. In any event, there is a document that is interesting for the light it sheds on that period's mentality — a letter sent to Fokine by Raffaele Grassi, the choreographer and director of La Scala's ballet school, protesting against some rather severe criticisms which Fokine had directed at La Scala and the ballet *Excelsior* (he had seen it at Teatro Dal Verme) in an interview in the *Corriere della Sera:*

"Monsieur Fokine:

"Your interview with the correspondent of the *Corriere della Sera* makes me realize the unhappy psychological state in which you are struggling. And I explain it this way: Either you are a victim of cerebral anemia, or you have unconsciously lied to that correspondent or you lied to me when we spoke in Milan, when you were sound in mind and body.

"You must recall the high praises that you gave me one day when you spoke of my students. And how have you

219

been able to change your opinion by just returning to your country?

"And there is much worse, still in connection with your anemia.

"With what right do you declare that you have had to give lessons to my students? Here, if you will permit me, I must explain something just to set matters straight. You may even be the reforming Messiah of the art of the dance, I do not think so, but, even if that were admitted, I must declare that there is no ballet school in the entire universe that would be prepared to execute your compositions *ipso facto,* which have nothing to do with true art, namely with that art which still reigns in St. Petersburg, Moscow, Vienna, Warsaw and Milan.

"And speaking of your compositions, I must tell you that you have invented nothing, since you cannot call new what Isadora Duncan has already done, and you are her imitator, and not always a correct one. Yet my students soon understood what you wanted and you told me, as I have already said, how happy you were with them.

"I do not take seriously the inept judgments which you have passed on Manzotti. These judgments have the same effect on me as would a baby who tried to demolish a colossus of granite with a straw.

"Our art can and must also develop, and you, though seeking them out, should leave the dead in peace and be a bit more grateful to the living, who have worked on your behalf.

"And now, Monsieur Fokine, you should realize that you have failed to be properly respectful to this ballet academy which I direct: an academy which was always admired and praised by great Italian and foreign choreographers. We shall all try to forget this, but unfortunately something is bound to remain with us. Your are still quite young; when you are a little older, I am sure you will see that you have made an irremediable mistake.

Raffaele Grassi"

Yet an interesting fact kept cropping up in the chronicles of the period: Diaghilev's ballets are described, when they appeared, as "Futurist." "Is this a new choreographic direction or a Futuristic plastic form?" asked the music critic D'Ormeville, a promoter and one of the freest and most interesting men of culture. The term "Futurist dancers" was quickly taken up without too much qualification. So Milan's inhabitants realized that this was a cultural discussion that went beyond ballet and they expressed this by a term that described one of the movements of the international avant garde. But they did not participate in it and clustered together beneath the shelter of Manzotti's phony granite, suspicious of Diaghilev and of Stravinsky when he arrived fifteen years later with *Petrushka;* and not very well disposed the year after in 1912 to welcome the ballerina and star Mata Hari in the ballet *Bacco e Gabrinus.*

From its beginning down to the present day, the 20th century is not a homogeneous period, or if anything in it is homogeneous and constant it may simply be the crazy, vertiginous, continuous changes that occur year after year, even hour after hour. Celebrations of great certainties have abruptly collided with the stark catastrophe of their demise. Wars, hard-earned conquests of freedom, whole peoples that history has wiped out, oppressions, dictatorships, Utopias and terrible disillusionments with them continuously change all political forms. Historic conditions favor the birth of great ideas, and in turn great ideas generate political ideologies and parties, and then these are wrecked or changed, courageous experiments struck down by the violence of power or transformed themselves into the essence of violent power. Marxism isolates the blood and tears of the poorest classes, puts the nationalistic vision in a crisis, reunites the peoples and divides them internally by an exhausting class struggle. Society is no longer a common idea; it is an idea that people search for, a model which has to be found by anxious efforts. And man is no longer all of one piece, like the hero of a Verdi opera, or someone who can recognize himself in a Wagnerian demi-god; he is the person whom psychoanalysis has discovered, split and dissociated so that he can be rebuilt and rediscovered at every moment; and the relationship with things has become a reality that must be subtly explored. Philosophy has given up offering a synthesis of the world and on the contrary tries to base itself on the perception of phenomena or denounces the dolorous and dissatisfied upsurge of a desire for the absolute. Painters, novelists and poets have all given up the illusion of a credible reality which can be captured in their works in precise and definitive forms; the truth is different from the arrangements of reality.... And the theater as a whole finds itself in a new role; it no longer has the prerogative of an unrivaled, unique spectacle, given the growth in importance and the spread of the radio, cinema and television. It is no longer the fount of experience, a social gathering-place, the message of a well-defined person to a well-defined social group which is known and predictable; the generations are too different from each other, the classes that come to power are more naive and at the same time more exigent in their demands than the old privileged classes. Magic no longer is born from the mere fact of making theater; but rather it is an aspect which the theater often rejects, and when it seeks it out it insists on finding it each time by starting from scratch.

In all these riptides of culture and history, La Scala presents us with different, changing periods; it expresses, reflects and proposes. However, it specifically shows us two different faces before and after the Second World War. The first face is that of a theater which is settling down to the search for success and a forthcoming encounter through two definite orientations: namely, the bringing up to date of the repertoire with the insertion of prestigious foreign composers and the revival of operas of the past which had not yet been too fortunate, all the way back to Monteverdi. In the two directions, the commitment is to that of a theater which is trying to systematize the traditional repertoire, chiefly in its theatrical and musical execution. The second face, which appeared immediately after World War II, is that of a La Scala now less concerned with looking for novelties, even foreign ones, and instead trying to find the up-to-date rationale for every opera and an interpretation that is in line not only with historical meaning, but also the relationship between this rationale and those of the culture and taste of our time. Yet what the 20th century's two faces have strikingly in common is the absence or, better, the scant importance of new Italian works, that is, of operas written for the occasion. Of the Italian composers who write for La Scala, many are staged but few stay on the program for several performances, or return year after year. Once the age of *Verismo* came to an end, perhaps only Ottorino Respighi (*La fiamma*); Italo Montemezzi (*L'Amore dei tre re*); and above all Ildebrando Pizzetti (1880-1968; at La Scala from 1915), severe innovator who treated classical themes or intense meditations in an antimelodic, richly orchestrated declamation, was successful with, among many operas, at least *Fedra* (1915), *Debora e Jaele* (1922) and *Assassinio nella Cattedrale* (*Murder in the Cathedral*) from T. S. Eliot's play (1958); and Ermanno Wolf-Ferrari (1876-1948), who, on the contrary, recreated the world of Goldoni with nostalgia and Austro-Venetian elegance, most interestingly in his opera *Il Campiello* (1936) and the various versions of *I quattro Rusteghi*. So the epoch of new operas had ended; for some time now the whole construction of "tonal" works had been in a crisis; and the dialectic between the predictable and the new, which had always animated music, was yielding to daring, conscientious experiments in new sonic structures, an itinerary which the public could no longer follow, impatient because it no longer found reference points in its memory which just as daringly and conscientiously brought order to its listening. To the difficulties of language, which a lazy Italy shocked by the newly aborning hermetic poetry had no intention of struggling with, there was added the tendency of some composers to attack the "facile" operas of the 19th century. And so it has gone to the present day — the taste for experimentation for its own sake, the reign of ideology and its exploitation on the part of certain power groups, while the economic possibilities which opened up, first with the phonograph record, later with the radio and, last of all, with television, gradually dug a gulf which now seems unbridgeable between cultivated and popular music, the latter now reduced to "light" music chained to repetitive models, the source of advertising slogans. Culture and its dogmas, the channels of information that propagate them, the sociological and esthetic significances which become more and more overpowering in our century, have paralyzed the opera composers' professional spontaneity. Which does not mean that art and custom have been gravely wounded but simply that the usual relationship to the opera theater, where the composer had the freedom to read and think, the adventurous gusto of searching in his own way in the culture, and faith that he would encounter expectation and joy in the listener, has been broken off. By now, save for not very important exceptions, there are no more opera composers; and the most interesting operas are nothing but the application to the theater of a musical language elaborated outside of it: the transposition of the theater into the world of Ravel, or that of Stravinsky. All the more easily is the opera of the past approachable on the plane of immediate encounter, on that of language; contrary to what happened up until and including the 19th century, the opera of the past in the 20th century begins to become present as an actual fact much more than the work of the 20th century itself; and just as in plays and non-theatrical music, the interpreter becomes pre-eminent, not so much in terms of his social role but precisely because of his artistic contribution, which is in a certain sense creative. It is the interpreter who begins to assume the responsibility not only to "do his part well" but to establish a relationship between the musical opera and the public, to reveal to the public the opera's integrity — in short, to range himself on the composer's side. This is the lesson of the great directors in the European theater; it is the lesson of the conducting of the orchestra in symphonic music, it is the lesson in chamber music of a meticulous search for a technique which insists upon the exact redition of the score; it is, in opera, the lesson of Arturo Toscanini.

Toscanini (1867-1957; at La Scala from 1896 to 1952) arrived at La Scala almost inevitably, because of a concatenation of circumstances and destiny. It was 1898, and after several seasons muddled through with some difficulty by several different impresarios (from Brunello and Zamperoni to Edoardo Sonzogno), La Scala had reached the point of financial collapse. From the very beginning, the help of private individuals had been encouraged by a public contribution — an opera theater specializing in producing operas is in fact and *per se* a theater in the red, since the costs of hiring so many people and using so much scenery and equipment do not permit the recovery of expenses. La Scala was naturally granted a proportional assistance, in view of the great role it played in public life, which was called the "dowry" and which ever since the period of Italian independence was allotted periodically by Milan's city government. There were of course always those who disagreed with the practice; but the standards prompted by a "feeling for art" and "civic decorum," even more than those of the spiritual and cultural services which the theater could render, usually won out. But suddenly in 1897 the "dowry" was denied at a meeting of the City Council, about half of the councilmen voting against it — 31 to 23 with 8 abstentions. On the evening of Saint Stephen's Day, 1897, Piermarini's auditorium was closed — for the first time. And for almost all of La Scala's historians and the lovers of theater and music it was a moment of shock and scandal, a feeling that there had been a serious failure

in common sense. However, in an unpublished essay Mario Labroca, describing the situation with the most acute attention, comments:

"La Scala's public, composed down the years of the subjects of the Royal Imperial government, of citizens of the Cisalpine Republic, of subjects of the Napoleonic Kingdom of Italy, and, again, of Austrian subjects, of Italians first led by the monarchy and later regimented by Fascism, then by Republicans and Democrats, did not, apart from isolated episodes, change much through all these epochs. La Scala was practically, and always, a fief of the well-to-do classes, that is, of those families which after every historic or social change still hold economic power. The result of this immobility was the inevitable lack of particular artistic interests, the horror of innovations and the consequent irremediable backwardness in respect to the events of culture and universal thought.

"La Scala's problem as 'the theater of the rich,' was faced openly for the first time by the City Council on July 1, 1897, when the municipal government denied the contribution to the theater, which was then closed for a year. A public communication from Pompeo Cambiasi declared that the decision had brought about 'the closing of the theater and of its annexes, the Schools of Singing and Ballet, causing grave damage to the fame of the city and to all those artistic and economic interests which, in a glorious, more than century-long life, had been grouped about La Scala'. The speech was almost convincing, but much more concretely those in opposition objected 'that the municipal government must not spend money for the amusement of the rich, for an expenditure of luxury, that the contributions of the people are intended to go for a much different purpose.' This argument was called a 'doctrinaire prejudice,' but it was more just than one could possibly imagine. The Teatro alla Scala was the property of the box owners who dominated the theater's life. The box owner possessed the key to his small domain and decorated and furnished it as he wished. (Even today some boxes still have special furnishings or a stove to heat them.)

"That La Scala was not a popular phenomenon or regarded with affection by the people was demonstrated by the referendum on December 15th, 1901, in which the people were asked if a subvention should be given to La Scala. The referendum had the following results:

| | |
|---|---|
| Voters | 56,983 |
| Those who voted | 18,908 |
| Yes | 7,214 |
| No | 11,460 |
| Blank ballots | 234 |

"In 1891, only ten years before, perhaps because of the rise of the new popular movements and before the criminal cannonade of Bava-Beccaris, standing room in the orchestra was abolished and 'numbered seats' were finally installed (not many years have passed since on the stairs leading down to the orchestra a plaster cherub disappeared which used to hold up an oval sign with the words 'seats' written on it.)

"What is more, fifteen central boxes of the fifth tier were transformed into a balcony and, during the season, some popular performances were presented at reduced prices (but one should not forget that even today the number of Milan's inhabitants who have never been inside La Scala is far from small.)"

In any case, the event proved to be propitious; for it brought about the first real turn towards a different conception of La Scala; and this was when Guido Visconti di Modrone, heading a group of generous and enlightened citizens, took over the management of the theater — a tradition continued after his death in 1902 and down to 1917 by his son Uberto. So Guido Visconti di Modrone munificently assumed the task of guiding La Scala; and he immediately chose two very suitable co-workers — as administrative director the enterprising, authoritative impresario Giulio Gatti Casazza (at La Scala from 1899 to 1907), who was not yet thirty, and as artistic director Arturo Toscanini, who had just had his thirtieth birthday.

The enthusiasm for Toscanini, the very myth that grew up around him, permits us to know step by step from its beginnings his important, fundamental activity in the life of La Scala through the reports in the newspapers, which moreover had just at this period acquired a much larger sphere of influence. So Toscanini inaugurated the first of his seasons on December 16, 1898 with Wagner's *Die Meistersinger von Nürnberg,* complete, without the usual cuts which were intended to "lighten" the audience's listening task — the first indication that here was a conductor who had come to do battle. And since he was the artistic director with full powers and the responsibility — as was then the custom with "permanent directors" — of directing the entire season, he immediately stirred up a scandal, for, after strenuous preparation of the next production, which should have been *Norma,* he finally cancelled it because he could not be sure of a performance that would be a satisfying artistic event worthy of the theater. This was utterly unexpected, a new approach and a new concept. And if his inaugural work as an opera conductor (two years earlier he had already conducted concerts) had given rise to debate, despite his recognized skill as an executant, under these special circumstances he set off an uproar. Here, for example, is the violent polemical assault on him printed in the newspaper *Il Corno:*

"To tell the truth, there is no point in boasting, yet our predictions have been proven literally correct. Who would have ever imagined that La Scala would become an artistic laughingstock under the sceptre of that Dwarf who answers to the name of Maestro Toscanini?...

"A man who has constructed his fame on absolute ignorance of the slightest form of good manners and on the dominance that a callous bully can always have over artists who, because of him, are rendered tremblingly unsure and submissive.

"We have said this time and again — if one really wants to save La Scala, one must not grant full powers to that abortion of an arrogant little Lucifer who, with so little foresight, has been chosen to control its artistic fate. Like any other conductor, Toscanini should be put on a contract, and then, if he ruins things by his weird requests, it should always be possible to dismiss him.

"And the events fully support our prognostications.

"Toscanini, the fortunate country bumpkin, borne by blind chance to the honor of a triumph, is La Scala's absolute financial and artistic ruination. Our statement may seem too harsh; but it is inspired by the great love we have for the most important theater of the most renowned artistic city, in that seed-bed of art which is our Italy.

"But let us pass in review the events which have led to this judgment, which, though severe, is nevertheless quite correct.

"As the first ukase under his Czarist regime, Toscanini protests against seven — I say seven — singers in supporting roles, who had already received a fourth of their monthly salaries. A financial blow that was far from insignificant and an act of indescribable artistic malice. Seven artists — the sort of people who have to struggle for their bread — have been ruined; a slap in the face to the famous synpicate of theatrical agents, which in this way has been shown up for not being able to find even a supporting singer. The Maestro prima donna then finds it amusing afterwards — the same man who made his debut as a very, very bad cellist — to quarrel with Magrini, the unquestioned master of the cello who deserves the fame of a Piatti or Braga.

"De Marchi the celebrated tenor became the target of the crude intolerance of the new Bluebeard, which then later struck the famous tenor Brogi.

"Here in fact my pen must make a Herculean effort to avoid putting down on paper the sort of invective which would be appropriate to the unspeakable behavior of an unspeakable scoundrel. It suffices, however, to mention one fact.

"The theater's carriage — the famous big carriage owned by La Scala — was late in picking up Brogi to take him to the rehearsal; the result was, as everyone can understand, that Brogi got there late, which earned him a scolding from Bluebeard and the tenor's irrefutable reply. Do you know, my friends, what that swollen toad of a Toscanini had the impudence to say in reply? I quote him word for word: 'I don't believe you; I believe the call-boy.' Brogi swore on his word of honor that it was so, and Toscanini replied: 'I don't believe you.' Brogi retorted: 'Then you're the liar!' and he threw the score at the head of the man who had insulted him — and he acted very badly... for he should have thrown something much more solid. Toscanini tried to jump on his attacker, but he was so upset that he fell to the floor, though he didn't — ah, the injustice of it all — hurt himself at all.

"After this great act of *lèse majesté,* Brogo was no longer called to the rehearsals and his part was given to the tenor Cosentino, one of Bluebeard's creatures, since he had already sung in his production of *Norma* at Turin.

"They rehearsed and rehearsed and *Norma* was withdrawn after two dress rehearsals.

"A fine piece of news! Malibran, Fricci, Galletti — to our misfortune and theirs — can no longer be found; now, since De Frate was a hit in Turin and Barcelona, one must not sign her up; if she were, one would have to leave the matter of judgment to the public. Meanwhile, since none of the singers have been discharged they must be paid and the opera still will not be staged. And yet the new tenor Cosentino was chosen in advance by the prima donna Bluebeard. We repeat: artistic and financial damages, all because of that swollen bag of wind, Bluebeard.

"In the meantime not only art and the public but also the stockholders suffer from all this... Toscanini, the ferocious Bluebeard, to show off his superiority, cannot

220. *Arturo Toscanini—artistic director from 1888 to 1903 and from 1920 to 1929. A tyrant who insisted on efficiency and a stickler who fought to give each production unity and coherence.*

*He changed the way people listened to opera and morally renewed the theater. He was criticized and fought but wound up victorious.*

conduct any operas but those that other people do not know — such as *Die Meistersinger von Nürnberg* — and he turns down the operas in the repertoire — such as *Norma* — in order not to reveal his insipid lack of taste." In fact, *Die Meistersinger* also left an uproar in its wake, for Toscanini forced a supporting singer to change his part, and the singer quarreled with an assistant Maestro. All of which, combined with the complicated legal situation surrounding *Norma,* permitted the *Gazzetta Teatrale Italiana* to print on its first page an article entitled "The Courts" which concluded: "What fine business deals for the Association of Impresarios!"

It was difficult for Toscanini to get people to understand his aims as an orchestra conductor: namely, to reestablish a creative and coherent unity for opera. The level of the disputes was always unpredictable; a long, unsigned article on March 16, 1901 in the *Gazzetta Teatrale Italiana* attacked Giovanni Pozza, the critic of the *Corriere della Sera,* in connection with that famous performance of *Mefistofele* with Caruso, Chaliapin and Emma Carelli (at La Scala from 1900 to 1901), the aggressive young woman who had grafted onto the flowing tones of a lyric soprano the harshness of *Verismo* feeling, commenting as follows: "The *Corriere della Sera* a few hours before the third edition of Boito's *Mefistofele* was staged in the greatest of our theaters, published these words: 'Boito's opera has never before now had an adequate cast of singers in the Milanese theaters. At its first performances, those in 1868, even the critics who were most severe attributed to the Maestro part of its lack of success. So, if singers were not lacking, there was still the need of a proper musical execution and a conductor of imperious and penetrating force, a lofty and poetic interpretative spirit, scrupulous precision, the lively movement and pictorial effectiveness of the scenic action.'

"This gentleman, the critic — who wants to appear young and so does not remember any of the previous productions — has published a huge piece of nonsense, but not only that, he has also given proof of a certain ignorance when he doesn't recall that at La Scala there existed — and they had long periods of glory — such concert masters as Alberto Mazzucato, Eugenio Terziani and Francesco Faccio, not to mention the fact that from time to time Mariani also held the baton there. And it should also be pointed out to our friend G. P. that during the time of these concert masters and conductors the orchestra at La Scala was not scraped together from musicians from Parma, Bologna, etc. but was a 'permanent' orchestra — such as people are now dreaming of as the great cure-all for the theater's troubles — and counted among them names that achieved a certain aura of fame, or still maintain their high value and teach at the Conservatory, such as Rampazzini, Zamperoni, Orsi, Borghetti, Bovio, Pio Nevi, Mariani, etc.

"To write that 'there was always lacking a proper orchestral accompaniment to *Mefistofele*' and in its execution

220

'a conductor with imperious and penetrating force,' is simply to insult Boito himself, who in 1868 wanted to replace Mazzucato to prepare the orchestral part of the opera and only proves that the critic is unaware of the fraternal friendship which tied Boito and Faccio, who was the concert master of the next more successful production in May, 1881, and the production in 1884."

It was only little by little that the critics began to understand the logic of Toscanini's efforts. The great surprise was his rediscovery of *Trovatore,* in which the Verdian grandeur appeared in the distribution and proportioned use of the different roles and the violent power of the ensembles, and was no longer entrusted to the possible "feats" of the individual singers, the "C" of "Di quella pira," the fascination of certain moments. Thus Toscanini's dry essentiality began to convince critics who spread on paper comments distinguished by neither dryness nor essentiality, such as Gustavo Macchi in *Il Tempo* of February 10, 1902:

"When the curtain fell on the last scene of the last act, I saw Maestro Toscanini radiant, as I imagine Napoleon III must have looked after the victorious day at Solferino, when he sent to Paris that laconic and eloquent telegram: 'Great battle, great victory!'... And Maestro Toscanini was right to be proud of his triumphant success, since a great part of that success was owed to him personally.

"A man has succeeded in imagining this inspired reconstruction of an opera that has been used and abused in all of the cheapest and lowest fairground stalls which arrogate to themselves the name of theaters, and no matter how honest and sincere the interpreters, and no matter how great and powerful the artist might have been, the fact remains that there has finally been revealed to the audience a work of art which until today was largely unknown."

In his "rereading" of Verdi, Toscanini also included *Un ballo in maschera,* which seemed to have been forgotten. And in Verdi as in Wagner, whose *Die Walküre* he also presented without cuts, though each had its own inner logic, he staked everything on the essential elements of the score, the clear exposition of the opera's unity. To achieve this, the other campaign which he launched immediately was the battle against encores, which made the audience lose sight of the close-linked unfolding and, even more, the indivisible unity of the performance. Thus, in 1902, at the première of Weber's *Euryanthe,* an opera which La Scala had never staged before, although it had been composed in 1823, there occurred what a not very acute and not at all respectful reporter for the *Lega Lombarda* described as an "hysterical evening" — and this is how the critic of *Lombardia,* Romeo Carugati, told the story of that April 3rd evening:

"... The overture, vibrant, classical, a masterpiece of its kind... almost stopped the whole production yesterday evening and in any case upset the evening's serenity. After the overture, the audience burst into an ovation to Toscanini and shouted loudly for an encore. Perhaps it was asking for too much; but the call for an encore is not proper any more, yet the theater audience still insists on it. Now, Toscanini did not want to replay the overture and just went ahead. But the audience, in its turn, redoubled its shouts for an encore, so the already lifted curtain had to be sent down again. The orchestra conduc-

tor was set on winning and resumed with the notes that announce the first chorus. More and louder cries for an encore. Then Toscanini with an angry gesture put down his baton, jumped from the podium and ran off, leaving the orchestra to fend for itself.

"The inexplicable event, the insult to the audience which had even acclaimed the young conductor, produced an enormous clamor.... Was it possible that a serious man, in such a high position — even when he does not sit on the choir stalls — could fling such a challenge to a whole audience from which he had just received signs of honor and respect? Had Toscanini become one of those old prima donnas subject to fits of hysteria who, because of her passing 'moods,' refused to offer the gift of her talent to the public?

"Signor Barilli, in the name of La Scala's management, took the stage to announce that the conductor had been seized by a sudden indisposition. The statement was greeted by some incredulity; but when it became known that Toscanini had worked very hard on the preparation of the opera and was also in a very low state of mind due to the fact that both his wife and children were ill, the nervous outburst was easily forgiven and as soon as he reappeared with the orchestra the audience welcomed him with benign good will. However, he had to play the overture again, and this was the evening's only encore.

"This incident had the misfortune of causing great agitation on stage and, as a result, the overall interpretation suffered."

One evening — it was April 14, 1903 — during a performance of *Ballo in maschera,* Toscanini's patience gave out. He crossed his arms when he heard vehement cries for an encore; he waited; and then he swiftly ran off the podium and left the theater. Maestro Sormani finished the performance for him. Cleofonte Campanini (1860-1919; at La Scala from 1889 to 1905) and Leopoldo Mugnone (1858-1941; at La Scala from 1889 to 1913) did the conducting until 1906, for until the 1906-1907 season Toscanini did not set foot in La Scala, save for the concerts which he had inaugurated in 1905 under the auspices of the Society for Symphonic Concerts, an association which down to 1915 welcomed as guest conductors such men as Vittorio Vanzo, Giuseppe Martucci, Tullio Serafin, Vittorio Gui, Pietro Mascagni, Oscar Fried, Antonio Guarnieri and Bernardino Molinari. After returning for the 1906-1907 season, Toscanini, depending on the operas to be performed, alternated as conductor with Panizza, Vitale, Gino Marinuzzi, Pietro Mascagni and others, and he continued to conduct until the tragic period of the war. But starting in 1906-1907, La Scala's management announced that a strict rule of the house prohibited the "repetition of passages," in short, encores were outlawed.

In the period right after the war, Toscanini resumed firm control of the theater's artistic direction; but a fact of extraordinary and decisive importance gave a new orientation not only to his conducting but also to the theater's entire life. This was the formation of the *Ente Autonomo* or "Independent Corporation," which from then on managed La Scala's affairs. All this occurred because the then Mayor of Milan, Emilio Caldara, and the City Council, in league with the box-owners, in 1919 worked out an agreement, approved in 1920, to give up

221-226. *During those years the conducting of the orchestra became pre-eminently important. Before and during Toscanini's time, Faccio, Mugnone, Panizza, Campanini, Serafin and Marinuzzi distinguished themselves: first-rate artists who could inspire their orchestras. Each performance proposes a specific interpretation; with Toscanini the myth was born that his was the "only" way, because of his obvious concern to conduct according to the letter of the score, which tradition had often overlooked.*

221

223

225

222

224

226

227-231. *Under Toscanini the singers were subjected to absolute discipline and had to get rid of the usual compromises. This is how it was for the bass De Angelis, the sopranos Claudia Muzio (shown here as Violetta and Norma) and Rosina Storchio. Toscanini himself was converted into a myth. But his main effort was to turn the public's attention to the composer. Below, a picture of the unveiling of the monument to Verdi at Busseto, which offers a humorous comment on that singular and contradictory period.*

their boxes at the end of nine years. And to provide further support, a collection of funds was organized by the *Corriere della Sera,* then under the direction of Senator Albertini. An executive committee, presided over by the Mayor and formed from representatives of the government, the box-owners, and certain donors (Annibale Albini, Luigi Repossi, Angelo Scandiani, Claudio Treves, Senator Borletti, Eugenio Balzan, Pietro Volpi Bassani, and Vittorio Ferrari), then wrote the constitution of the *Ente,* which on December 29, 1921, on the basis of a Royal decree of the same date, was set up as a corporation. The *Ente Autonomo* ran the theater with complete juridical, administrative and artistic independence; it was supported financially by the government and local contributions. Arturo Toscanini remained the artistic director — he had already been appointed to this post in March, 1920 — and he decided to make La Scala into a repertory theater; that is, a theater which was in the position and, according to its concrete possibilities, had the task of preparing all the operas that could be performed again in the coming season, together with a certain number of new works or exceptional programs. Now La Scala's new grandeur did not rest so much on the enhanced possibility to stage operas and carry through excellent operatic seasons. Extraordinary things had already been done in the preceding seasons; it should suffice to recall the 1908-1909 season, with Mussorgsky's *Boris Godunov* and Strauss's *Elektra* and the inaugural presentation of Spontini's *Vestale,* which in January had been taken to Paris — both singers and scenery — for a gala benefit evening for the inhabitants of Calabria and Sicily, which had just been struck by one of many earthquakes. This was a great triumph, both financially and critically, with a company in which the featured singers were the impetuous, almost savage Ester Mazzoleni (at La Scala from 1908 to 1917), the dazzling tenor Emilio De Marchi (at La Scala from 1898 to 1909), the noble, inspired baritone, with his splendid vocal range, Riccardo Stracciari (at La Scala from 1905 to 1924) and the intense, sharply clear, colorful, tempestuous, meditative, and powerfully resonant basso Nazzareno de Angelis (at La Scala from 1907 to 1933), the last two singers becoming La Scala mainstays during the first quarter of the century—or the 1913 season, commemorative of the centenary of the births of Verdi and Wagner, which, besides Toscanini and the usual excellent conductors, was entrusted to singers of the stature of Ines Maria Ferraris, Bernard De Muro, and Mario Sammarco. It also witnessed the first big successes of two exceptional singers, Carlo Galeffi (at La Scala from 1911 to 1940) and Claudia Muzio (at La Scala from 1911 to 1930): both artists of a suave and enchanting charm, with voices particularly expressive in the nuances, the shadings, rendering by their vocal feats the psychological intuitions that made the parts they portrayed brilliantly recognizable, but above all characterized by their desire to ennoble their roles by beauty, attaining

this both by their voices and their stupendous acting. Galeffi was a singer who, in the course of many, many years of a glorious career, could portray a Rigoletto whose tragedy sprang from his human vulnerability, while Muzio could create a Violetta in *Traviata* capable of maintaining through all the phases of her character a sense of erotic intensity, inner sweetness and hidden sorrow. For in this period, too, the singers, whose history is interwoven with all the other aspects of the theater, so complex and tangled in the new century's dizzying tempo, present us with a history of taste and interpretation of capital importance. And it is significant that La Muzio and Galeffi practically by themselves took both Italian opera and La Scala out of the sphere of rhetorical, above-the-stave, vocal athleticism in the vibrant *Verismo* style, which had its great exceptions only in the amorous old-style singing of the aristocratic, idolized baritone Mattia Battistini (at La Scala from 1888 to 1917) and the intimate, melting, resplendent, lunar tones of the soprano Rosina Storchio (at La Scala from 1895 to 1917). But the new grandeur of La Scala's *Ente Autonomo* under the direction of Arturo Toscanini could be found in its having brought to the theater a new, decisive, moral, organizational and esthetic discipline that helped to change the audience's habits and, in fact, repeated precisely in an executive setting what Verdi had long ago creatively defined. The audience, which listened to the opera in complete darkness and silence, knew that an orderly and total artistic commitment reigned in the theater. Toscanini's art of conducting, animated by those famous, dangerously offensive outbursts of anger, though always for reasons of artistic impatience and never as the expression of personal, prima donna-like tantrums, lay above all in his prepotent desire to achieve the unitary equilibrium of the score in regard to every written note, while preserving both the necessary objectivity and the simplifying, lightning-like clarity of his personal reading of the score. But his figure represented, as Franco Serpi insists in his authoritative discussions of Toscanini, the symbol of an esthetic ideal and, to the most attentive observers, the point of convergence of different processes of development on the plane of taste, the plane of problems connected with the interpretation, and, finally, the plane of orchestral technique. And La Scala identified itself with Toscanini, as it had identified itself with Rossini, Viganò, Bellini, the last Verdi and the last Puccini.

How important and successful the Toscanini-*Ente Autonomo* association was could be seen from the very beginning when, La Scala's orchestra having completed a long, very highly praised and applauded tour through Italy and America with Toscanini conducting, he opened the season on December 21, 1921 with *Falstaff* and Mariano Stabile (at La Scala from 1921 to 1955) in the main role, a singer whose long and triumphant career demonstrated the results attained by the rigorous musical sense which he had learned in the long rehearsals with Tosca-

227

228

230

229

231

nini, and whose voice with its quality of colloquial directness could make the listener's imagination soar. Gaetano Cesari's review, in typical authoritative *Corriere della Sera* style, gives us a good idea of the atmosphere of the evening:

"The word solemnity, so worn out by its use in descriptions of the lyrical stage, should acquire again its genuine meaning of a great, fortunate and resplendent event when one wishes to express the complex significance of the magnificent spectacle which has taken place at La Scala's reopening."

And a passage from Andrea della Corte, music critic for *La Stampa,* sets forth precisely the results of that commitment which Toscanini, with his fits of bad temper and his ability to be patient, had aimed at:

"Indelibly stamped on our memory is the amazement we experienced at the technical and spiritual novelty of this production of *Falstaff.* More than one person remembers that in the first period of this century performances of *Falstaff* during normal seasons with conductors like Mascheroni and Mugnone of good and great fame, who knew Verdi well and were loved by the public, were not very successful. Some would repeat the stupid opinion 'it doesn't make you laugh,' while others maintained that it was too fine a thing for our audience's palate. Toscanini has critically demonstrated that *Falstaff* does not intend to make us laugh, for this comic drama is substantially melancholy and pessimistic, and all one has to do is bring this substance into prominence to render the opera intelligible and pleasing to any audience, whether it be Italian or foreign. So he has revealed in this opera the poetry which he himself discovered in his maturity, and so lucidly and enchantingly did he present its fine qualities that the audience, swept along by the dramatic tide, no longer shouted for encores of *'Quand'ero paggio'* — in fact for a 'double encore' which, as we recall, he granted twenty years before, when this opera seemed different to him, too."

This was the beginning of a radical operation, obstinately pursued for eight years with the support of Engineer Scandani and his excellent secretary Anita Colombo. "A golden period which deserves a chapter by itself," Armani and Bascapé have written,[44] "because of his — Toscanini's— presence in every element of that delicate and complicated machinery which is an operatic spectacle." In the large volume published in 1972 and entitled *Toscanini and the Scala,*[45] the musicologist and historian Guglielmo Barblan thus synthesizes and explains Toscanini's position, which was clear from the start:

"At the moment when Stabile had his first timid audition, singing — according to the Toscaninian prescription — the entire first scene and monologue of the last act of *Falstaff,* La Scala seemed 'all topsy-turvy' because of the radical reforms, which were both spiritually and practically dominated by Toscanini, who was all over the place, arranging, keeping an eye out, prodding, inciting,

so as to be certain that the artistic plans of the new Scala era were being punctually carried out. In previous decades he had 'moralized' the environment of the operatic theater by means of the measures we have seen (complete darkness in the auditorium, the abolition of encores, etc.); now, however, he worked not only to achieve perfection in the vocal and instrumental interpretation of the score... and to insure the minute preparation of the entire spectacle (scenery, costumes, lights and staging), but also to complete the organization of the complex confluence and interaction of all the various components which converge in the presentation of a lyrical work. His goal was the 'unity of the spectacle'; and he did not merely assume the task of attaining this ideal but, with a kind of rigorous punctilio, actually insisted on assuming all the responsibilities. This was quite exceptional, particularly among men for whom shifting the responsibility was the normal thing. Besides, Toscanini... in the period right after the First World War, studied the new organizational systems which were being used to reconstruct Italy (and it wouldn't be the last time!), and applied the same standards employed by a business executive in a big, present-day firm to the preparation of the operatic spectacle. Above all, prior coordination among the heads of the various sectors: the people in charge of the management of the theater, those directing the choruses and singers, the technical department, those in charge of the scenery and costumes, and, finally, those who had to stage the opera. Each section had to work out its own plan of action, establishing in advance even the time required to achieve it. As for the orchestra, chorus and individual interpreters, they were all rehearsed separately, and the rehearsals of the various groups only began when each section declared itself ready. Thus the spectacle matured through an elaborate 'assembly line' over which Toscanini presided, which 'not only led to notable economies but also to a discipline in the preparation which until that time had not existed.' This was at bottom the usual banal discovery that everyone had known in advance, a true 'Columbus' egg,' but one needed the appearance of Columbus in the field of opera, too."

As for the execution, in those years the available singers were quite numerous but also typed. The school of *Verismo* had greatly emphasized the importance of the soprano and tenor because the passionate, elementary dramas typical of the genre usually centered around them. So there was the very dramatic Eugenia Burzio (at La Scala from 1906 to 1915) as well as the robust and incisive Tina Poli-Randaccio, or the very beautiful and sensual Salomea Krusceniski, who was, with Toscanini conducting, La Scala's first Salomé in 1906. The contralto had almost vanished, since it was regarded as the voice that typified the period of Verdi's maturity. On the other hand, the mezzo-soprano had become important, as was exemplified in the careers of Fanny Anitua and the subtle, fascinating Gabriella Besanzoni (at La Scala from 1923

Milano 1936
Al Sig.r Alfonso Casati per ricordo di Falstaff.
Mariano Stabile
TEATRO ALLA SCALA
MARIANO STABILE
in "Falstaff"

233

to 1933), who had been born a soprano and, what is more, a light soprano. Among the tenors, the notable personalities had greatly diverse traits; but many of them had by now left La Scala, such as Edoardo Garbin (at La Scala from 1893 to 1918), a typical, delicate light tenor, or Giuseppe Borgatti (at La Scala from 1896 to 1914), who was the interpreter of the most notable characters of *Verismo* opera and had a lot to do with Wagner's success, or the ringing, generous tenor Giovanni Zenatello (at La Scala from 1903 to 1913). Whereas a certain type of baritone, and not necessarily singing the "bad parts," often did take the limelight, and because of this Giuseppe De Luca (at La Scala 1904-1937) was a great success. However, the great difference between the singers before and after Toscanini's time can be traced to the fact that under his regime there was an end to the cult of stardom at the expense of the opera itself. One might speak of a leveling, but in the sense of renouncing those easy effects that are applause-getters, and nothing more; and also of the high level to which the entire company, and even the secondary roles, were lifted. So one saw an excellent mezzo-soprano like Elvira Casazza (at La Scala from 1916 to 1942) adapt herself to the task of portraying parts which at other times would have been considered of little interest; she played not only an Ulrica but also an admirable Dame Quickly, and ended her career at La Scala as late as 1942 as the Marzipan Witch in Humperdinck's *Hänsel und Gretel,* which since 1902, when it was brought to the theater by Toscanini, has always been a favorite. Faithful to the tasks demanded of her, Gilda Dalla Rizza (at La Scala from 1916 to 1934) moved with versatility through the different roles of a repertoire which ranged from *Verismo* operas to *Traviata,* displaying that process by which the exigencies of the theater, repertoire and spectacle assume an over-all pre-eminence. Precise, enormously exciting, and with extraordinary diction, Giulia Tess (at La Scala from 1922 to 1936) revealed the wonders of Pizzetti's declamation at the première of his opera *Debora e Jaele* in 1922; and Ezio Pinza (at La Scala from 1922 to 1934) also participated in this opera with his virtues of will and discipline, as he did in others, such as Alfano's *La leggenda di Sakuntala* and Boito's *Nerone,* a basso who in other times could have staked everything simply on the fine qualities of his large, wide-ranging, warmly toned voice and on a repertoire more concerned with striking effects. In this discipline of artistic precision, under Toscanini there was also a tenor like Francesco Merli (at La Scala from 1918 to 1946), whose incisive pronunciation and expert musicality throughout his long career always kept exactly to the score, particularly in his part in *Turandot,* and the tenor Miguel Fleta (at La Scala from 1924 to 1926), who was generally liked until his great success, due entirely to his skill at ecstatically prolonging *sotto voce* notes. Many singers became part of the new consciousness who later would preserve the lesson learned, such as Benvenuto Franci

234

235

237

236

238

239. *Aureliano Pertile (here as Edgardo in Donizetti's Lucia):
an extraordinary example of a singer's enlightened and inspired
fidelity to the score.*

239

(at La Scala from 1923 to 1940), an impetuous baritone
with a fiery, violent style, or the cordial, typical "buffo"
of that period Salvatore Baccaloni (at La Scala from 1926
to 1952). But when Toscanini rehearsed the singers, and
even the orchestra, he would sometimes say: "Sing, sing
it the way Pertile does!" Aureliano Pertile, "Toscanini's
tenor" (at La Scala from 1916 to 1936; at La Scala's
Teatro Sociale of Como in 1944), incarnated the singing
style, the art, the moral commitment to melody, the solid
humanity without breaks, slackness or self-indulgence
that Toscanini had always dreamed of. The words of
the libretto, made the object of human concentration and
restored to the complete logic of the music and the
character, awakened unexpected harmonies, manifesting
a secret profundity and releasing a truth which helped
as never before to recover the opera's total coherence.
One saw this most of all in the tenor, that is, the interpreter most easily led to concentrate only on isolated
passages, but now become the proof that the operas of
the great composers lived a continuous life that must
not be sacrificed. Thus, as the phonograph record had
begun spreading the gay mania of "romances" and "arias"
separated from their context (and each record had a
limited duration), Aureliano Pertile restored to the recitatives and arias their creative reality and appropriate
accent. And meanwhile a new comprehension and art
was evident in La Scala's chorus, which had passed
through the hands of such finely educated masters as
Emanuele Zarini (at La Scala from 1862 to 1876), Giuseppe Cairati (at La Scala from 1880 to 1891) and Aristide
Venturi (at La Scala from 1894 to 1913) and, since the
formation of the *Ente Autonomo,* had been entrusted to
the wise, enlightened human simplicity of Maestro Vittore Veneziani. The same care, the same importance,
the same coherence in regard to the staging led to the
same results on the plane of language; the audience
realized that the opera was a theatrical event of images
and presences with its own logic. On the esthetic plane,
the artistic quality of the result was much less important.
What was beginning to be called the stage direction was
confined to a graceful and insistent desire to give scenic
credibility to the action and, chiefly, to characterize the
types and personalities. Above all, the orchestra conductor
made the acting his concern, at least in Toscanini's case;
as for the over-all mounting of the opera, the light cues,
the coordination of the acting, there was a director of
the *mise en scène,* and among those who occupied this
post the most outstanding was a typical figure in the
respectacle theater world of Milan and Italy of the years
between the two wars, Giovacchino Forzano (at La Scala
from 1922), also a playwright and author, permanent
stage director during the period of Toscanini, who began
his career with Puccini's *Trittico* in January 1922, and
who wrote the librettos for two of the one-act operas
in this trilogy, *Suor Angelica* and *Gianni Schicchi.*
The scenery, in line with this quiet, sure taste, was almost
always composed of flats or large, painted scenes, which
were in the bright, corny style of the illustrations seen
in the magazines of the time; that is, realistic with a
faint Impressionist nuance when the subject widened
into an evocation of landscapes, and with a remote hint
of Art Nouveau when the furnishings of the set required
a certain number of lines and objects. Alongside the
successors to Ferrario, that is, Parravicini, Rota, Sala,

240. *For Toscanini, the staging was a centrally important part of the opera. He himself often taught the proper gestures to his singers and coordinated the movements of the chorus. He was not an innovator in the field of scenic taste, yet he was modern in his concern for coherence. This wish to "shape the characters" arose out of a tenacious desire to obtain scenic truth but also from an innate and playful feeling of exuberance. In this unusual photograph Toscanini (at the right) is enjoying himself with friends, inventing a scene from* Bohème ...

240

241-243. *The other side of Toscanini—the idol surrounded by adoring people. Many pictures were taken on his tours which show us this side, especially the tours with La Scala's orchestra. One day in 1929 Toscanini left on a tour but with the intention of also leaving La Scala and Italy. In 1921, La Scala became an independent corporation or, as it was called, Ente Autonomo, which was free in its management, the choice of conductors and operas. But Italy was now Fascist and freedom was fast disappearing.*

241

242

243

and Songa, Antonio Rovescalli (at La Scala from 1912 to 1943), became well known thanks to his craftsmanlike touch and his felicitous experience; while for its costumes La Scala usually turned, like almost all of the cinema, which had just come into existence, and Italy's plays, to the first-rate workmanship of the Casa d'Arte directed by Luigi Sapelli, known as "Caramba" (at La Scala from 1911 to 1937), a man who had a vast knowledge of the history of costumes and great imagination in creating different versions of them adapted to changing theatrical needs, though always with a pleasant talent which with brilliant effectiveness met the average expectations of middle class taste, combining history, realism, and Art Nouveau. However, really bold initiative in scene design was not appreciated. One innovator of the modern stage setting, Adolphe Appia, aroused more protests than comprehension with his famous setting for *Tristan und Isolde,* which was reproduced at La Scala on December 20, 1923 by Lert and Caramba, and in which the invitation to live in the spaces created by an exclusively theatrical universe without the least effort at verisimilitude and without the usual painted, easily accessible illusions collided with the somewhat fixed and obtuse perplexity of an audience never disposed to adventures and new discoveries. What is more, the set was imperfectly realized by its imitators. And also the attempt of the scene and costume designer Hohenstein in January, 1899, for the opera *Iris,* employing the purest, most attractive Art Nouveau style, did not gain adherents or produce any imitators, though he used this approach in splendid theatrical manifestations from *Tosca* to *Francesca da Rimini.* Toscanini was open to certain new attempts in scenic inventions; but if he saw a scant effect in the immediate results he preferred to forget the attempt in order to carry out with assurance the task which he felt most strongly about — the reduction of all the components of the spectacle to a unified form, which in fact was accepted and welcomed without too much debate and discussion.

Between Toscanini's first and second periods, European opera had assumed a pre-eminent position, which had become even more commanding with Toscanini's return for the 1906-1907 season (fourteen performances of Bizet's *Carmen,* sixteen of Strauss's *Salomé,* ten of Wagner's *Tristan und Isolde* and two of Gluck's *Orfeo ed Euridice*); and in 1908 there appeared, conducted by Toscanini, Debussy's *Pelléas et Mélisande,* and La Scala finally produced Mozart's *Magic Flute* in 1923, with seven performances, all conducted by Toscanini, after the opera's absence for more than a century; and in 1927 it also repeated Spontini's *Vestale,* which, together with Cherubini's *Médée,* presented for the first time at La Scala in 1909, completed an essential knowledge of French operas written by Italian composers during the neo-classical period. Alongside these illustrious names of old and contemporary composers, several minor Italian composers also helped to create ephemeral novelties; Lattuada, Bianchi, Lualdi, Montemezzi and Vittadini all tried their hands at opera, as did others who are now covered by oblivion. However, La Scala had success with operas like Charpentier's *Louise* (at La Scala from 1907), which was given many performances over the years, and with the very fortunate encounter with the children's world and those who love it, in Humperdinck's *Hänsel und Gretel.* There did not exist a true seasonal forecast of the program but rather summary indications; the operas were presented depending on whether certain definite conditions were within reach. It was run like a repertory theater, aimed at a privileged group in society, people free to dispose of their evenings and not at all interested in knowing in advance how the season's spectacles would unfold and what sort of culture would be met with during the year. Nothing gave the impression that the *Ente Autonomo* would be overtaken by a crisis. However, the political course of events pushed matters in another direction. The economic management was faulty, and the chosen remedy was the decision progressively to abandon the concept of an independent corporation and to enter the orbit of the State, which by now, since the tragic events of 1922, was the Fascist State with its full panoply of claims, rhetoric, centrifugal forces and the will to gather everything in the Roman capital, now hailed as the capital of the world. First came a decree-law in February 1928, expropriating certain private boxes to "guarantee the constant and perpetual existence of the Teatro alla Scala in Milan, which has assumed the character of a National Institute for lyrical art"; and later, in the July of the succeeding year, a law granted a loan to the *Ente Autonomo;* and in October, another decree dissolved the directing council and named Senator Borletti the commissioner. This constituted an economic advantage, for a month later another decree arranged for the transfer to the *Ente* of the fiscal and domanial rights to all spectacles staged at La Scala, but the *Ente* was now in a condition of subordination, for the Ministry of National Education installed a representative and the Head of the State selected its president. So in May, 1929, after having celebrated his thirtieth year at La Scala with the production of *Die Meistersinger* and a memorable end to the season — *Aida* with a cast that included Elisabeth Rethberg, Elvira Casazza, Francesco Merli and Carlo Galeffi — Toscanini left La Scala. He would conduct only at Berlin while on tour with the theater's companies in a triumphant series of Italian operas, and he returned only in May, 1930 with the new orchestra of which he became the permanent conductor, the New York Philharmonic Symphony Orchestra. Toscanini would no longer work in Fascist Italy.

In any event, such was the lesson of Arturo Toscanini; and if other orchestra conductors were as great as he, in the history of La Scala and radiating out from La Scala to affect the history of the interpretation of opera throughout the world it was Toscanini who, because of his iron-willed and dominating personality and his rigorous methods of work, brought the authenticity of opera respect, recognition and gave it a living meaning and impact. So while the esthetic system of Benedetto Croce seemed to put a distance between Italian intellectuals and the great creative and popular patrimony of the Romantic musical theater, La Scala with Toscanini's assistance recaptured their interest in an unexpected way: not as a composite spectacle made up of concomitant events but as a unitary and complex act of life, the ever-renewed creation of each and every performance.

244-247. *La Scala was destroyed by the war. It was reopened a year after the war ended. Once again it was given priority, just as it had been when it was first built. Arturo Toscanini was asked to conduct the first concert. It was a memorable day, May 11, 1946. La Scala regained its Maestro, its freedom and its life.*

244

245

246

Toscanini would return to La Scala's podium in 1946 and would again conduct concerts right down to the last, remarkable concert of Wagner's music in 1952, which was his farewell. Between the active period of his great thirty-year reign and this mythical one of farewell, the war had taken place; and in Italy not only the war but the fall of Fascism, the German occupation, the Resistance, and the American occupation, regarded by Italians as a new alliance. Since Toscanini's withdrawal and his opposition to the dictatorship, the situation had become worse and worse and the world outside seemed to plunge deeper and deeper into the darkness. As the poet T. S. Eliot wrote in his second "Quartet" in 1940:

As, in a theater
The lights are extinguished, for the scene to be changed
With a hollow rumble of wings, with a movement
— of darkness on darkness,
And we know that the hills and trees, the distant panorama
And the bold imposing façade are all being rolled away...
I said to my soul, be still, and wait without hope...

And Bertolt Brecht admonished that to talk about trees at that tragic time of oppression was a crime. But the musical theater in Italy did not get the chance to offer a reply or present the grave signs of revolt. The culture of the historical avant-garde had not even stirred up the gust of restlessness which the "Scapigliatura" had produced in its time; Futurism had glided unthinkingly and bombastically into Fascism, supporting and adding its color to the ideology of power. To die or preserve its illusions was La Scala's fate. And so from the beginning of the 30's down to the 50's, in terms of artistic substance, music and theater at La Scala formed a homogeneous twenty-year period — the period of Fascist rule — without too many jolts or upheavals. By now the orchestra conductors had complete control over the spectacles; and if the meager musical culture and the bizarre behavior of the singers could continually endanger the equilibrium of the whole and display an alarming lack of taste, there was, however, a greater alertness and surveillance than in the past, and in the audience an attention which more intelligently followed the fundamental lines of the interpretation. But this was not a matter of a school of singing able to grasp and express the profound stylistic differences of the various scores in the history of opera, nor to recover the technical and express exigencies of the diverse historic and creative moments. To sing the "melodrama" of Bellini and Donizetti one did not employ a coloratura soprano, a dramatic singer of pyrotechnical skill, as was done when the work originated. For Verdi's opera the baritone did not differ much in his bravura flights and sad passages from those he used in the *Verismo* style. Instead, everything was entrusted to the good taste and artistic intuition of the conductor and the individual singers, above all in a personal identification with the role which left vocal training aside. In this milieu and with results which

were at times amazingly felicitous, circulated the great names of singers who by now an ever more precise recording technique restores to us as much as is possible, in both entire operas and isolated pieces. And in this gallery the peak is attained by the powerful tenor of Giacomo Lauri-Volpi (at La Scala from 1918 to 1947), or the extraordinary sympathy of the strong vocal and human personality of Gino Bechi (at La Scala from 1940 to 1953). A region of taste which above all loved unconscious beauty, the savoring of a song that stunned and made one dream of lost paradises, was seen in the lyric soprano Toti Del Monte (at La Scala from 1916 to 1939), one of the most popular singers in our century; and an entire epoch which trusted in eloquence and the natural prodigies of a beautiful, melodious voice was reflected in the success of *Norma* in 1932 with Bianca Scacciati and Ebe Stignani, or of *Turandot* with Gina Cigna (at La Scala from 1929 to 1945), who sang the leading role in 1935 and 1944. The stage of La Scala was occupied by the stupendous presence and great scenic animation of interpreters who were also vocally fascinating: one heard Massenet's *Manon* as it was lived and suffered by the incomparable Mafalda Favero (at La Scala from 1928 to 1949) or *Carmen* with Gianna Pederzini (at La Scala from 1930 to 1956). Margherita Carosio (at La Scala from 1929 to 1954) opened the heavens of that song which lives in the soul and in the frivolity of the open personality finds the truth of the character, whether it be in a light vein or portraying a Violetta. Cloe Elmo (at La Scala from 1936 to 1954) traversed the entire parabola possible to a mezzo-soprano, from dramatic roles to delightful portrayals of comic figures; and such singers as Francesco Merli, Giovanni Malipiero, Giuseppina Cobelli, Maria Caniglia, Iris Adami Corradetti, and Gabriella Besanzoni also starred and the full-bodied, noble bass voice of Tancredi Pasero became famous. Tito Schipa (at La Scala from 1916 to 1949), in an almost continual lesson, proved how precise, penetrating and emotionally exciting the voice of a tenor could be in phrases lyrically sung and poetically confided with those light tenor's enchanting flights in which Rodolfo Celletti heard "nuanced and aerial hues," "almost metaphysical transparencies," an artfully conscious gradation of tempos, rhythms and tones, and witty agility or affecting pathos. And meanwhile Beniamino Gigli (at La Scala from 1921 to 1947) offered the audience his overwhelming emotional power, his tenor's generosity, his ecstatic, languishingly tearful approach to the most lyrical arias, and the audience rediscovered the voice which it had learned to love in the romances and songs and knew very well because of his records and radio broadcasts; it forgave and forgot his meager acting ability and responded to him with extraordinary affection. Outside the theater, the dictatorship was a danger to be forgotten, a reality that had to be accepted and tolerated; the war was a nightmare to be driven away, a tragedy in

248-253. *Three great tenors: Enrico Caruso, who sang at La Scala only during Toscanini's first season; Beniamino Gigli (249), idolized through a long career at La Scala; and Giacomo Lauri Volpi (250), with his noble, luminous, and plangent voice. The baritone Carlo Galeffi, in the costume of Barnaba, preserved in La Scala's Museum, the very symbol of an epoch of great singers. Toti Dal Monte and the "buffo" bass Melchiorre Luise shown in typical poses.*

248

250

252

249

251

253

the full and complete sense that would go on to its inevitable end; the post-war and the post-dictatorship were problems that had to be confronted: Beniamino Gigli was the voice that accompanied and comforted them, testifying to deep affections, making his the allurements of a dangerous, ambiguous Italian spirit which, however, was rooted in a powerful truth — an illusion perhaps, but not of dreams, rather of the hope that everything could still go on, that one could still live. The spectacles remained substantially those of the time of Toscanini, save for certain presences which ensured a more conscientiously elevated level of staging, as on the few occasions that Guido Salvini (at La Scala from 1930 to 1961) directed. The regular stage director was Mario Frigerio, who had been in that post from 1930 to the present day, a kind of symbol of the old Scala: a strict supervisor of scenic dignity, a skillful director who could create spectacles under all sorts of changing conditions, a useful man who inspired confidence. Yet gradually the methods of staging changed, especially with Nicola Benois's (at La Scala from 1938 to 1970) entry and the importance he assumed both as scene designer and stage manager. His professional skill continued at a distance the line of stupendous invention of his father, Alexandre (at La Scala from 1938), the scene designer of the Ballets Russes, who more than anyone else knew how to put the old suggestions of the archaic world and the new lessons of painting (from Bakst's Orient to Chagall's subjective fantasy) at the service of the spectacle, releasing emotions of high theatrical intensity, such as the famous scene in the second act of the ballet *Giselle* which seemed an incomparable summing up of the Romantic mode on La Scala's stage and which the ballet still uses. Nicola's versatility, however, was more an eclecticism which ranges indifferently between painted scenes and partially constructed ones; but what he contributed above all was the constant exaltation of themes and places, of an ordered and rational glorification of situations and spaces; so that one can point to many happy instances of his work, chiefly with Verdi's operas, but more than anything else a general conception of the opera in which the value and scope of La Scala's scene design could be seen: not so much an interpretative operation on the score as an encounter between La Scala and the several worlds of the operas. But this hallmark of composed spectacular solemnity was important in the history of La Scala, since La Scala was identified with it when it came to style, taste, mentality, at least between the period after Toscanini's withdrawal and the 50's, when the theatrical spectacle of the new era would be born. And even in the last years of supremacy, when by now it seemed clear that other scene designers could better express the contribution of new ideas and new images, when scene design no longer appeared the art of the certainties which a theater offered to the score, the world, and the lives that it welcomed, but rather the search for a truth internal to the individual operas and their present-day significance, Nicola Benois still succeeded in constructing ultimate, fascinating syntheses, above all for the taste of yesterday's typical La Scala spectator, inclined to celebration and enchantment, well disposed to the mysteries and culture learned in the classical lycée; as, for example, in the opening scene of Pizzetti's *Fedra* in 1959, directed by Luigi Squarzina,

*254-255. Extraordinary artists, with voices that had inimitable inflections, a fine sensitivity to the lyrics, such as Mafalda Favero, here portraying a delighted, resplendent Nannetta in* Falstaff, *or Tito Gobbi, here as Rossini's Figaro, both veterans at La Scala.*

254

255

256-257. *Dark mezzo-soprano voices, of quite different character, succeeded each other: Ebe Stignani's velvety, authoritative voice (here in* La Favorita*), and Gianna Pederzini's exuberant, colorful voice (here in* Carmen*).*

which was described by the fascinated scholar of La Scala Carlo Enrico Rava as follows: "Rooted, one might say, in the bowels of the earth, from which emerged, confused with the rocks, almost formless cyclopean masses carved with mysterious reliefs, trunks of lopped-off columns nesting in the shadow and crushed by the barely squared forms of immense capitals; and from those shadows which seemed to contain the most distant origins of myth, between jagged and rusty stone dripping with the blood of sacrifices and crimes, red stairs rose from the darkness, ascending towards the distant glare of a Doric colonnade innundated with light. When the singular and astonishing opening curtain (painted on a transparency) which depicted with great perspectival daring the central scene, 'seen from below and up,' of the four gigantic columns of a Doric propylaeum, gradually dissolved, letting the scene behind appear and gradually define itself in its volume, it seemed truly to have overcome miraculously every theatrical 'fiction,' giving form and authentic substance to the royal palace of the Troezens, with a sense of implacable 'presence' which almost made one gasp."[46]

Providentially putting on trial the convenient and absolutist faith in Toscanini, which had given rise to the facile myth of the "objectivity" of his performances, as though every interpretation of his could be definitively stored in the realm of untouchable absolutes, the artistic talents of other great conductors intervened. And not so much that of Antonio Guarnieri (at La Scala from 1922 to 1948), splendidly musical and a rather disenchantde improviser, a man of the highest talent; nor that of Vittorio Gui (at La Scala from 1924), inspired and enlightened apostle of the rebirth of Rossini, the cordial, charming liaison man between European culture and the Italian public; nor that of the wise, vigorous, impassioned conductor Tullio Serafin (at La Scala from 1910 to 1947), permanent La Scala conductor from 1910-11 to 1913, directing the first performances at La Scala of several European operas, such as Strauss's *Der Rosenkavalier* (1911), Dukas's *Ariane et Barbe-Blue* (1911), Rimsky-Korsakov's *Pskovityanka* (1912) and Strauss's *Feuersnot* (1912) and, more important than all the rest, Wagner's *Parsifal,* which after its opening on January 9, 1913, was given twenty-seven performances. A combative figure and a connoisseur, not only of the singers for whom he became the most famous of advisers but also of quite banal things in the world of the operatic spectacle, Serafin could, for example, discover that one of the electrical switches needed to transmit the conductor's tempo to the choruses hidden in the "cupolas" for the performance of *Parsifal* (the stage director was Fuchs, from the Bayreuth theater) had been broken before a rehearsal; indeed, even more, he could then gather all the assistant conductors, inspectors and electricians in his dressing room before the first performance and, showing them a revolver which he meant to put in his pants pocket, declare: "If anything like what happened yesterday evening occurs, I know where to shoot and I'll hit the mark."[47] But beyond all these fine musicians the personality who served notice on Toscanini's lazy successors, together with all those who did not want to reopen the perennial problem of what path musical interpretation should take, was Maestro Victor De Sabata (1892-1968; at La Scala from 1929 to 1953), a conductor with incomparable native gifts,

256

257

197

an absolute sensitivity to timbre and intonation, and an infallible memory. With a sensibility which expanded in an almost physical perception of the musical event and an intuitive control of all the possibilities of evoking sensations and emotions, having been trained in the French Impressionist milieu, he immediately made his mark with his productions of *La fanciulla del West* and *La Damnation de Faust,* in which Puccini and Berlioz suddenly seemed caught up in a symphonic song with infinite, secret refractions but at the same time fluvial and compelling. But he really astounded everyone in January, 1932, with his performance of *Tristan und Isolde,* the opera which he would later repeat many times, always to an enormously enthusiastic audience. Gradually, he mastered a repertoire; at first much criticized due to the special angle from which he saw the works, intent on subordinating the singers' interpretations to a disquieting, convulsively eloquent, agitated musical context. He also aroused discussion and debate with his concerts, when he attacked Beethoven with the violent impatience of someone who wants to extract a total participation, synthesized immediately in the intellect and at the same time felt on the thinnest part of the skin. But he was a conquistador. The real period of De Sabata's reign came immediately after the end of the war with a remarkable *Otello,* the innovative rediscovery of the orchestral ornamentation and frivolities in Puccini's operas, *Bohème* included, and many other interpretations. But in 1953, having taken over the job of La Scala's "artistic superintendent," he no longer conducted regularly: heart trouble forbade his mounting the podium. He did return, however, to make a fleeting appearance at Toscanini's funeral, rehearsing and conducting the *Marche Funèbre* of Beethoven's "Eroica" Symphony, which was broadcast in the streets and over television. It was the orchestra of so many incandescent evenings which commemorated the departed Maestro under the baton of the Maestro who for one last time had returned; the orchestra of Minetti and Valdinoci, containing so many great instrumentalists who were also bringing a happy epoch to a close, an epoch of passions without vindictiveness, of dedication without rivalry, of skill without arrogance. Soon there would come the period of the struggles for the conquest of rights, the justified union struggles, the unrenounceable quest for more humane conditions in a society which had always found it difficult to realize itself and in times that became more and more anxious: a hard-fought battle to live justly and fully; but in which, unfortunately, the discussion of rights coincided with a certain decline in the entire Italian instrumental school and with a mentality alien to the exciting or laborious emergencies on which a theater lives, and averse to accepting the unpredictability of exceptional schedules and occasions out of a love of the theater. It was a historic phase, and it did not begin that evening, just as for some time now there had been forming that other historic phase of new perspectives and new ideas. But the very next day it was obvious that a whole epoch had come to an end.

Before that moment, the orchestra had been able to improve its skill in the sphere of concerts with a number of quite successful seasons and programs and conductors of the highest international prestige. From 1921 onwards, one can only register the names of the most famous

258

*258. In the dim light of the orchestra Toscanini talks with De Sabata. This famous photograph reunited two men who had opened an epoch, the epoch that made the conducting of the orchestra La Scala's new myth.*

259-268. *Victor De Sabata, at La Scala from 1929 to 1953, immediately reopened the interpretative discussion. He was quite different from Toscanini: restless, agitated, a conductor whose physical sensitivity to the music created a compelling atmosphere which overwhelmed the listener. Eloquent gestures, at first restrained and later as though immersed in the vortex of the music, he personally put each musician in the orchestra to the test. Completely submerged in the logic of the sound, De Sabata demonstrated his impressionistic training and his personality. Argued over and revered, De Sabata responded to the music with*

259

260

262

261

263

lightning-like intellectual syntheses and every nerve in his body. He conducted Beethoven's Funeral March from the "Eroica" Symphony for the last time to an empty auditorium, before a microphone that carried the music to the street, while the long, impressive funeral procession for Toscanini stopped on the piazza outside. Many of the men in the orchestra wept; and people in their homes also wept, while listening to the radio or watching television.

264

266

267

265

268

269-271. *The punctilious calibration of Hermann Scherchen, the man who revealed so many contemporary scores and was also an inspired interpreter of music from every period. Wilhelm Furtwängler's unwavering gifts which made him do everything with authority and measure.*

among the great musicians who were heard at La Scala and who did not turn down a chance to appear here on display and to respond seriously to an ever-growing interest. De Sabata from 1927, Hermann Scherchen already since 1926, Fritz Busch from 1929, Pablo Casals from 1930, Vittorio Gui from 1930, Wilhelm Furtwängler from 1932, Kleiber and Dobrowen from 1933, and in 1935 a memorable Beethoven series conducted by Otto Klemperer; Richard Strauss from 1938, Igor Stravinsky from 1939, and Herbert von Karajan from 1940. And with the orchestra there appeared such great solists as Pablo Casals, Arturo Benedetti Michelangeli (from 1940), Edwin Fischer (from 1941), Walter Gieseking (from 1941), Gioconda De Vito (from 1942), Wilhelm Kempff (from 1942), Yehudi Menuhin (from 1946), Alfred Cortot (from 1946), Wilhelm Backhaus (from 1947), and Arthur Rubinstein (from 1947). In 1950 Leonard Bernstein made his first appearance as conductor and pianist. These are simply dry lists but the names could be multiplied. One would like to gauge the contribution of such talented musicians as Bernardino Molinari and Willy Ferrero. One would like to discover the diverse importance which the entire musical phenomenon assumed in Italian civilization, when during its concert seasons an orchestra like La Scala's devoted itself to the revelation of worlds and ideas, of sonic and spiritual reality. But in La Scala's overall history, this aspect of the concerts always remains a trifle apart; as a kind of admirable exercise of what was a received school more than a matured discourse. Since its origins, La Scala has been a theater of opera and ballet; as we have seen, it later became for a long time an opera theater with a good series of ballet evenings, and only in very recent times has it returned to being a complete musical theater which presents both opera and ballet. It became a place for concerts and has had and continues to have a wealth of stimulating activities and programs; but its natural, genuine life is that of the theater. The symphonic concerts and recitals are somewhat like the breath of music without which there is no life, the moment perhaps of someone greatly loved who produces the most brilliant and suggestive results. But it is not the central life of the theater and it forms a kind of luminous niche in its history.

And yet the most memorable event in the entire 20th century was actually a concert. And this took place on May 11, 1946, when Arturo Toscanini returned triumphantly to the podium at the reopening of the theater after the war in order to conduct a composite and fascinating program. Renata Tebaldi, Jolanda Gardino, Giovanni Malpiero, Tancredi Pasero, Mafalda Favero, Giuseppe Nessi, Mariano Stabile, Carlo Forti also participated; and the chorus was trained by Vittore Veneziani. It was, however, a program of opera without theatrical gestures or stage equipment; a compendium of meditations and memories. It opened with the overture to *La gazza ladra,* the opera which Rossini had composed that gave rise

269

270

271

272

273

274

to and invented the myth of La Scala, and nothing could be more suitable to this new consecration of the theater. It continued with two other pieces of Rossini's: the wedding chorus and dance from *Guillaume Tell,* the opera that celebrated the folk uprising and was redolent of both nature and history, and the famous prayer from *Mosè in Egitto: Dal tuo stellato soglio/Signor ti volgi a noi,* ("From your starry threshold/Oh Lord, turn to us"), and from there it passed to Verdi with his overture to *I Vespri Siciliani,* which called up the entire Risorgimento and made one feel that it was still alive and present in the hall. Then Verdi's *Te Deum:* his farewell to La Scala, his Lombardian, Manzonian, obstinate synthesis. Then Puccini: the intermezzo and third act from *Manon Lescaut,* the affirmation of the new school of opera at La Scala, after the distrust of both *Verismo* and Puccini himself. And finally, what was more than ever tied not only to the battles won at the beginning by Toscanini but also the final moment of innovative Lombard hopes, when official literary culture had reached out to La Scala: the prologue of Boito's *Mefistofele,* which was also a beautiful, greatly effective finale to an electrifying evening. Thus the choices were carefully weighed, wise and honest. It was a kind of reunion after the war, and it was a strong declaration of La Scala and what it meant to everyone, an all-inclusive testimonial. La Scala had just been reconstructed a short while back over the heap of rubble left by the bombs; and so they had celebrated its rebirth, which went arm in arm with the rebirth of freedom.

In fact, on the night of August 16, 1943, La Scala was destroyed by bombs. The war had been going on for three years, and it would continue for another two; and already for some months now the city of Milan was dying: its people, its houses and its streets. A theater is not its walls, its red stalls, its long white columns, gilt ornaments, and stuccoes, the seats ranked in its balconies. The Scala of triumphs and struggles, filled with gestures and songs, had become more and more distant with the passage of every day. The new Scala, crushed, offended, ruined like the poorest houses of Milan beneath the destructive fire, was in its darkest and most tragic hour the true and just La Scala of Milan's citizens. And so every wall that crumbled, every red upholstered chair that was buried under rubble, every space invaded by beams and piles of plaster, every seat torn apart, and all the columns, ornaments and stuccoes which for the first time seemed so important and necessary, secretly lived on in Milan's tears of pain and its desire for redemption.

275-281. *Guido Cantelli, a young man with a future. At the rehearsals, attentive, intense, peremptory, inspired, evoking the music as he felt it within himself: eruptive, impassioned, great. He became permanent conductor at La Scala at thirty-six, in 1956.*

275

277

276

278

When he conducted a performance, he seemed intent on controlling and checking the music which he had unleashed; even to the point of being astounded, almost frightened, by so much power. He died in an airplane crash a few months after being appointed permanent conductor.

279

280

281

282-290. *Herbert von Karajan, magnetic center of sonic and spiritual tensions, shaping the music with his gestures and presence, imparting a beauty of sound and line at the border between the abandonment to musical joy and something sorrowful.*

*A theatrical director (above to right, with members of the chorus) and a television director (below on the left, with Jon Vickers, Peter Glossop and Raina Kabaivanska in* Pagliacci*), and director of recordings (to the right, talking to the chorus*

282

284

283

285

286

*master Roberto Benaglio)—in him present-day civilization has the most successful promoter and spreader of music on records and film. La Scala has participated with him in these productions on several occasions.*

287

289

288

290

291-297. *Gianandrea Gavazzeni, refined intellectual and musician immersed in opera's passionate violence. A contradictory figure of notable consequence in the history of La Scala today, he has performed many feats by his inspired readings of old scores.*
*Here he is at work with the stage director De Lullo and the mezzo-soprano Fiorenza Cossotto for "Condotta ell' era in ceppi" from*

293

291

294

295

292

296

Trovatore: *a clearcut and precious documentation of the way, by their very different gestures, the conductor can evoke song and the director the action.*

298

299

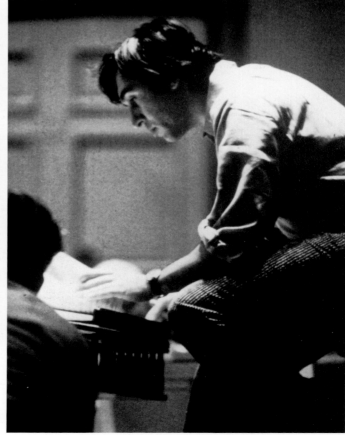

301

300

302

298-303. *Claudio Abbado, at present permanent conductor and musical director at La Scala. He has introduced the precise analytical rationality of the new generation, and with this the fascination of rediscovery, piecemeal, of the repertoire.*
*Rooted in a family of musicians, Abbado is very attentive to the spectacle as a whole; as one of La Scala's directors he works actively with the artistic management. He is modern, but he also has a touch of the old-fashioned, which makes him a classical interpreter.*

303

304

305

306

304-306. *Other conductors who have made notable contributions to La Scala. Carlo Maria Giulini, nobly inspired by an almost sacred conception of music. Zubin Mehta, from India, skillful animator of orchestral life. Leonard Bernstein, American, who shocked directors and members of the orchestra by his nonchalant, easygoing manner, but he dominates on the podium, to which he brings an unbridled spontaneity, a force of conviction and involvement of rare power.*

307-309. *Sergiu Celibidache—he has given us a new lesson in music. Georges Prêtre, French enchanter of the orchestra and audience, has tied his name to an interpretation of opera in which brilliance and color are put at the service of psychology.*

307

308

309

310

The new Scala was born in haste, as an urgent problem that had to be solved the day after the liberation of Milan in the spring of 1945. From December 1943 until the summer of 1945, its shows were continued at the Teatro Sociale of Como, the Teatro Donizetti in Bergamo and the Teatro Lirico in Milan, where it would have to stay until December 1946, that is, until the *Nabucco* conducted by Tullio Serafin resumed performances and the official seasons in the reconstructed auditorium. Milan's mayor, Antonio Greppi, had appointed Antonio Ghiringhelli as Extraordinary Commissioner, Engineer Luigi L. Secchi was put in charge of the work of reconstruction and rebuilt the roof with iron, remodeled and refurbished the architectonic proportions in line with the designs of Piermarini and Sanquirico, reproduced the ceiling vault decorated in 1879 and the central Bohemian crystal chandelier with its 365 lights. Technically, the work was unanimously judged to be perfect; the acoustics were not worsened and in any event proved almost miraculous, according to all the historians, despite the rather ticklish problems posed by the largeness of the building and its particular type of construction, designed at the beginning to provide good sound only for those who wanted it, that is, for those who sat in the boxes or got a good seat in the orchestra filled with unfastened chairs. La Scala's organization on the practical plane has developed gradually, and a pamphlet published by the theater's publicity department in October 1972 sums up the situation as follows:

311

"Today the Scala has insured the stability of the orchestra, chorus, ballet, and technicians; it possesses in Bovisa, an outlying section of Milan, perfectly efficient storehouses and workshops (they contain more than 70,000 costumes and the scenery for 150 complete spectacles). It has installed a switchboard with 318 circuits for the lighting of the stage; it has been given an air conditioning system, a closed-circuit television apparatus and electronic equipment which help to perfect the performances. In 1956 it inaugurated the new lobby and the new foyer for the orchestra, and in 1955 it provided the balconies with their own foyers, carrying through work that has also an obvious social significance. And, finally, to conclude this summary of the principle work done, it has reorganized and improved the offices, the rehearsal halls, the dressing rooms for the singers, choruses, and extras, etc."

312

The credit for all this activity, together with the general conviction that La Scala should be preserved and brought up to date because of its undeniable historic role, can go to the generous management of Antonio Ghiringhelli, the Superintendent from 1948 to 1972 who transformed the theater and installed a system of modern efficiency in its prudent administration, which during Fascist times had been able to weather difficulties thanks to Anita Colombo, Maestro Trentinaglia, Jener Mataloni and Maestro Carlo Gatti, who had succeeded each other over the years. But in the meantime, there had come into exi-

313

310-313. *20th century operas: by now a limited phenomenon. La Scala presented them in prestigious productions. Here are Schwarzkopf and Picchi in Stravinsky's* The Rake's Progress *(1951), Berg's* Lulu *(311-312) (director Rennert, Hamburg Opera Company, 1962), Ravel's* L'Heure Espagnole *(director Crochot, 1958).*

314-316. *Two world premières: Poulenc's* Dialogues des Carmélites *(after Bernanos, director Wallmann, scenery by Wakhevitch, 1957); and Pizzetti's* Assassinio nella Cattedrale *(after T. S. Eliot, director Wallmann); and here the famous scene designed by Zuffi in the form of a cross, with Nicola Rossi Lemeni.*

314

315

316

stence a new set of problems, which became urgent in the postwar period and had grown progressively until they exploded at the end of the 1960's—cultural, social and moral problems that were so entangled as to render necessary a continuous search for coherent, unitary solutions and choices made from an all-embracing operational standpoint.

The main problem was that of the nature of the audience at La Scala, which was a public theater and therefore was intended to furnish a service to the entire city. Until the end of Ghiringhelli's management, La Scala's choice was to make a gradual attempt to enlarge its middle-class audience, while the middle class itself was being transformed and its level of education and power was climbing and slowly changing. The truth is that La Scala at its resplendent "first nights" remained a fief of the rich bourgeoisie and aristocracy; but it no longer had the same dependence on them as in the past. It pursued its own artistic and cultural goals, sought out a dialogue that went far beyond the interests of the inner circle. But musical and theatrical education in Italy was at a desperately low point, and so the available education and cultivation that a musical theater demands did not permit a broadly sympathetic base; and this was all the more true since present-day custom channels the majority to other spectacles, such as the movies, sports and television. La Scala's public, even in its progressive growth (of course, not proportional to the growth of the city's population, which reached more than a million and a half in the 50's, and now, twenty years later, stands at about two million) remained a curious mixture of interest and blindness, of fanaticism and laziness, of furious hopes and the serene love of music. Certainly the struggles between interpreters, the rival factions, did not help to change habits; and so what prospered was what might be called the "balcony birds," those balconies in which are nested, as is customary in Italy, the true experts of opera, who have no suspect desire to hobnob with the stylish and elegant society folk in the boxes and orchestra, and from their high, dominating positions can be heard by everyone and, if necessary, can even intimidate — which can happen above all at first nights and can make itself felt chiefly at those times when a period of interpretive transition combines with the spread of nonchalant, sloppy behavior. But leaving aside these rather colorful and at times genuinely impassioned manifestations, which might be generally considered inevitable, if not to say providential, it was precisely the common taste which had its shortcomings, the stable reference points which were crumbling. La Scala's entire audience, whether brazen, timid, or haughty, had little faith in the innovations in the sphere of opera and, in general, in the new musical languages. Alongside the apostles of the new music and those interested enough to understand its reasons for being, there still can be found at La Scala the immovably pious and utterly respectable, mixed up with the radical and perplexed.

One of the fundamental characteristics of the thirty-year period after the Second World War was unquestionably the decrease in authentic new works and the recourse to operas of a more assured accessibility. In truth, the merit of Antonio Ghiringhelli and his associates was to have chosen this road with an overall and coherent purpose, that is, without too often having recourse to new operas that were facilely melodious and had obviously angled, spectator-baited plots. But generally every significant attempt to present a new work, whatever its true novelty might be, encountered strange, fierce or picturesque opposition. To cite the more clamorous instances of operas of recognized value, Britten's *Peter Grimes* was presented in 1947 without too much damage, Prokofiev's *Love for Three Oranges* was heard at the end of the same year and Stravinsky's *Oedipus Rex* in April, 1948 (the month before they had staged, with De Sabata conducting, Ravel's touching, fascinating *L'enfant et les sortilèges*). Honegger's opera *Jeanne d'Arc au Bûcher* (already presented in 1947) required the presence of the international movie star Ingrid Bergman in the seven performances which were tumultuously awaited, together with the famous Venetian actor Memo Benassi and the stage direction of that champion of cinematic Neorealism, Roberto Rossellini; a circumstance which for some unknown reason scandalized the adepts in the field of music criticism and was symptomatic of the conservative position normally taken by the specialist press. And when Giancarlo Menotti's *The Consul* was produced in January, 1951, one of the most talented musicologists and critics, Giulio Confalonieri, went up in the balcony and hissed throughout the performance, offended by the movie-style Neorealism of the opera's political plot, which, however, is flavored by a very traditional, openly impassioned lyricism. In 1952 a frigid audience greeted *Proserpina e lo straniero*, an opera with a rather uncertain musical style by Juan José Castro, winner of the Giuseppe Verdi International Contest. In March, 1954, at the close of a completely new and pleasing opera, Peragallo's *La gita in campagna*, a shoe was hurled down from the balcony to punish the composer for having brought on stage a Fiat "Topolino" car. That same year Rossini's *Cenerentola* reached five performances, Puccini's *Tosca* nine; the thermometer read tradition as the generation formed by *Verismo* tastes understands this word, even Verdi's *Don Carlos* reaching only five performances. But the real measure of critical conscience and public taste can be seen in the famous case of *Wozzeck*.

It was June 5, 1952. Berg's opera, with its stormy subversion of traditional musical language and its charge of explosive denunciation set in the anguished world of the oppressed soldier, was being presented for the first time at La Scala in a memorable production: the conductor was Mitropoulos, the interpreters, among others, were Dorothy Dow, Tito Gobbi, Peter Munteanu, Mirto Picchi, the stage director was Herbert Graf, sets by Ratti and costumes by Ebe Colchiaghi. The audience was not familiar with the work; perhaps it was not informed, although it had had thirty years to become so, perhaps it wanted to oppose it; in any case, the fact remains that the audience rejected it from the opening beat, disturbing the performance. Dimitri Mitropoulos then turned and asked for silence, the necessary concentration for so dif-

*317-323. Every significant 20th century composer has been represented at La Scala in the last twenty years. Here are two scenes from Gershwin's* Porgy and Bess, *and scenes from Stravinsky's* Oedipus Rex, *Prokofiev's* Angel of Fire, *Berg's*

317

318

319

Wozzeck, *and Schönberg's* Moses und Aron. *These productions exemplify very different views of operatic staging, ranging in directors from Puecher (Prokofiev) to De Filippo (Shostakovich) and De Lullo (Stravinsky), and in designers from Damiani (Prokofiev) to Svoboda (Berg) and Pizzi (Stravinsky).*

*324-326. The lesson of the contemporary theater is also reflected in the way scene design interprets the classics. Here are three sketches for the 1973* Walküre *(direction and sets by Ronconi and Pizzi, respectively) which openly displayed historical emblems and theatrical machines.*

320

321

322

323

324

325

326

217

*327-331. One of the prominent exponents of contemporary music was Dimitri Mitropoulos, a conductor with an exciting sensibility and singular talent, whose name was bound up with La Scala and who died on its podium during a rehearsal on November 2, 1960.*

328

327

329

330

A historic moment: June 5, 1952, Mitropoulos is conducting the premiere at La Scala of Wozzeck. He hears a buzz of voices and a protest against the opera's difficult and anguished language, turns to the audience and asks it to be silent to the end. Phyrric victory for the "new".

331

ficult a score, right to the end; after that, he said, they could hiss all they wanted to. And this unusual and daring move on the conductor's part changed the situation; and the opera sailed safely into port. Now, this episode is usually seen as proof of the public's incomprehension of anything new. However, the audience did not leave the opera house (as part of it did, however, in 1970, when there was a new production) and a theatrical but genuine act of a fine artist like Mitropoulos sufficed to change, if not the audience's evaluation, the atmosphere of the evening; which also shows a certain openness and availability on the audience's part. But, certainly, if one looks beyond the episode itself, La Scala after the war did not simply reject Alban Berg's free thematic and formal associations, but a particular opera dealing with rebellion and anguish which it was not able to discover during the grave years when war loomed and at last broke out. But Italian customs in this regard are hard to evaluate; after all, the audience found it very difficult to participate in the operatic world that was suddenly presented to it and somehow felt excluded or excluded itself. As for Dimitri Mitropoulos, he returned to La Scala for Busoni's *Arlecchino* (1954), and for many greatly acclaimed concerts, and, in fact, died at La Scala, collapsing on the podium during a rehearsal on November 2, 1960.

332-340. Two sets of conditions will change the theatrical spectacles at La Scala in the 50's: the birth of stage direction no longer as a fact of decorum but as an interpretative choice; and the presence of an actress and singer like Maria Callas.

The birth of great stage direction—which already had made excellent contributions with Strehler, Visconti, Zeffirelli, Pavlova and others—became an explosive issue in May 1955 with the production of Traviata.

332

335

333

336

334

337

These well-known images testify to the atmosphere of that production: Lila De Nobili's sets and costumes, which placed the action toward the end of the 19th century, with a fascinating effect of decadence and of intense naturalness in the characters. What was striking above all was the acting of Maria Callas, who played beside Di Stefano and Bastianini. Guided by Visconti, she captured a balanced melodramatic style, not emphatic or rhetorical but bold, a synthesis of emotions in a fully conscious human presence.

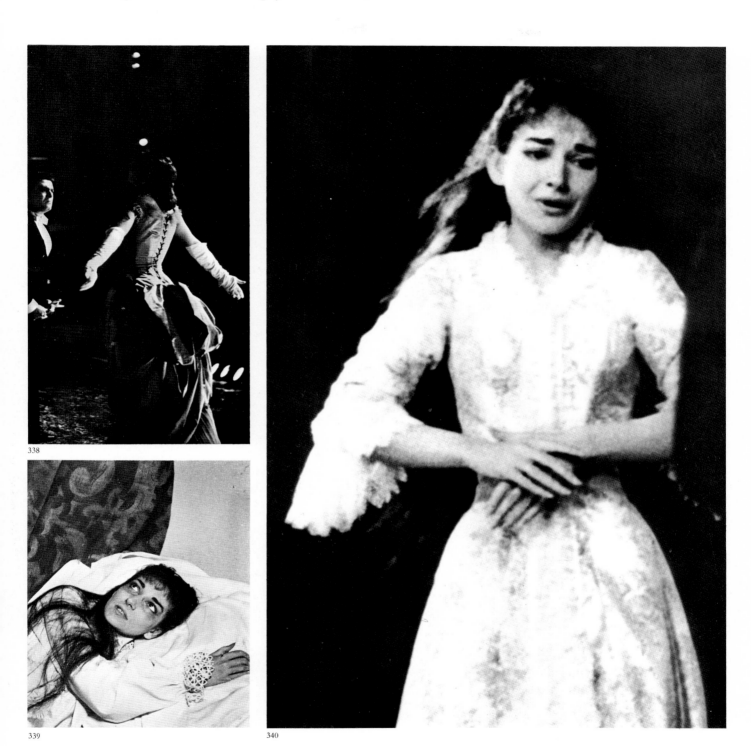

338

339

340

341

342

343

sets, which evoke, however, a sense of constant solitude around the unlucky queen.

And Callas's gestures: her hands, her face which seems clearly etched among the shadows, the composure of a romantically eloquent expression and the shattering of that composure in an anguished faint.

344

345

346

347

348

*Maria Callas, making evident everything that the character experiences, is torn between amusement and distress, until she takes thought and meditates sadly but proudly. She has made up her mind. This is the birth of a new acting style for the operatic stage.*

349

350

351

352

353-362. *In this sequence (to be followed vertically from top to bottom) with Franco Corelli in* Fedora, *Callas's art of creating tragically intense images which, for the spectator, seem also to embrace the tenor, even when he confines himself to being a* smooth, handsome presence. *In the large photograph she is seen in* Un ballo in maschera *with the tenor Di Stefano. Here again her performance confers credibility on the conventional acting of the other singers in the cast.*

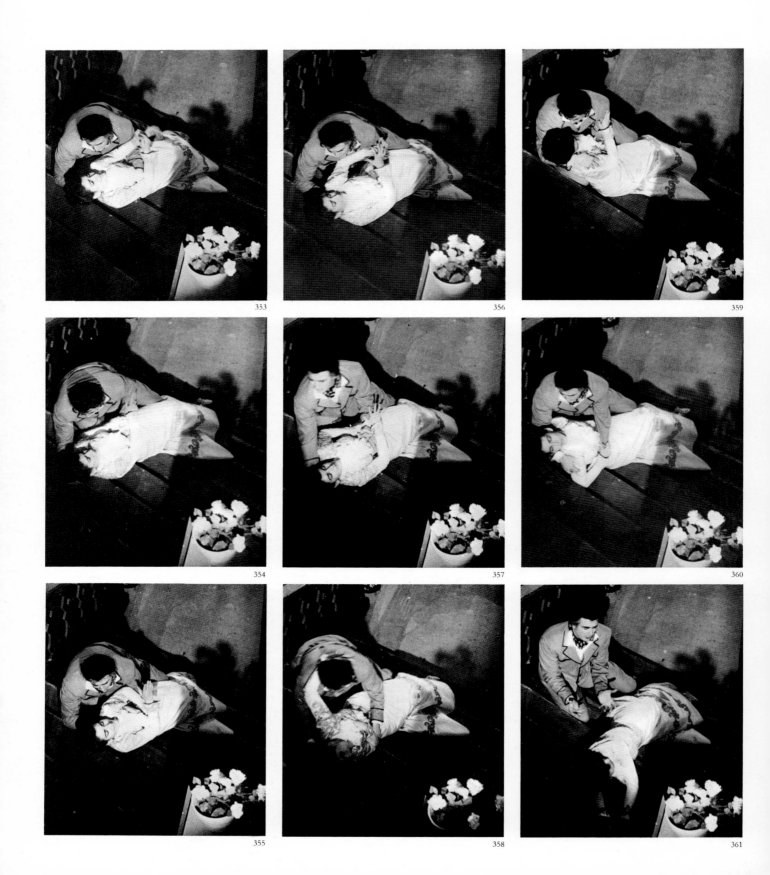

353

356

359

354

357

360

355

358

361

363-369. *Since its origins, opera was concerned with classical tragedy. This dimension was brought to its greatest effectiveness by Maria Callas, a Greek, chiefly in operas with classical subjects but in Romantic tragedies, too. In the large photograph her magnificent classical composure in Gluck's* Alceste; *while in the top series is shown the mad scene from Donizetti's* Lucia di Lammermoor. *The pictures below are three moments from Cherubini's* Medea.

364

366

368

365

367

369

These last twenty years have been our own history — from
one point of view unrecoverable, and certainly not to
be misrepresented by partial lists. Our discussion becomes
fragmentary, the historian is transformed into a frightened
witness, and nothing is clarified save for a few fixed
points of orientation; and we can trust only these points.
As for singing, there is one orientation and a blatantly
obvious one; this is the revival of the old singing styles,
rather than a mere adherence to the taste of our own
time, the obvious attempt to carry the public back to
the language of the epoch in which the opera was composed. And the crucial name here is evident: Maria Callas.
For the technicians of singing, the whole experience with
Callas (at La Scala from 1950) was revolutionary. She
transfused the technique of the coloratura into the art
of the dramatic soprano, and in her dark, emotional voice,
so far from the warm, full-bodied tones of the Italian
tradition, she revived wonders and suggestive powers
which had been forgotten for decades, qualities which,
in her pre-Verdian repertoire, earned her a comparison
to Maria Malibran, and which led her to solve all the
problems of the score, whatever its period, by colorfulness,
eloquence and virtuosity. But the effectiveness of her
mode of singing, the example she proposed, became an
established style because of its overwhelming, enormous,
incredible popular success, which even overcame, despite
her impatient, violently prima donnaish personality (which
had its tender, slyly ironic side, too) the image of the
"tigress" which fashionable opinion in the gossip columns
and the press tried to impose on her. A phenomenon
of this sort is not easily explained, and certainly not in
terms of a predestined personality: she was Callas, and
that was explanation enough. Her model was the exemplary
singer Rosa Ponselle, who in some respects was her pre-
cursor. With innate acting ability, she was a true Greek
tragedian, which gave her a powerful control over gestures,
spaces, words and phrases; and, what is more, she was
guided by wise conductors and intelligent stage directors.
In short, this aggressive, fragile, nervous, egocentric
woman for the first time in many years magnetized the
interest of the entire world, which was not accustomed
to listening to or attending opera; but she was not (as
Beniamino Gigli was) someone about whom it was interesting for everyone to know what she did in life since
she sang so well. For Callas, it was interesting for everyone
to know what she did in life in order to discover why she
sang in so revolutionary a manner, what her secrets were,
why the traditionalists were opposed to her, why her
premières at La Scala became long-drawn-out battles, why
the conviction grew stronger and stronger that after
Maria Callas singers would no longer be able to sing as
they had done before her advent. The battles, caused by
human emotions and by many other matters connected
with good and bad operatic customs, sprang in truth
from a really new creative event: Maria Callas sought
expressiveness not in abandonment to immediate eloquence

370

371

*A great interpretative tradition was also born in acting. After Maria Callas's version, here in* Norma *in sets by Salvatore Fiume, is Leyla Gencer, brandishing a sword in a fury and rapt in her destiny of love and expiation (immediately below, with her, Giulietta Simionato).*

372

373

and the grand phrase but in the character's inner motivations which could be found in the score. Thus she revealed that the marks contained in the five-line stave, which few artists respected as much as she, did not limit the personality of the interpreter but released it, and that a theatrical technique which captures the audience can take the place of inner concentration without detriment to the voice. But here, too, it was fortunate to be Maria Callas. She began at La Scala as Lady Macbeth in Verdi's opera, after a performance of *Aida* in which she had substituted for the main singer of the evening; and she continued with so large a number of roles that she invaded the entire repertoire: an unforgettable *Medea* to Cherubini's music (first conducted by Leonard Bernstein in 1953, later by Thomas Schippers in 1962), *Lucia di Lammermoor* (conducted by Herbert von Karajan in 1954), Fiorilla in Rossini's *Turco in Italia* (conducted by Gianandrea Bavazzeni in 1955), and many other roles, from Amelia in *Ballo in maschera* to Amina in *Sonnambula* (conducted by Antonio Votto in 1959); and so on down to Rosina in *Il Barbiere*. It was an epoch; and it lasted for close to ten years, until 1962.

One also saw that the angelic lightness and powerful emotional amplitude of Renata Tebaldi's singing (at La Scala from 1946) was unrepeatable, incredible artistry. And the same judgment applied to other important figures, who were now at the margins of the new history, such as Magda Olivero (at La Scala from 1939), Antonietta Stella (at La Scala from 1954), and Clara Petrella (at La Scala from 1948), though one admired in these artists the musicality of the first, the astounding equality of register of the second, and of the last the incisive diction which made her the best interpreter of contemporary opera, which is so intimately tied to declamation. Then new great singers, each in accordance with her particular taste, voice and talent, immediately moved in a direction which was much different from the generic, instinctive simplification with its *Verismo* aura and sought to attain a new stylistic precision. Generally, they were foreigners, also an interesting sign, for during the postwar period the school of Italian singing had been forced to mark time and in some areas of the repertoire it was natural to resort, for singing Mozart and Beethoven, to the intelligent bravura of Sena Jurinac (at La Scala from 1949), or for Wagner to the overwhelming musical powers of Birgit Nilsson (at La Scala from 1960), the heiress of the great Kirsten Flagstad (at La Scala from 1947) and, for Puccini's *Turandot,* the heir and renewer of *Verismo* through the white, crystalline absoluteness of passionate dramatic song. Indeed, it now seemed evident that the prima donnas who came from abroad had precisely taken possession of the most inimitable Italian repertoire by employing a pertinent interpretation and a precise singing style. And so, thanks to a rich, well-modulated technical perfection, that stupendous Australian singer Joan Sutherland (at La Scala from 1961) made a great hit, presenting a new version of Donizetti's *Lucia,* in the same stage setting which had seen Maria Callas triumph. And she found her bearings in that region of vocalism which would soon gain followers outside of Europe — all singers intent on the revival of that taste for *fioriture* typical of baroque civilization; a taste which had its magnificent, fascinating celebration at La Scala with the production of Rossini's *L'Assedio di Corinto* (conducted

*374-375. In 1973, Mario Ceroli's sets for* Norma, *starkly simplified wooden structures, took up some of the design motifs of previous productions, but in another atmosphere. The wonderful Montserrat Caballé, the protagonist, with Gianni Raimondi at her side.*

*376-377. Two ways of experiencing Gounod's* Faust*: Renata Scotto in the noble stage set by Alexandre Benois (director Maestrini, 1962); and Mirella Freni in Jean-Louis Barrault's production (1963).*

by Thomas Schippers in 1970), in which the American soprano Beverly Sills and the American mezzo-soprano Marilyn Horne vied in vocal skills, with the expected embellishments and elegancies of expression. However, also in the sphere of a rigorous stylistic approach there were different solutions and directions, indeed opposed solutions and directions; and so the violent personality of the Turkish soprano Leyla Gencer (at La Scala from 1957) accentuated her expressive temperament by establishing an instant relationship between her vocal style and the lyrics, the phrase and the weight of the orchestra, working to transform into a theatrical event phrases rescued from their apparent negligibility, immersing them forcibly in the drama, and not only in the Romantic repertoire but also in operas that move toward Romanticism — as in Gluck's *Alceste* (conducted by Gavazzeni in 1972), where a brief recitative assumed the same importance and revelatory intensity as a long aria. These new lessons had also been learned by another great singer, the Spanish soprano Montserrat Caballé (at La Scala from 1970); her *Norma* (conducted by Gavazzeni in 1973), so lyrical, so immobile, so completely summed up in the internal tragic line of the song, never remotely metallic and never fiery but always wrapped in the shadow of mystery, seemed to be connected directly with the original Bellinian sensibility and at the same time seemed to respond to certain feelings of our time which question the perennial music drama. The most famous Italian singers, however, completed their more leisurely and enthralling parabolas. Renata Scotto (at La Scala from 1953), a lyric soprano, enchanting because of the sweet expansion of her voice, her way of accenting phrases and words (her entrance in Gounod's *Faust,* conducted in 1962 by Gavazzeni, was particularly remarkable), now sought her dramatic presence in roles which traditionally demand a more robust voice, relying instead on the emotional force of her phrasing. While Mirella Freni (at La Scala from 1962), who had begun as a light soprano, got the chance to express her technical ability and the lyrical beauty of her singing in roles usually entrusted to dramatic sopranos, not so much by an adaptation of her vocal means as by a courageously unusual interpretation. Yet the case of Mirella Freni is a special one; a Mozartian singer, aware of the stylistic lessons of an Irmgard Seefried (at La Scala from 1948), as well as a Hilde Gueden (at La Scala from 1948) but possessing a warm-timbred Emilian voice that was always more intense in the center, she has always had an affectionate, direct contact with the audience. The exact opposite of the traditional diva, she is a small, blond, simple girl with a face that Rodolfo has described as that of "the perfect comic opera primadonna," who brings on to the stage a species of our special nostalgia, heightened by our instant identification with her and the miraculous beauty of her singing.

Besides the striking change in the various kinds of

374

375

378

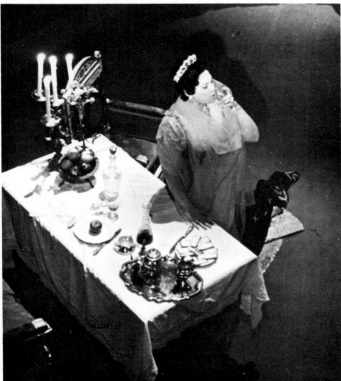

379

sopranos, something analogous has affected singing in all the other parts. Chiefly in the parts for mezzo-sopranos, where suddenly it seemed that the generous, dramatic effectiveness, in the *Verismo* manner, of an Adriana Lazzarini (at La Scala from 1958) or of a Fedora Barbieri (at La Scala from 1946) — who has always, however, been an inimitable Mistress Quickly in *Falstaff* — has been relegated to the past. Yet thanks to the exact, flawless artistry of a style that was appropriate to every score she sang, Giulietta Simionato (at La Scala from 1937), who had also begun with pre-eminently Rossinian and Mozartian roles and then exhibited her gifts throughout the repertoire, for example, bringing to Rossini's *Cenerentola* a tender, charming wit always in the clearest of tones, and to Mascagni's Santuzza the fatal, meditated feeling of someone who without undue strain or effort can express her destiny in all of its lights and shadows. In her wake, Fiorenza Cossotto (at La Scala from 1957) has shaped her strong, splendid voice, now burnished, now crystalline, to the demands of style and inner order, associating her name with many parts, starting with her highly acclaimed Amneris in the fourth act of *Aida*. And among other unforgettable guests, Christa Ludwig (at La Scala from 1960) has brought testimony to the civilization and high style of Strauss's *Rosenkavalier,* conducted by Karl Boehm (1961), who for this opera also engaged Anneliese Rothenberger and the great soprano Elisabeth Schwarzkopf (at La Scala from 1948), whose repeated appearances at La Scala have always been an example of and key to the musical theater of the high Viennese tradition of impeccable classicism, because of her voice's inflections, her musical grace and her smooth acting. But singers had not abandoned the traditional classical purity, even the stupendous actress, woman and singer Shirley Verrett (at La Scala from 1969), who, with the quivering responsiveness of her black woman's nature and her compelling sensitivity as a musician, has given evidence of a vocal inspiration and a completely unique intensity, both in the subtle voluptuousness of *Samson et Dalila* and the sudden, motivated psychological transitions of Eboli in Verdi's *Don Carlos.* However, the change in vocal tastes in tenors has been less striking. A few months after Beniamino Gigli's farewell, Giuseppe Di Stefano (at La Scala from 1947) made his debut in a fine production of *Manon;* and Mario Del Monaco had already been at La Scala since 1945. These two men were singers of great authority, capable of exciting enthusiasm and emotion: Del Monaco because of his strong, sharply accented, violent and impetuous vocal immersion in the part, with a kind of stentorian assurance; and Di Stefano because of his instinctive and prepotent, impassioned and enthralling manner of presenting all of his singing, with the same native ease with which before, and even after, his opera career he had sung songs of every kind. Del Monaco's power, Di Stefano's elegant diction and his charming fashion of molding a phrase, did nothing on the plane of style to further the art of singing, but rather perpetuated the resurgent presence of singing in the Italian style — that is forthright and clear. Ten years later Franco Corelli (at La Scala from 1954) became part of the small group of great tenors; and he too did not take the road of renewal that might have founded new schools or established new styles; yet his voice, with a strong, full richness, a dark hue and an underlying,

380

381

382

383

mysterious melancholy, so in keeping with his tall, slim figure and romantic face, was more inclined to attain it; and study gradually led him to achieve a notable fidelity to the score, at least in its expressive sings, but his vocal abilities were not adequate to his ambitions. This transitional phase (and all phases are) combined quite well, in its own way, with the revolution that Maria Callas had been carrying through. For alongside the new myth of the prima donna in the romantic manner, these new interpreters personified the eternal myth of the tenor; and precisely at Callas's side the intuition of a Di Stefano helped to create an excellent *Ballo in maschera* (1957, with a fantastic company of singers at the peak of their talents: Callas, Di Stefano, Simionato, Bastianini, and Ratti, conducted by Gavazzeni), and it was while singing a duet with Simionato that Franco Corelli received one of the longest ovations in the immediate postwar period, in Meyerbeer's *Les Huguenots,* another astounding production (Corelli, Cossotto, Ganzarolli, Ghiaurov, Maionica, Sutherland and Tozzi, with Gavazzeni conducting, stage direction by Enriquez, sets and costumes by Nicola Benois). Meanwhile, as Ferruccio Tagliavini (at La Scala from 1942 to 1953) was ending his happy career as a light tenor, there began to be known and welcomed the pure, beautiful voice, with its pellucid diction, of the dramatic-lyrical tenor Gianni Raimondi (at La Scala from 1956), who was destined for a long career at La Scala. For some years, however, alongside these dominant tenors, two artists with admirable voices have caused a shift in taste toward a more subtly differentiated interpretative logic: Placido Domingo (at La Scala from 1970) with native spontaneity and Jon Vickers (at La Scala from 1960) with the tragic strength that expresses itself with resonant emotional force in both the sound and the words, not only a fine singer but also a formidable actor who in Wagner managed to attain an intimate tone combined with that expansive, fuller abandon to the orchestral sweep and its attractions to which the great Wagnerian interpreters have accustomed us. Speaking of such interpreters one could also hear at La Scala the classic Wolfgang Windgassen (at La Scala from 1952), while in Italian opera the coloring and phrasing was emphasized in an effort to achieve a deeper sense of the psychology of the characters. Yet the recovery of the taste for stylistic precision has been more fully achieved among the light tenors, now completely, or almost completely distinguished from "lyrical" or "dramatic" tenors; and even if a lyrical tenor such as Luciano Pavarotti has until now had his most flattering successes at La Scala in the roles sung by the light or lyrical-light tenor (Donizetti's *La Fille du Régiment* and *L'elisir d'amore*), thanks to his spellbinding voice, the tradition of light tenors has a separate story of its own at La Scala, if one thinks of the tender and witty ebullience of Cesare Valetti (at La Scala from 1950), the penetrating grace of Nicola Monti (at La Scala from 1951) and Luigi Alva.
This new feeling for song and style has no real parallel among voices in the lower registers, for there stylistic and interpretative differences have been smaller over the course of the years. Two such different baritones as Tito Gobbi (at La Scala from 1941) and Ettore Bastianini (at La Scala from 1948 to 1960) have become an integral part of La Scala's legend: Gobbi, an artist born in the circle of a civilization where opera ("*la lirica,*" it was

called, as if its whole meaning lay in the singing) was popularly a fact of custom, and also a movie actor, someone who followed ideas still part of the glorious past of theatrical craftsmanship, in which the actor seeks out in the details (even of his makeup) the secrets of the character he is interpreting, and, finally, endowed with a voice of limited means from which he could draw, as Giacomo Lauri Volpi has said,[48] "unimaginable sonorities and rash yet conquering resolutions"; Bastianini, composed and aristocratic in his movements and postures, with a dark, deep, very melodious and admirably full, finely balanced voice, which almost with its beauty was able in *Ballo in maschera* to set echoing the forces of vendetta and regret and in Donizetti's *La Favorita* made one feel the solar wonders of the Gardens of the Alcazar and the secret melancholy of his love for Leonora. There also entered the legendary bassos Boris Christoff (at La Scala from 1947), a great interpreter with a regally incisive phrase, and Nicola Rossi Lemeni (at La Scala from 1947), extraordinary in *Boris* or the part of Phillip II in *Don Carlos,* but chiefly the unforgettable creator of certain characters through which his talents as an actor and elocutionist could be powerfully expressed, for example, Kaspar in *Der Freischütz* and, above all, Thomas Beckett in Pizzetti's *Assassinio nella Cattedrale.* With the advent of the 60's, there appeared a new phenomenon, the vocal lightening of deeper voices; voices less easily reached the lowest notes and developed more consummately the higher register, becoming more agile than full-bodied. It is a characteristic which recurs also among mezzo-sopranos who are closer to soprano than contralto; and which also to some extent can be matched among singers with authoritative vocal powers. For example, the baritone Gian Giacomo Guelfi (at La Scala from 1952), who in *Macbeth* proved that when he wished he had a keen critical sense, but above all was memorable as the thundering Compar Alfio in *Cavalleria Rusticana,* has chest tones which are hard to find among the young baritones, including the most famous of the last generation, Piero Cappuccilli (at La Scala from 1968), a very lively interpreter of Verdi, also capable of reaching the summits of acting skill and profound psychological maturity, as he proved in *Simon Boccanegra.* Also among the basses, Cesare Siepi (at La Scala from 1946), apart from the elegant distinction of his manner, had the ability of releasing a stupendous flight of notes that rose from a deep, dark bass register; and Giulio Neri (at La Scala from 1941 to 1948) was a torrent of homogeneous sound. Today the great Nicolai Ghiaurov is also more at his ease in the middle and higher registers, even if this does not prevent him from interpreting nearly any part with splendor and almost incomparable vocal power, striking physical presence and skill as an actor and the rare ability to express all of a character's intensity without spoiling the carefully molded precision of the melodic line; while the excellent Ruggero Raimondi (at La Scala from 1971), though gaining recognition in Verdi's operas, is practically a bass-baritone, a quality which he exploits with an agile, modern interpretative openness. However, in comic opera basses and baritones are usually lumped together under the heading of *basso buffo;* and even if at the level of an involvement outside the circle of stock character parts, it is clear that Fernando Corena (at La Scala from 1949) is an excellent comic opera bass and

*384-387.* *In the 50's, Ettore Bastianini was a noble baritone with a dark, potent voice. Here in* La Favorita *he is seen with the leading lady Giulietta Simionato, an artist with great style, intensity, exceptional intelligence and charm. Fiorenza Cossotto, as Azucena, was second to Simionato in fame as the leading*

384

385

386

387

Renato Capecchi (at La Scala from 1950) an inspired and lovely baritone, while when it comes to roles where the voice must manage a kind of recitative while treading the razor edge of the melody, there are glorious *buffo* specialists such as Carlo Badioli (at La Scala from 1946) or Melchiorre Luise (at La Scala from 1938); even if nowadays the new critical feeling aims at rediscovering and reinserting the most difficult arias which were usually cut in the past, such as Don Bartolo's quite typical aria in *Il Barbiere,* which demands a strong vocal personality and effective means. But there are also singers who overcome the distinction between the comic and the serious; as was true of one of the most sympathetic voices and faces at La Scala, Rolando Panerai (at La Scala from 1952), a fine singer because of his nonchalance and strong expressiveness, both in the parts of Doctor Malatesta in Donizetti's *Don Pasquale* and the Consul in *Madama Butterfly.*

In time these facts also conferred a diverse physiognomy on La Scala. But the most crucial, most original and shocking event can be seen in the revolutionary parabola which stage direction drew over these years; or, more accurately, the new approach to the spectacle, and the new way of understanding it. For the entire conception of opera took a radical turn during the last twenty years, going through so consistent and continual a revolution as to put La Scala on the road of a perpetual crisis, that is, of a continuous and tormented search for itself in the changing relationship with a reality in which everything was being transformed. So, instead of the beautiful certainties of a comforting spectacle, there was the continuous questioning of reality, chiefly in terms of the coherence, logic and beauty of the spectacle.

Stage direction, therefore; it bore this name already in the days of Giovacchino Forzano; and ever since opera began there was a person whose concern was to direct and mount the spectacular side of opera, overseeing every aspect of the *mise en scène.* But we have seen at La Scala about the middle of the 19th century what the logic behind the spectacle was: a botched movement of entrances and exits, and more because of convention than for motives internal to the opera's action. "An operatic parody," by Antonio Ghislanzoni, the librettist of *Aida,* which was published in his book *Scritti Piacevoli* in 1859, in an amusing anticlerical pamphlet entitled "*La festa dello Statuto ovvero I misteri di un Te Deum,*" ("The Holiday of a Statute, or The Mysteries of a *Te Deum*"), presents the humorous stage directions for a scenic realization which was imagined according to the then existing criteria:

Don Pertusio:
Very well! I agree... Take this note.
Now in exchange return my letters.
Sandrino:
I give you my promise
After you will have sung...
I await you in front of the church....
*Sandrino gives the sheet of paper to Mascherpa, who leaves swiftly to take it to the Mayor. Sandrino takes a few steps to leave but then Ninetta arrives, and he returns to take her with him. The actors will try to prolong the scene in order to give enough time to Mascherpa to deliver the note to the Mayor, and for the Mayor to tell the entire population about the Te Deum. To give greater verisimilitude to the situation, Sandrino*

388-390. *Images of an already consolidated taste, and intelligent beauty: the last scene of* Lucia di Lammermoor, *with Pier Luigi Pizzi's costumes and De Lullo's stage direction in 1967, starring Gianni Raimondi and La Scotto. Leyla Gencer* sorrowfully immersed in two great characters of the music theater: Alceste and Elizabeth of Spain. Her characterization was not only psychological and dramatic but responsive to a whole general logic in the ambiance and style.

388

389

390

*and Ninetta could dance a few steps, thus expressing their inner jubilation. Don Pertusio could take advantage of this incident to pick up his prayer book again and recite the office....*
All the records seem to agree that at the end of the 19th century, save for a few productions prepared by Verdi with furious attention and inspired concern for detail, and some other instances, the stage spectacle fell far short of being dramatically convincing and moving. So it can be understood that the most urgent problem in respect to the spectacle, when the sensitivity to it was undergoing a vivid rebirth in a society that was trying to reorganize itself, having left behind the emergencies and tumultuous life of the Risorgimento, was that of finding a firm relationship between the music and the action, the music and the actor's gestures, the music and space in the opera; and that this relationship should remain stable in an immediate sense. Musical *Verismo*, whose ideas insisted that the score must not theoretically give rise to actions but instead reproduce them, not only resulted in fixing a definite choice of milieux, movements and gestures, but also led to conceiving of the score itself in terms of preordained movements and spaces. For example, when Puccini composed *Madame Butterfly* for La Scala, he musically characterized the protagonist when she asks her maid Suzuki for the white garment in preparation for the wedding night, so that the thematic repetition has significance when tied to these particular gestures and no others; and again when she receives it and changes, as she looks coquettishly in her mirror, primping her hair; and again when the night's purifying tenderness descends and bewitches Pinkerton ("*Notte completa: cielo purissimo e stellato,*" "Deep night: pure and starry sky"), and the orchestra's *andante sostenuto* is accompanied by Butterfly's movement (*slowly approaching Pinkerton, seated on the garden bench*), even to the extent that she will wait until she is close to him before she sings (*she kneels at Pinkerton's feet and gazes at him tenderly, almost imploringly*), and only then will she say in a low voice: "*Vogliatemi bene, un bene piccolino, un bene da bambino quale a me si conviene*" ("Ah, love me a little, oh just a little, as you would love a baby").
To present another example, the entire action of the second act of Giordano's *Madame Sans-Gêne* is rigidly controlled by this relationship; if the movements on the stage are not performed, the music becomes descriptive and sounds like the accompaniment to something that is not actually happening. In other words, it no longer has any meaning. The same order in the established relationship between action and score existed between space and score, scenery and score. The scene in Puccini's *Il Tabarro* is described minutely, and contains not only the precise epidermic sensation which accompanies listening to the opera but also the ingredients that will propel the action, and explain why the distances, the conversations and the empty, solitary spaces have their precise arrangement and composition:
"A bend in the Seine on the outskirts of Paris, where Michele's barge is moored. The barge occupies almost the entire front of the stage and is connected to the quay by a gangplank.
"The Seine stretches away as far as the eye can reach. In the distance one can see the outline of old Paris and, chiefly, the majestic bulk of Notre Dame stands out against the sky, which has a marvelous red hue. Also

in the background, to the right, are tenement houses which border the right bank and, much closer, lushly luxuriant plane trees stand tall.
"The barge looks like but another of those many barges which navigate the Seine. The helm can be seen above the tiny cabin; and the cabin itself is neat and gaily painted, with green windows, a small chimney and a low roof, which is somewhat like an altar, on which stand some pots of geraniums. On a clothes line, stretched across the deck, wash has been hung out to dry. A bird cage is set above the cabin door. It is sunset."
In the postwar period at La Scala it seemed that the important problem was to give all opera the same scenic credibility that opera had actually had in the period of the *Verismo* and in a certain sense to ennoble the action by calling in directorial experts to guide the singers. Ennoblement had already been tried successfully at the Florence Maggio Musicale in the years immediately after the war, when the artistic director Francesco Sicialini commissioned great Italian painters of the period, from De Chirico to Sironi and Casorati, to paint the backdrops. And already before 1943 La Scala had profited from the contribution of such noted painters as Casorati, De Chirico, Vellani, Marchi, Cascella, Carpi, Marussig, Prampolini, Neher and Kautsky, with varying results as to beauty and suggestiveness.
In short it seemed above all a fact of style and custom; and with the arrival of Giorgio Strehler (at La Scala from 1947) and his direction of *La Traviata* (settings by Gianni Ratto), together with other operas including Prokofiev's *Flaming Angel,* and later, Luchino Visconti (at La Scala from 1954), with his production of Spontini's *La Vestale* (scenery and costumes by Piero Zuffi, Maria Callas in the leading role, Franco Corelli's debut and, among the many singers, Ebe Stignani and Nicola Rossi Lemeni, the conductor Antonio Votto and, for the first time, Norberto Mola the chorus master, taking the place of Vittorio Veneziani), the question did not seem to go far beyond these terms. Indeed, for many years, if one read the reviews, it would seem that the substance of the problem remained abstract and limited: Can stage direction upset the sacred traditions of lyric opera? Can it make us believe that until now we have been mistaken? Can it disturb the singer, forcing him to think of acting movements and gestures when his task is principally singing? Can it "distract us from the music"? (And the traditionalists, out of resentment, would praise as tradition that which did not "disturb" the parades of banners and standards, the processions of extras and choristers, the precipitous exit of people carrying halberds, the absence of a logic which can distinguish between the gestures of singers in some antiquated *mise en scène,* or, even, elegantly disposed in a graceful, harmonious choreography by Margherita Wallmann.) But the reality of the innovation was something quite different. It could be seen — by those who wanted to see — in the most sensational event, the staging of *La Traviata* by Luchino Visconti, where, assisted by the astounding pictorial elegance of Lila De Nobili's scenery and costumes, the stage action was shifted from its original period to the late 19th century so as to present it in a decadent image and setting. With that brilliant move, which also put at the center of the critical polemics Maria Callas's performance, which aimed entirely at being psy-

chologically convincing and theatrically arresting even at the cost of breaking with the passively handed down tradition of a robust, tubercular Violetta standing forever at the footlights, Visconti demonstrated that he sought not the special theatrical equivalent to Verdi's music but one equivalent among many; that is, he was not intent on discovering the sole and definitive image of *Traviata* but rather a way of experiencing it; and the apparition of the decadent world did not intend to make us believe that this was the solution most suited to Verdi but rather to understand, through these images and presences, the meaning of the society in which the music sought for its space and its characters acted out their destinies, enclosed in themselves or lost in the easy, ample expansion of ephemeral beauty. So this spectacle was an astounding breakthrough; and if people were shocked because attention had shifted to the stage director at the expense of the orchestra conductor, who was one of the most prestigious, cultivated and interesting, Carlo Maria Giulini (at La Scala from 1951), that did not alter the fact that the stage direction did not actually overwhelm or diminish the music. The truth was that an inventive intelligence was employed in a more unpredictable manner on the stage than in the orchestra, and the singers on the stage, above all the protagonist, were supported by the opera's staging instead of being left to their own resources. But the decisive step in this first phase of the renewal of the forms and significance of the spectacle was the production of a Donizetti opera, *Anna Bolena* (April 14, 1957), which had dropped out of the repertoire for some time. Here the new approach lay in having tried to achieve not a kind of singing equivalent of the stage direction of a prose play, though adapted to the exigencies of music, but rather stage direction that found its moral and logical motivations in the music drama itself. The results were unquestionably exceptional. The artistic director Francesco Siciliani, who had been at La Scala for a year, would later declare that there had been established by that production a kind of "Scala hallmark" which represented an initial milestone, a constant point of reference in the long-continuing effort of theatrical experimentation, which would undoubtedly have an unpredictable history. The review written on April 27 by Fedele d'Amico in *Il contemporaneo* explained the reasons for that exceptionality, centering attention on Gianandrea Gavazzeni's conducting, the skill and elegance of a cast that included Gianni Raimondi, Nicola Rossi Lemeni, the great Giulietta Simionato and, of course, the talents of Maria Callas and Luchino Visconti.

"As for the protagonist, that Callas was naturally in her part was clear beforehand.... And once more, both her irate accents as well as her whispered confessions — *'au confessional du coeur'* — were those of a singer who remains one of the most dazzling apparitions of the modern theater. The only singer, certainly, capable of rediscovering instinctively the atmosphere of Italian opera in the first part of the 19th century, the opera which was still permeated with florid, pyrotechnical singing and yet variously strained toward the dramatic feats of Romanticism... Her way of realizing and transfiguring the musical line of the coloratura with a kind of lyrical sigh, recomposing it in a web of transcendental prosody articulated by an incredible richness of accents..., or, analogously, transforming it in a prolonged passionate interjection,

*391-397. This group of photographs could bear the fond title: "the director's vigil." It is in fact the theater seen from a technical, artisan's standpoint—*Aida *with the extras and the chorus with their faces smeared with shoe blacking; snacks backstage*

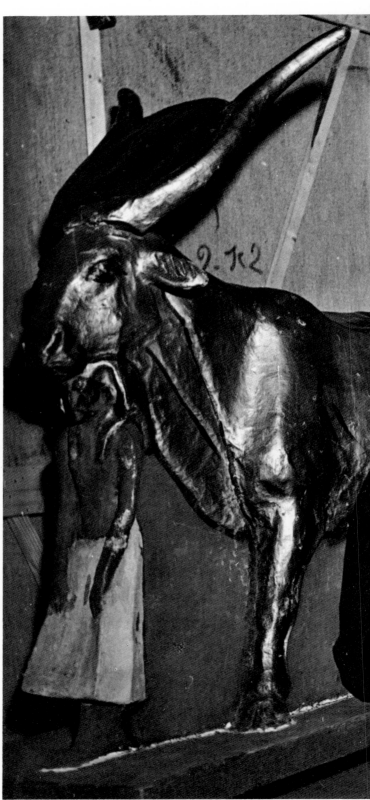

from bags sent up by Milan's cafés amid idols and carelessly propped fans, in a shot that reminds one of a Fellini movie. The time of striking effects put over in a slapdash manner, with soldiers and real horses at the rehearsals; and artists who were to become first-rate are involved in this naive and improbable world, as in the shots from 395 to 397, where one can see Gian Giacomo Guelfi, Ferruccio Tagliavini and Carlo Bergonzi.

393

394

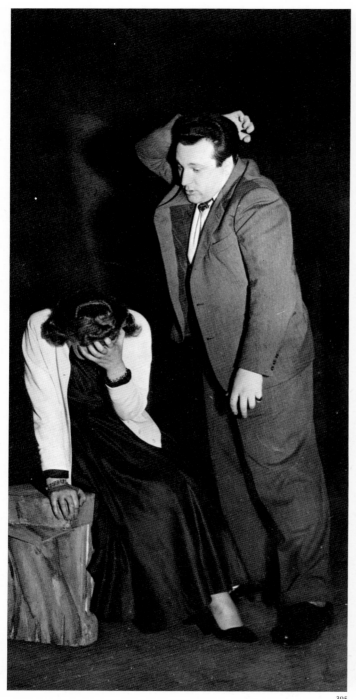

395

396

397

reveals an essential aspect of that music; and precisely that which time has buried and we can no longer find on the written page. We had obscurely imagined that this is what the presence of Pasta or Malibran would have meant; but only Callas has definitively accredited this belief of ours.

"Gavazzeni's very acute conducting, which aimed at letting the individual singers' resources emerge within the limits of a refined, exquisitely minute concentration, was perfectly matched by the spectacle achieved by the stage direction of Luchino Visconti and the scenery and costumes of Nicola Benois. Equally distant from 'melodramatic' rhetoric as from attempts to revive it through the *Verismo* style, Visconti was concerned to preserve, in the encounters between the choruses and soloists, their naturally monumental aspect, aided by symbols of folk clarity (the sudden entrance of Seymour, the Queen's rival, wearing a costume of flaming red against a gray setting; the king who continually appears and disappears through hidden doors, like a conspirator in his own castle). There was no overt insistence, no overemphasis, no moments of indulgence — everything was apparently channelled into the conventions; and yet not a trace of clumsiness — everything was alive and functional; the original nobility of the opera's folk mythology was captured directly, without comments. And there was perfect attunement to the dialectic of the music: the placement of the characters in the ensemble scenes, and Callas's arms in the delirium scene like the wings of some nocturnal bird."

Many stage directors and scene designers who have worked in collaboration will continue to play a big role in this renewal of stage direction. Also the conducting of the orchestra is by now a complete participant in the movement, whenever the conductor wishes to collaborate or is in a position to do so. Gianandrea Gavazzeni (at La Scala from 1943), a fervent, combative, inspired intellectual and an impassioned conductor with an inimitable Bergamasque temperament, was in fact brought to the very center of the movement precisely with *Anna Bolena* and helped to carry it to its immediate consequences. He sought the logic of the spectacle not only in the orchestration but in the reading of the score, attempting, where the opera was bound up with conventional and provisory criteria (the score simply represented a copy of the first production, along with the familiar tangle of accretions caused by changing circumstances, right down to Verdi's time), to perform a series of cuts which followed modern standards of restoration. That is, the cuts were made not, as was often done before this, so that the theatrical passages would become even more prominent, or excluding completely those which were considered "weak" in themselves, but rather by starting from a historical understanding of everything that was certainly intended and essential and everything that was accessory and owed to the forms of those old performances, in order to attain a firm realization of the artistic unity of the present-day spectacle.

A quite similar operation was performed by Gavazzeni on Meyerbeer's *Les Huguenots* and the world of French Grand Opera, resurrected by the fascinating direction of Franco Enriquez and achieving an unusual concentration. The most daring work attempted by Gavazzeni, accompanied by a stormy discussion among the music

247

critics and a great success with the public took place some time later in 1970, with the transposition of the pretended Middle Ages of Verdi's *Vespri Siciliani* to the date of the opera's actual composition, that is, the thick of the 19th century — as had been suggested to Gavazzeni by the set designer Pier Luigi Pizzi (at La Scala from 1963) and brilliantly realized by the stage director Giorgio De Lullo (at La Scala from 1963). These two artists, with Claudio Abbado on the podium, have given life to an elegant and pellucid stylization of the Romantic world in a number of vividly conceived spectacles, which limit the intermissions to an essential one (a necessity by now which is also felt in Italy, following the German example) and which, with transparencies, lights and images for the essential scenic signs but with a kind of substantial suggestivity and a pronounced narrative bent, drew the operatic plot very clearly and boldly. Their rereadings of old scores culminated in their stark, severe *Aida* (1972), in which the presence of the overhanging, mysterious rock alerts us almost physically to the enfolding shadows through which the characters move in symbolically meaningful costumes. Also Franco Enriquez, at La Scala from 1955), a source of theatrical liveliness and a disorderly, reckless talent capable of embodying certain key ideas, gave us, together with various conductors, a number of notable contributions: as in the *Cavalleria Rusticana* of 1964, with Gianni Polidori's scenery, all gray, black and white, livid and tragic, breaking violently with an irritating, tenacious tradition which from the start had set this opera in a highly colored, magazine illustration milieu that smacked of a corny postcard, and on the contrary in this new setting with its bleak stone steps permitted the drama to explode with cruder veracity. In the operas, as in the symphonic concerts with their tradition of a high cultural level, La Scala welcomed prestigious orchestra conductors and continued the series started by Toscanini with the customary Italian guest conductors. These last had above all in common besides their high level of professional experience, a sobriety which avoided rhetorical attitudes and that total abandonment to the sung phrase which characterized Pietro Mascagni's conducting of the orchestra, especially his own operas. Which had also given rise to the misunderstanding that this was the only way to execute them, rather than the personal choice of the composer at the moment he was conducting them, responding to the exigencies of his own rhythm of conducting, the temptations of taste, and his desire to hear himself calmly. Mascagni's conducting was not bad, but it appeared to the younger generations as an example to be avoided. On the other hand, other cultural and artistic reference points could be found as the guidelines accepted by some of the new conductors. Antonio Votto (at La Scala from 1923) was the substitute for Toscanini and conducted almost in his name, even though his taste led him to a certain dwelling on the phrase when accompanying the singers and a peculiar dryness in the orchestral sound. Francesco Molinari Pradelli (at La Scala from 1946), a student of Bernardino Molinari, was impatient, rapid, and tumultuous. Nino Sanzogno (at La Scala from 1941) came out of the Venetian milieu of Gian Francesco Malipiero and Bruno Maderna which was completely open to the new, and dedicated himself with an absolute predilection to the new works, helped by a flair and a

mental skill that could immediately read the most complicated scores and bring to them the light of instant clarification. In the great auditorium of the Teatro alla Scala, these conductors have not perhaps tied their names to particular memorable productions. Yet this did happen when Leonard Bernstein (at La Scala from 1950) presented his version of *Medea* (1953), sung by Maria Callas in scenes designed by Salvatore Fiume (yet Schippers' version of the same opera with a *mise en scène* by the Greek stage director Alexis Minotis and with Callas again the protagonist was a flop in 1961). In 1964 Hermann Scherchen (at La Scala from 1960) also conducted a much discussed and very lucid production of Verdi's *Macbeth,* beautifully simplified by the delicately refined direction of Jean Vilar, which was a great success. However, other guest conductors have done much to further the inner logic of their relationship to the theatrical spectacle. Knappertsbusch (at La Scala from 1957) conducted Wagner with the stage direction of Rott and the scenery of Kautsky; Georges Prêtre (at La Scala from 1962), by now an established and acclaimed guest at La Scala, presented *Faust* as his most important spectacle, with Jean-Louis Barrault's direction and Jacques Dupont's scenery, where the stage space seemed split apart and apparently multiplied in a stupendous synthesis. In this presentation the direction began the experiment afterwards prolonged and perfected in *Carmen,* with a style that was at once breezy and simple but psychologically acute and stripped of all grandiose effects, making a conscious effort at reviving the taste and manner of the old *Opéra-Comique.*
But the conductor who from the start made his restless presence felt most deeply, his personal feeling for innovation and organization, was Herbert von Karajan (at La Scala from 1948). The exciting tension of the new season, the ardent adherence to both the Austrian and Italian worlds, the decadent, amorous beauty of his world of sounds, emotions and a wisdom at once contradicted and rediscovered in the on-going season, together with his almost monstrous ability to coordinate a spectacle through all of its phrases — conducting the orchestra, stage managing the action, making the record and filming the opera, which by now habitually accompanies all of his productions — made him immediately successful, always awaited with emotion, and acclaimed with almost furious fervor and gratitude. Accepted enthusiastically as a Mozartian (and in truth in his Mozart there flashed inspired intuitions, supported by his stage direction, such as the constant tragic note that ran as a clear undercurrent all through his *Don Giovanni,* or the air of nocturnal mystery which surrounded Graziella Sciutti in his *Marriage of Figaro,* even from the recitative before the aria "*Deh, vieni, non tardar*"), acclaimed for his *Fidelio* chiefly because of the exultant, passionate execution of "Leonora No. 3," which is played as a symphonic interlude, and, finally, easily conquering the audience thanks to his *Lucia di Lammermoor,* which isolated the figure of Maria Callas and her actions against nearly black backgrounds and in which both as stage and musical director he managed to involve the entire cast and orchestra in its emotional and tragic intensity. His productions of Verdi were discussed and debated a great deal: his *Falstaff* left the conventional annoyed but not bored, while his *Traviata* flopped on the first night in an atmosphere of agitated nerves (with Mirella Freni singing the main role and the stage direction

398-400. *Two of the most famous La Scala sets in recent years: Lila De Nobili's set for* Aïda, *and Zeffirelli's set for* Bohème, *both of which productions he also directed. Two "second acts" of impressive, refined beauty, arranged with great talent. The* next large photograph shows a rehearsal of the Trovatore *already mentioned a number of times, conducted by Gavazzeni, directed by De Lullo, and with sets by Pizzi. The extras, chorists, assistant* maestri *and director's aides cluster together in the wings.*

398

399

401-403. *Luchino Visconti's lesson. He disposes the large groups, regulates their movements, works with the interpreters, showing them the most revelatory gestures. Visconti's nobility and obstinacy were affirmed at a difficult and propitious historic moment, but they were affirmed definitively.*

402

403

*404-407.* Simone Boccanegra, *1973-1974 season. Giorgio Strehler's lesson. A rehearsal of* Simone Boccanegra *where he delves deeply into the different characters and explains the reasons for their movements and gestures. The imaginative perfection of the opera's theatrical presentation is accompanied by the singers' feeling of inner conviction.*

404

405

406

407

408-420. Color introduces Pepi Merisio's photo-reportage on opera in today's Scala. From the orchestra and from behind the wings his camera has caught Verdi's Simone Boccanegra. Here we see the whole process, in color and in black and white, from the period of rehearsals all the way to the audience's grateful

409

410

411    412

*applause. The cast: Mirella Freni, Gianfranco Cecchele, Piero Cappuccilli, Ruggero Raimondi, conductor Claudio Abbado, stage director Giorgio Strehler, sets and costumes by Ezio Frigerio.*

of Franco Zeffirelli). Nevertheless, with both Franco Zeffirelli (at La Scala from 1953) and Mirella Freni he went on to the great success of *La Bohème;* a production pervaded with an affectionate tenderness for this story of precarious youth that slowly fades away, and with the famous setting (also by Zeffirelli, costumes by Escoffier) of the second act divided into two levels, the Momus Café below and, above, the crowd which strolls along, bumps into each other and never stops swarming past, oblivious to the opera's main action), Gianni Raimondi's voice of ringing purity and Mirelli Freni in her first famous international appearance. Karajan was also responsible for the memorable conducting of Verdi's *Messa da Requiem,* repeated several times after July 8, 1963 (this was the first time that Roberto Benaglio worked as chorus master, a task he performed with great human expressiveness and powerful stylistic impact until the 1972-73 season, when his post was taken by the excellent young musician Romano Gandolfi). And among the many operas Karajan conducted one recalls with surprise, because of his skill in revealing unexpected orchestral possibilities pushed to the limit of stylistic embellishment but with a compelling execution, his production of *Cavalleria Rusticana* (1965), with the direction of Giorgio Strehler and the scenery of Luciano Damiani (at La Scala from 1956).

This production of *Cavalleria Rusticana* seemed to many a kind of operatic "summit meeting": two great interpreters, among the most important of music and the theater; an absolutely first-rate company of singers (Fiorenza Cossotto, Gianfranco Cecchele, Gian Giacomo Guelfi, and the sinuous, very dramatic Grace Bumbry in the leading role), and one of the most talented, refined scene designers, Luciano Damiani. It was another typical reference point for the official Scala, and the whole operation became a kind of race between the stage director and the conductor to depart from remote cultural regions which would somehow ennoble or justify the choice of so popular a drama with music now so distant theoretically from present-day society and culture. So Karajan brought to the score the lesson of the Austrian classic orchestra, remembering also how Gustav Mahler used to conduct; Damiani set the *Verismo* scenes in the distance, placing them at the far corners of the stage set so that from the center of the orchestra one could hardly catch a glimpse of them; the church on the left and Mamma Lucia's vine-trellis and wine-shop on the right. In the pantomime of the religious procession, with the statues jolting on the peasants' shoulders, Strehler emphasized the roots of an ancient Sicilian ritualism, and in the chessboard-like, very controlled movements of the characters, standing out sharply against a few gray houses in the distance and a clear, bright sky, there was a Greek classicism that transformed the bloody climax between Compar Alfio and Compar Turridu into a ritual. Once again this was the conception, which always reappears, of La Scala as the place that welcomes the operas born elsewhere and in another manner. But Giorgio Strehler reversed this procedure with his direction of *Simone Boccanegra* in 1972. The somewhat mysterious and confused story of the Genoan Doge who kidnaps a woman, rediscovers his own daughter, is continually assaulted in his family feelings of affection and attacked for his political efforts at pacification, gave birth to a fond act of faith in the fantasy world of musical opera and its extravagant paraphernalia, and in the truth that it proposes. Not accepting the clichés of the traditional production but rather rendering it all eloquent by a narrative style that tells the story of a privateer called to power by the people and poisoned by a traitor, presenting it in bold figures and emotionally charged images that appeal to cultural memories (the scene and costume designer, Ezio Frigerio), the whole production was inspired by the music's syntheses and amplifications. The triumphant outcome of this production established a new point of reference, indeed one that was much more significant for the future than the equally prestigious *Cavalleria*: Piero Cappuccilli, Mirella Freni, Gianni Raimondi, Nicolai Ghiaurov (in the 1973-4 revival, Gianfranco Cecchele and Ruggero Raimondi) brought the performance to life with a completely natural identification with their parts; and what the stage director had explained during the rehearsals, partly reproduced in the program notes in 1973, became quite clear: "The libretto makes all the events quite complex and even obscure. The marvelous idea to unite the political theme with that of personal affections, the weariness with power and Simone's human loneliness, is resolved by falling back on the old paraphernalia of the fairy-tale plot: the almost casual moment of recognition between father and daughter, the false names, the disguises, the flashing of daggers, the hired murderer of the traitor who poisons the Doge....

"In order to orient ourselves it is necessary to set up essential guidelines. One must follow the drama of the Doge who is very good and seeks peace, surrounded by the others who behave as though he were terrible and cruel. Everything can seem confused, a jagged jumble, but it has meaning in Simone's soul: the prologue, amid torches and cloaks, which is like a series of flashes emerging from the darkness, moments disconnected, broken and superimposed by the memory, the empty palace, the kidnapped girl found dead, the crowd that acclaims the Doge: all this without its real space, its objective order.... The presence of the rediscovered daughter, with its flavor of innocence, at the beginning of the real action, like a legend which comes from afar, blond and gentle at the base of a great sail.... Then the constant struggle to impose and save himself in the hall of the Council, in the Doge's house with its treacherous walls, until he leaves the palace and power and goes to die on the sea amid the rigging of his ship of the past, dressed as he was then, a plebeian among his men.... And to follow the behavior of the different parts of the story: the people of Genoa who gather loyally around Simone the Doge... the struggles among the factions, which suddenly erupt with violence, the Guelph counter-revolution that is subdued, the sailors on the ship at the back of the stage, who lower the sail over their dying Doge."

On the podium for *Simone Boccanegra* stood Claudio Abbado (at La Scala from 1960) La Scala's permanent orchestra conductor and the extraordinary creator of many operas, besides being a successful conductor of its concerts. Abbado came to opera from a mentality and sensibility educated by chamber and symphonic music. Among Italian conductors who have left their mark on La Scala, he is the first who was not born in opera as in a natural breeding ground, a spontaneous theatrical culture, but who rediscovered it by reading scores and

becoming enchanted by the expanses those scores opened up for him. From this came the precise sense of the musical line and a very felicitous baton capable of obtaining both light and sharp sounds, which delved ever deeper into operatic emotion and became a confident possessor of theatrical feeling, combined with a rigorous and fascinating interpretative freedom. Abbado now searched for the most permanent relationship possible with his collaborators; he started with Strehler and tried to gather together a group of first-rate singers who would become accustomed to working in concert. One can see how far he succeeded in his most characteristic cultural and theatrical operation: the revival of Rossini's *opere buffe* in a critical version (*Il Barbiere di Siviglia* entrusted to Alberto Zedda, and *L'Italiana in Algeri* to Azio Corghi), that is, with scores shorn of the incrustations which stale performing habits and faulty transmission of the material have accumulated in the course of about one hundred and fifty years of musical life. For three different operas the company remained almost unchanged: the mezzo-soprano Teresa Berganza (at La Scala from 1958) a singer of fine stylistic intuition and the highest ability, the tenor Luigi Alva and the bass Paolo Montarsolo were the pillars of the production (but with them were the very young Lucia Velentini, La Guglielmi, La Zannini, Capecchi, Ugo Benelli, Enzo Dara and Angelo Romero). Thus the extremely refined cultivation of the first two singers was contrasted with Montarsolo's intelligent, comic Neapolitan verve, a *buffo basso* with a hidden vein of vulnerable melancholy. The entire theatrical side of the productions was in the hands of Jean-Pierre Ponnelle, who had a refined taste in images and a popular taste for stage business — which included his curiously 19th century insistence on the most explosive and gratuitous "gags" — and a rare talent for gaining the company's lively participation in the stage action. This particular way of doing Rossini, which always has an astonishing lightness in the orchestra yet at times can be molded to very different interpretative ends, is naturally but one way of doing Rossini, that is, one way of understanding the faithfully recreated score. But the fascination of these performances was not only due to the experiment, it was also due to the faith which was put in the company, which could be seen quite effectively in its affectionate harmony.

This trend toward stable companies was the most vivid lesson of the striking and suggestive new initiative taken by La Scala in 1955, which constructed next to the theater a small, elegant building called the Piccola Scala or "Small Scala." According to the already quoted *Cenni storici* published by La Scala in 1972, this is: "A theater of about five hundred seats, with a stage that has a surface of about 160 square meters, whose upper floors house the study halls for the Ballet School and chorus, rehearsal halls, etc. It has been aptly called 'La Scala's daughter.' In concrete terms it is a theater conceived in order to reevaluate and bring into living contact with the public, through an authentic desire to increase knowledge and enjoyment, a whole part of the operatic patrimony of the 17th and 18th centuries which was created for theaters of small dimensions or which lends itself, due to its intrinsic structure, to being staged again. And also to present to the public, stimulating its taste for and sensitivity to contemporary music, those

417

418

419

420

421. The Piccola Scala, the small theater which stands next to La Scala. Alva, Sciutti, Maestro Sanzogno, Ratti, Badioli, Simionato, Calabrese take their bows after a performance of Cimarosa's Matrimonio segreto, the inaugural opera in 1955.

422-423. Eduardo De Filippo, director of Paisiello's Barbiere di Siviglia at the Piccola Scala in 1960. The Colonel's scene, with Oncina and Lidonni in a serenade beneath Graziella Sciutti's balcony.

works of the 20th century which, since they require small orchestras and limited stage space, would find here an appropriate place for their presentation. It is a matter of reviving operas already placed historically and esthetically in the musical panorama of the first half of this century, or of encouraging young and talented composers to attempt the path of the musical theater..."

So avant garde experimentation was carried out and is still being carried out. However, most operas were never destined to go beyond their first performances, as is the habit in the present-day world, where the musical theater searches for its forms elsewhere, or at least that part of the musical theater which counts as much as the other parts — that is, the public. And so, aside from the dazzling success of Nino Rota's felicitous little opera *Il cappello di paglia di Firenze*, with Giorgio Strehler's stage direction, Damiani's scenery and Frigerio's costumes, conducted by Nino Sanzogno with an over-all elegance, and aside from the revival of small operas which now seem doomed to disappear, save for Berio's *Passaggio* in 1963 and Manzoni's *Atomtod* in 1964, which was also staged elsewhere, it was not possible to make a lasting contact with the audience except through operas of the past. But, in truth, even the revivals did not have great success in recent years, if one excludes a few, very fortunate instances, such as the intriguing production of Claudio Monteverdi's *Il ritorno di Ulisse in patria* (1973), conducted by Nicholas Harnoncourt and with the illuminating, affectionate stage direction of Giulio Chazalettes (the stars Angelo Romero and Norma Lerer, with sets designed by Ulisse Santicchi). The glorious period of the Piccola Scala could be confined to its first five or six years, when public fervor and interest swirled around a group of singers gathered together in a kind of permanent company, well-trained, stylistically refined, invited to perform everywhere, whose nucleus was composed of the "Cadets of the Scala," which had the scholarly, artistic Giulio Confalonieri as its Maestro. During this period, the small stage of the Piccola Scala was used in succession by such great directors as Giorgio Strehler and Franco Zeffirelli, when they were still gaining recognition, Franco Enriquez and even Eduardo De Filippo. It made a success of the 20th century masterpiece, Stravinsky's *L'Histoire du soldat* (Strehler as director and narrator, Cranko choreographer, sets and costumes by Nicola Benois, the singers Giancarlo Cobelli and Carmen Puthod, and the conductor Sanzogno, 1957), and also the contemporary work of Gianfrancesco Malipiero with his *Sette canzoni* (stage direction by Enriquez and scenery by Lorenzo Ghiglia, 1960) and *Torneo notturno* (stage direction by Beppe Menegatti and scenery by Falleni, 1961), in very suggestive and exciting spectacles. Of the European 20th century there was also an exemplary interpretation of *The Rise and Fall of the City of Mahagonny* by Brecht and Weill in 1964, conducted, as were all the operas previously mentioned, by Nino Sanzogno, directed by Giorgio

422

423

424-426. *Sesto Bruscantini, amusing and extremely gifted artist, beneath the table in Rossini's* Scala di Seta. *Below, two scenes of a memorable production of Nino Rota's* Il Cappello di paglia di Firenze, *the director Strehler, sets by Damiani and costumes by Frigerio.*

427-429. *Strehler as commentator and director of Stravinsky's* L'Histoire du Soldat. *In two years, 1962 and 1963, this work was conducted first by Bruno Maderna, famous musician, and later by Nino Sanzogno. The leading part was sung by Giancarlo Cobelli. This show concluded the Piccola Scala's fervid first period.*

424

427

425

428

426

429

430

431

432

433

430-433. *A few events during the last years of the Piccola Scala. Brecht and Weill's* The Rise and Fall of the City of Mahagonny *(Strehler's direction, 1964); Britten's* Turn of the Screw *(Puecher's direction, sets made from photographs by Mulas, 1972), Monteverdi's* Il ritorno di Ulisse *(Chazalettes, director, Santicchi's sets, 1973).*

Strehler, and with sets by Damiani and Gloria Davy in the leading role.

But the most typical and delightfully unique characteristic of the Piccola Scala during those years was the joyous rediscovery of the European 18th and early 19th centuries: from Handel's *Serse* in 1962, conducted by Bellugi and with Enriquez's imaginative stage direction and manificent sets by an excellent artist, Attilio Colonnello, who had also designed the rich costumes for Rossini's *Scala di seta* in 1962, conducted by Bruno Bartoletti (at La Scala from 1960), a young conductor who would make valid contributions to the theater's life, and with Corrado Pavolini's stage direction, Polidori's sets and costumes, and the singers Sciutti and Alva. These were complemented by the elegance and charm of the stupendous baritone Sesto Bruscantini (at La Scala from 1948), who had always been enormously successful at La Scala because of the measure and precise tempos of his comic style, and whose amiable voice could also be convincing in serious roles, though it was not keyed to the Romantic repertoire, and at whose side one saw in succession Giulietta Simionato, Fiorenza Cossotto, or the graceful Bianca Maria Casoni, and sopranos of the excellence of Eugenia Ratti, Marcella Adani, Ilva Ligabue, and a bass of the stature of Franco Calabrese. In fact Alva and Sciutti were an established pair in the great spectacles of the Piccola Scala, ever since the inaugural production of Cimarosa's *Matrimonio segreto* on December 26, 1956, conducted by Sanzogno, with a cast that included Badioli, Calabrese, Simionato, and Ratti, directed by Strehler, sets by Damiani and costumes by Frigerio, which was repeated many times with great success in the same theater. They were also on hand for the festive revival of Piccinni's *La Cecchina* (1958), Cimarosa's *Le astuzie femminili* (1960), both entrusted to Sanzogno and Zeffirelli; Paisiello's *Nina ossia la pazza per amore* (1961, conductor Sanzogno, stage director Puecher, with scenery by Damiani) and many other productions, including Cimarosa's *Marito disperato* (1974, conductor Pier Luigi Urbini, stage direction Chazalettes, costumes Jurge Henze, with Emilia Ravaglia, Elena Zilio, Rolando Panerai, Walter Monachesi and Leonardo Monreale) which marked their highly successful return after ten years' absence. The immense cultivation of Sciutti's and Alva's singing is among the most delicate and lovable to be encountered in the theater: the lyrics enunciated perfectly with a feeling for all the nuances of the melody, certain pauses, certain sighs, the cleanly etched peremptory opening, abandoning themselves to the affection of the audience, suspended and implicit intentions and those openly expressed, the bewitching, miraculous beauty of the voice's range guided by an alert and sympathetic mind enriched by a graceful and exquisite presence, with a dash of ironic naughtiness that divests them of all possibility of affectation. And if Alva in his ability to enchant and his tenderness conceals a comic vitality

434. *The delirium scene in Paisiello's* Nina, la pazza per amore, *with Martino and Ganzarolli, in sets and costumes by Damiani, direction by Puecher. Graziella Sciutti, the regular prima donna at the Piccola Scala, is seen here with Luigi Alva.*

*Sciutti and Alva at the Piccola Scala formed a pair of great cultivation and admirable, delightful art: the operas that sprang from their singing and acting had an air of authentic, affectionate life, making them live again but with modern intensity.*

that explodes in joyous, irresistible forms, Graziella Sciutti, brilliant and captivating soubrette of the 18th century musical play and opera, with her unerring musical intuition, the beauty of her voice's timbre, as though suspended over a mystery, seems to assume her roles on the very threshold of infinity. And all the more in Mozart's tender and profound music, when they both participated in the Piccola Scala's most memorable production of *Così fan tutte,* which was presented for the first of seven performances on January 27, 1956, with Elisabeth Schwarzkopf, Nan Merriman, Rolando Panerai, and Franco Calabrese, sets and costumes by Berman, Guido Cantelli (at La Scala from 1945, in concerts) conducting and also directing. Cantelli, one of the major talents in the field of musical interpretation, rehearsed his cast for a longer period than usual. He created a spectacle of indelibly memorable beauty that crackled with excitement. He was Toscanini's favorite conductor, a young man with incredible powers of concentration and a potent musical instinct, a musician who was conquering the public by giving it with rigorous assurance the gift of art and receiving its affection and enthusiasm in return. That year he was appointed La Scala's permanent conductor. A few months later he died in an airplane crash, at the age of thirty-six; a dream extinguished in sorrow and resurrected in myth.

Until the outbreak of the First World War, the audience also used to dance at La Scala. There were luxurious, officially voluptuous balls under exceptional circumstances, such as during Carnival Week. There were the *"veglioni"* or all-night balls on the eves of the important holidays, and it is both sad and amusing to think of this well-off bourgeoisie all rigged out in costumes at this crucial period of history, so incapable of watching over itself and so happy and eager to watch all night for the dawn of a festivity. But taking over La Scala did not so much mean abandonment to the joys of dance as it did participation in an art or game which each person, whether bourgeois or classical dancer, celebrated in his own fashion; that is, there always remained a great gulf between the classical dance and the dances of the Carnival balls, especially in terms of mentality and psychology. It had been different only during the period of Austrian domination, even if the gay, frivolous gyrations, the joys of harmonious movement dear to the people of Vienna suffered a certain immersion in irony in Milan. Yet between the dancing of the audience and the dancing on the stage there remained in common the idea that at bottom the music must be simply stimulating, functional, posing no big problems for the listener and, at the most, be an indicator of action, not a summation of significances. The scant attention which was given, except in the most enlightened sections of intellectual society, to Igor Stravinsky's arrival at La Scala in 1926 is quite indicative; but much more so is the list of composers in which, from the last years of the 19th century, one could find Marenco, Bayer, Mader, Minkus, Hellmesberger, Ganne, Collino, Bacchini, Byng, Drigo and Chiti, right down to Vittadini, the composer of a nostalgic, rather slipshod grand ballet, a fond evocation of the city somewhat in the key of *Excelsior,* invented by Adami for the choreography of Giovanni Pratesi, *Vecchia Milano* (1926), which, with its forty-three performances, was the most frequently staged ballet of the 20th century, surpassing even *Luce* by Pratesi and Marenco and rivaled only by the repeat performances of ballets by Manzotti, *Amor* and *Sport.* But in the meantime Delibes and Tchaikovsky had also made their appearances, with *Coppélia* and *The Sleeping Beauty,* which in 1896 were staged by Saracco, who used the original choreography by Nuitter, Saint-Léon and Petipa with middling success (twelve to fourteen performances); in fact, this was a decisive precedent, for it demonstrated that music for the dance, without losing any of its rhythm, its classicism and functionalism, could also be good music. But the rebirth of the importance of the ballet music scores (which in Italy could simply be called a birth, above all at La Scala, since in Viganò's time it was a matter of collages of the celebrated passages of the great composers, and after Viganò the music was always compositions without any pretentions) took place, as always, not only with the rediscovery of the past but with the decision to attempt something new. All this

435

436

occurred when Toscanini, by his presence at La Scala, had created a different mentality in every sector of the opera house, and it has a precise date, the reopening of the theater in 1918 with the ballet *Il carillon magico* by the fine Bohemian musician who had become a naturalized Italian, Riccardo Pick-Mangiagalli (at La Scala from 1914); his music, which revealed a tonally rich and felicitous palette, close to the world of Strauss and Ravel, was conducted by Tullio Serafin. From that time until 1931, except for the insertion of Vittadini's ballet (which, however, was conducted by Gabriele Santini, who from 1925 to 1964 was the fervid animator of many opera productions at La Scala and in the major theaters), the composers were of great prestige: the innovative master of Italian music Alfredo Casella (1883-1947; at La Scala from 1916 as a conductor of its concerts) with *Il convento veneziano* (1925), together with Sauguet, Ravel, De Sabata and others; while the conductors were Panizza, Stravinsky, Votto, the great Ernest Ansermet, who appeared on the tours of Diaghilev, and Richard Strauss, who came in 1928 to conduct the Italian première of his ballet *Josephslegende*. The tradition of ballet had by now been revolutionized; and there will appear on the programs De Falla and Respighi, Rimsky-Korsakov and Prokofiev, Busoni and Petrassi; while usually the orchestra conductor for ballets was a minor maestro of more limited prestige. The distance between classical dance and dancing for the people will increase even more, but this time with a much different significance: classical dance becomes a great artistic fact, which it had not been for decades.

The choreography at La Scala lived for a long time on the ephemeral laurels won by Manzotti's talents; however, the ballet school had lost the grandeur which Blasis had given it in his day. It was indeed Toscanini who revived its splendor, for in 1925 he called to direct it the great dancer and teacher Enrico Cecchetti (1850-1928; at La Scala from 1870 to 1927) who at that time, first in the great Russian theaters, later in cooperation with Diaghilev, had taught the dance to the world's foremost ballet dancers, who still came to him for advice and lessons and submitted to his rigorous discipline. Cecchetti, who was an Italian, the son of a dancer and choreographer who had been a student of Blasis's, made his debut at La Scala in one of Borri's ballets, *La dea del Vahalla,* the beginning of a fabulous career in which he succeeded in redeeming the autonomous value of the leading male dancer, no longer simply the partner of the star female dancer but also a prime figure, and briefly made his contribution to La Scala; but it was just a flick of the whip. During the three years he was there before he died, one felt again the strength of his training based on the structure of academic dance preserved in its abstract fundamental principles, that is, in everything which down through time had demonstrated the substantial impact of classicism on the dance. Cecchetti appeared one last time on the stage in 1927, as the old Charlatan in Stravinsky's *Petrouchka,* alongside his student Vincenzo Celli (at La Scala from 1923) who was destined to become an influential teacher in Europe and principally in North America, and also with his favorite female student, Cia Fornaroli, who after the Maestro's death became the director of the ballet school, also destined to only three years of teaching (after the brief interlude

438

439

438-441. *La Scala sought an international balance in ballet. Here are Spessivtseva and Lifar; Antonio with Elettra Morin in De Falla's* Three-Cornered Hat *with Picasso's sets; Stravinsky's* Rite of Spring *with Massine's choreography.*

442. *La Scala's star ballet dancers today: the delightful and stylish Liliana Cosi and her masterly and effective partner Roberto Fascilla. Ballet at La Scala has had great success in the 70's, even equal to that of opera.*

440

441

442

444

445

*443-445. A wonderful picture of a great guest star, Yvette Chauviré; two ballerinas at La Scala: Vera Colombo in Stravinsky's* Firebird *and Lucina Savignano in a typical dance of the* Albatro *with Ghedini's music.*

of Jia Ruskaya followed by Ettorina Mazzucchelli) and some splendid international contributions. So the life of ballet at La Scala went through a phase of adjustment, of changing tastes and techniques. The audience was offered the refined, abstract choreographies of Margherita Walmann, the cordially expressive dance and intelligent choreographic creations of Nives Poli (in 1941 and 1942 these will be called "Symphonic Ballets," on the basis of a formula invented by Massine to describe an imaginative interpretation of symphonic music), the art of Bianca Gallizia, Attila Radice, and the elegant Luciana Novaro, a dancer and choreographer of intense and unerring inspiration. During these years there were several distinguished choreographic contributions, especially by Aurelio Millos (from 1942).

The entire period after the Second World War was marked by the discomfort and uncertainty of a ballet corps which had to deal with the preparation of ballets within the operas that call for them and also the independent ballets. The leading female dancer most eclectically suited to these exigencies was perhaps Vera Colombo (at La Scala from 1947), with a rare solidity of technique, who could, when needed, be both flaring and sublime. But while she was filling in the gaps during her active years there also came to maturity the thrilling Elettra Morini, the extravagant Giuliana Barabaschi, the exquisitely elegant, precise grace of Liliana Cosi (at La Scala from 1957) and the highly stylized presence of Luciana Savignano, sensual and abstract as some figure taken from an ancient decoration. Together with them, such male dancers as Ugo Dell'Ara, also a fine choreographer, Giulio Perugini and Roberto Fascilla became important. And Amedeo Amodio (at La Scala from 1956) made an impression with his unmistakable élan and his athlete's physique, a face wreathed with curls and a restless disposition, like a boy of today with dreams of the future and a remembrance of the past. And meanwhile world-famous male and female dancers of unquestioned stardom from all over the world appeared on its stage: Yvette Chauviré (at La Scala from 1950) and Violetta Elvin (at La Scala from 1950), both unforgettable personalities, and Maya Plissetskaya, with her violent expressiveness and incredible arm movements, returned several times to great acclaim, and in 1973 her choreography of *Anna Karenina* was also staged. Margot Fonteyn's (at La Scala from 1950) tours began, astonishing balletomanes with her perfection. Balanchine (at La Scala from 1927), the genius of abstract dance rarified in chaste and imaginative forms, came to La Scala to stage his masterpieces, using La Scala's ballet corps, and with important results for Milan. In 1953, Jerome Robbins, the other great figure of American ballet, brought the company of the New York City Ballet and left behind a wake of furious debates after putting on his fine ballet *The Age of Anxiety* with the music of Leonard Bernstein. It was another world. Times were ripening, however, for avant garde ballet; and the fruits

446

were gathered in the seasons from 1972 on by the company of that talented man of the theater, Maurice Béjart.

Ballet grew in importance and congeniality in a society by now accustomed to peace, and in a civilization of images which gradually turned its ever-mounting interest to a theater based less on words and more on gestures. But the real propelling force in ballet was not simply the images but the presences. In 1964, a political defector from Russia, Rudolf Nureyev, came to La Scala; and he immediately had an extraordinary triumph. Dancing with him was Fonteyn, who was at the peak of her romantic beauty and inner refinement. Nureyev was especially brilliant in the pas de deux from *Le Corsaire,* but he was magnificent and stupendous in all of his interpretations; that face and body of a Tartar, that lion-like pounce, those soaring, hovering splits and leaps, the violence of each of his unleashed moments, the meditative and disquieting presence now of an actor of supreme talent (that entrance with flowers for the grave of the betrayed girl in *Giselle* remains a legendary moment in the theater above and beyond the dancing itself) now a splendid theater animal — all these moments project the world of ballet into our lives, beyond all communication and through the simple code of academic dance. It was Nureyev who smoothed the way for broad popular comprehension of ballet, whether one admired the amazing elegance of Paolo Bortoluzzi, or appreciated the intelligence and theatrical presence of Attilio Labis, or became enthusiastic over the infrequent appearances of the sensational Russian male dancer Vladimir Vasiliev, first in the splendid test of strength in the kitsch-ballet *Spartacus* with the Bolshoi company (which had some fantastic ensemble dancing in which the great dancer Liepa stood out), later with his wife Ekaterina Maximova during the summer at the Sforzesco Castle (a very recent tradition at La Scala), and finally at La Scala itself, dancing with Carla Fracci during the memorable evening in honor of Charlie Chaplin. Carla Fracci (at La Scala from 1954), a dancer who came out of La Scala's Ballet School as a Milanese promise, at first the graceful embodiment of its hopes, afterwards the proof that a girl from the people can transform herself into a fabulous personage of the world's great theaters, and finally the presence of "someone like ourselves" in the mysterious world of the dance, personally living the human truths which are hidden from us, a dancer who today incarnates the myth of the interpreter in La Scala's life. Every one of her recitals is completely sold out, for example, the fifteen performances of *Swan Lake* during the 1973-74 season, when she made her debut in this ballet. Every moment of her existence is the object of close attention; and she already has behind her a series of important experiences at La Scala, too: whether she danced in Prokofiev's ballet *Romeo and Juliet* which was created for her in 1958 by John Cranko, or interpreted the ballets of Italian composers at their first performances, such as *Fantasmi al Grand-Hotel,* with a libretto by Buzzati, music by Chailly, and choreographed by the famous Leonide Massine (1960); or *La Strada,* taken from Fellini's film, with music by Nino Rota and the choreography created by Mario Pistoni, one of the dancers most tied both as an interpreter and creator of ballets to La Scala's life. Fracci has appeared as many different characters, all interpreted from within, often shaped by some gesture invented with her

447-449. *Maya Plissetskaya with her unforgettable power in Tchaikovsky's* Swan Lake; *Margot Fonteyn (here with Attilio Labis), the queen of international ballet due to her classic perfection; Galina Ulanova, mythical ballet figure of striking native violence.*

447

448

449

450-452. *Modern ballet has of course a large and growing place at La Scala. Maurice Béjart has been the chief mover and shaker, the inventor of inimitable and inspired ballet spectacles.*
*New symmetries in today's dance, new gestures: such as the* pathetic, *extraordinarily intense movements of the mime Marcel Marceau, who seems to sum up both the old and new styles with his amazing ability to appeal directly to the audience.*

451

452

special imaginative gift; and she has approached many areas of taste and culture, often guided by her husband Beppe Menegatti, a tenacious proponent of the necessity of staging in ballet, who is concerned with the molding of the spectacle; but above all she has personified the most famous figures in ballet, beginning with *Giselle,* which, after having brought to maturity while dancing with Erik Bruhn, with his noble art and impeccable technique, she was later able to bring to absolute perfection. And in this perfection were evident not only the light play of her legs, the poise of her neck, the abandonment to the music of her arms which trace miraculous, fantastic shapes, but also the profound coherence of the character she is portraying, the absolute immersion in it of her face, body and soul, together with the tension that springs from this and produces an exultant success. Indeed this is the significance of Fracci's presence in the present-day life of La Scala: the ability to infuse ballet with an intense appeal, making it into a complete theatrical experience; and not simply the theater where one looks, listens and admires, but the theater where everyone is directly involved and is compelled to feel and think.

454

455

*holiday performance; ending with that exhausted, marvelous moment when the performance is over, just behind the barely closed curtain. All has been offered, even the last bows. Nothing remains but a little joy, silence and the future.*

456

457

458

459

460

462

463

464     465

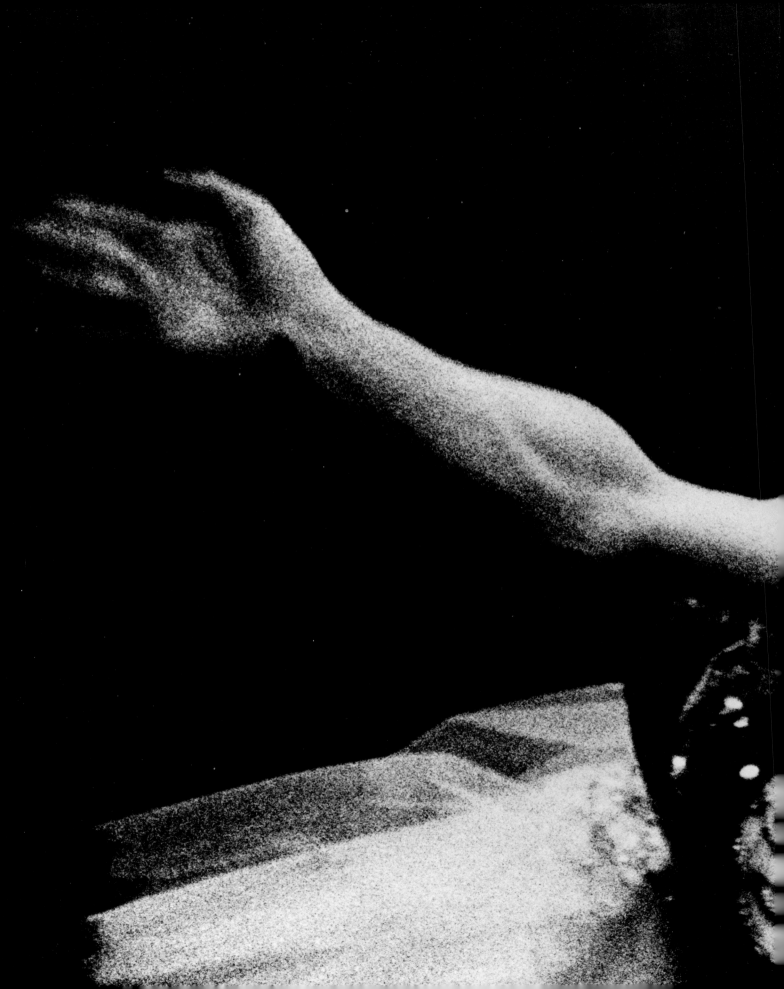

469

The important role is to listen, think and feel. True enough. But who fits this role? It is of course the audience that is called upon to fit it, but who the audience actually is happens to be not only a subject for research but also a matter for the organizers and promoters — with the hope that the entire city will eventually participate in La Scala's life. That is how modern logic runs, especially when it sees La Scala making an extraordinary contribution as a public theater, and when it theorizes about the social obligations of the theater in general. This is how, certainly, the new Superintendent Paolo Grassi, who has been active since 1972, thinks and indeed acts. The push in this social direction given by Paolo Grassi is the really new event: the multiplication of initiatives, the opening of the theater's productions to groups of spectators organized directly by the trade unions, together with many other efforts to make La Scala's presence felt in the entire city's life. This is a more arduous enterprise than in the past, since it is taking place just when La Scala cannot offer a culture that is the man of today's but rather the man of today's meditation on the creations of yesterday, save for some rare exceptions; and when it must fight its battle at the highest level of artistic accomplishment and effort. All this demands organization at a moment and in a country not exactly suited to putting through long-range plans, particularly because of laws which tend to keep every new effort under close control not merely in terms of projects but also of results, and during a phase of delicate transition, when the group of men who managed La Scala in the postwar period have concluded their work. So the attempt at renewal is bound to run into many problems and difficulties.

Paolo Grassi brings to his work his experience of twenty-seven years as director of the glorious Piccolo Teatro of the city of Milan, and also his popularity as a figure in the arts. It is not for nothing that when a singer does not hit a high note properly there is always some denizen of the top balcony who whispers or shouts: "It's all Paolo Grassi's fault," in just the same way that when the orchestra played badly after 1929, the old subscribers would often shake their heads and murmur: "You can see that Toscanini's days are over." In fact, once when a violinist's string broke, there were people who maintained that it would never have broken in Toscanini's time. In short we are living in different times, searching for a new La Scala which will be both of our day and the future. Certainly tradition counts for a lot, and La Scala preserves a great deal of it, perhaps ritualistically. To mention a few: the opening on St. Ambrose's day, the holiday of Milan's patron saint, absolute punctuality about curtain times, the cordial dignity of its ushers and usherettes. But certainly it is hard to say in advance what new roads will be opend by La Scala. A theater is also made up of this — a search and a quest.

And so this account of the history of La Scala breaks off suddenly in the spring of 1974, without being able to say anything about the future and, for the same reason, about the present, which is too mobile in an unpredictable world. All that remains for us is to return to the past, both recent and far-off, to try to resume the discussion, round it out with neglected names, even important ones, with useful and suggestive events so as to understand what weight art and customs, culture and life generally had on La Scala, which gathered these things in and spread them abroad. The weight of the past: that weight which is still so overpowering if one looks at Piermarini's great auditorium, when it seems so natural and inevitable to say what Riccardo Bacchelli said: "Here are joined together in the memory remembrances handed down and musical motifs, words and actions on the stage: and remembering them conjures up in the mind, imagination and emotions an ideal scene. It is enough to mention it, and in the empty theater, with all the lights out, the instruments stir in their boxes or move beside their music stands: the very footlights flash on by themselves!" The past — the past which vibrates in the words of Giulio Ricordi, who defended La Scala about a century ago from the faction which claimed that its task had ended. It was a fighting speech, as we say: "Gentlemen, La Scala is a great theater but it is also a great and glorious temple of art; and I say glorious because the accusation of decadence which has been hurled at it with so little sagacity and, permit me to say so, so much light-mindedness, is not true and is not founded... Indeed so true is this that, while some today are regretting the glories of the past if one looks at the newspapers of forty or fifty years ago one can read the very same sentences being spouted today. Then, too, they deplored the scarcity of new singers; then, too, they deplored the scarcity of new operas; and yet the composers of that epoch were called Rossini, Bellini, Donizetti, Mercadante."

That took place in 1885. Less than two years later, on February 5th, Massenet, Reyer, Bellaigue, Muzio, Clemenceau, Du Locle, Gailhard, Carvalho, Fogazzaro, Giacosa, Tosti, Checchi, Panzacchi, Matilde Serao, Michetti, Torelli, Pascarella, Depanis, Turco, Sivori, D'Arcais and many other well-known names in the world's history, together with three thousand people who packed La Scala, heard the first of *Otello's* twenty-five performances. As night was falling, the entire audience gathered beneath the windows of Verdi's hotel. And when the old Maestro came out on the balcony, the tenor Tamagno, who had been on the stage before and now was there below waiting for him, intoned at the top of his ringing, plangent voice, as if he were reading it from the score: "*Esultate!*"

1. F. Armani and G. Bascapè, *La Scala, breve biografia*, Milan, 1951, p. 60.
2. Published posthumously in 1838.
3. *Carteggio di Pietro e Alessandro Verri dal 1766 al 1797*, edited by Novati, Greppi, Giulini, Seregni, I, Milan, 1919, vol. 1, p. 212.
4. For example, Gino Monaldi in *Le regine della danza del Secolo XIX*, Turin, 1910, and Giuseppe Rovani in *Cento anni*, Milan, 1859, chapters 1 and 3, report conflicting judgments. The polemic is summed up also by Luigi Rossi in *Il ballo alla Scala*, Milan, 1972, chapters 1 and 2.
5. These events are put in their proper context in the *Enciclopedia dello Spettacolo* under the entries dealing with the various performers and written by Andrea della Corte and Rodolfo Celletti.
6. *Teatro della Scala nella vita e nell'arte dalle origini ad oggi*, Milan, 1921, p. 18.
7. *Storia di un teatro e di una città*, in *La Nostra Scala, Quaderni della Città di Milano*, 1961.
8. For the events of Milan's history see *Storia di Milano*, vols. 12-16, Milan, 1956-1962.
9. G. Rovani, *Cento anni*, edited by G. Gutierrez, Milan, 1934, p. 94.
10. An untranslatable play on words, since in Italian "fiasco" not only means a theatrical flop but also a large bottle of wine. (Translator's note)
11. Letter of February 12, 1717.
12. That is, the composer Mayr's.
13. *Op. cit.*, pp. 54-55.
14. *Commentarii della vita e delle opere coreodrammatiche di S. V.*, Milan, 1838. All of Rossi's quotations are taken from this book.
15. Milan, 1968. The exhibit was organized by La Scala Museum.
16. *La "Gazza ladra" a Roma. Un'astronave carica di note*, in L'Espresso, 9.12.1973.
17. We advise consulting the 1973 edition of this essay published in Milan with an introduction by Franco Catalano, which is a useful source of testimony and reflections on La Scala's history in Milan seen in a broad context. The quotation above appears on pages 41-42 of this edition.
18. The attempts to explain the relationship between opera and the public's ideas were usually made at this time from the standpoint of the Risorgimento, just as today they are made from a social or socialistic standpoint; hence the rather naive simplifications, for example the ardent eloquence of Giuseppe Mazzini's *Filosofia della musica*, which is nevertheless a precious document.
19. *Il gruppo del 'Conciliatore' e la cultura italiana dell'Ottocento*, Milan, 1969.
20. In the article on Tamburini in the *Enciclopedia dello Spettacolo*.
21. Pseudonym of Edoardo Perelli, the critic of the *Gazzetta Musicale*.
22. The article appeared on February 26, 1829. The opera had been staged on the 14th; on the 19th the first article by Francesco Pezzi was published.
23. For example: *Alfonso di Ferrara, Eustorgia da Romano, Giovanna I di Napoli, La rinnegata, Elisa Fosco, Nizza di Granata* and *Dalinda*.
24. Letter to Antonio Vasselli, October 24, 1841: "For *Lucrezia*, Lanari's score is bound to have Lucrezia's cabaletta at the end, as they all have; but you follow the rule that after the death of the tenor all stand up at the Duke's arrival and then drop the curtain". And a few days later: "You and all the Romans are cretins. So you want the cabaletta at the end? All right, you'll see how it goes."
25. Cited in F. Pastura's book *Bellini secondo la storia*, Parma, 1959, p. 295.
26. In her essay *"Prospettive della librettistica nell'età romantica,"* published in the volume of studies on the Italian theater, *Vita e Pensiero*, Milan, 1968, p. 226. But for the relationship between Bellini, Donizetti and their various sources, see the volumes by the same author entitled *Indagini sulle fonti francesi dei libretti di G. D. ... e di V. B.*, Milan, 1966 and 1968.
27. G. Gavazzeni, *Donizetti*, Milan, 1937, pp. 32-33.
28. This is an Italian version of A. Pougin's *Verdi, vita anedottica*, with additions by Folchetto, Milan, 1881.
29. There is a whole series of mistakes, which might have been made by Verdi as he told the story; in any case, the spirit of the account is what Verdi felt or let one believe he felt, even if the narration may accentuate some details in a highly romantic fashion. The mistakes are chronological: the composition of the comic opera *Un giorno di regno* began in the first days of March, 1840, and at that time the children were already dead, first Virginia (August 12, 1838) and then Icilio (October 22, 1839). His wife, Margherita Barezzi, died on June 18th. (The première of *Un giorno di regno* was on April 5, 1840.)
30. Beginning of a conversation with Piero Rattalino, *Leone Fortis, il "poeta del teatro,"* which will soon be published by RAI, in a volume which collects reviews written in 1893 and other writings by Fortis.
31. *I problemi della scenografia e l'Ottocento*, in *Tempi e aspetti della scenografia*, Turin, 1954, p. 162.
32. Programs from 1864 to 1964 were published in *Cento anni della Società del Quartetto*, Milan, 1964.
33. In the article devoted to Faccio in *Enciclopedia dello Spettacolo*.
34. *"Come scrive e come prova G. V.,"* an article by Giulio Ricordi in the special issue of *L'Illustrazione Italiana* devoted to *Falstaff*, Milan, 1897.
35. In his biography *Caruso*, Milan, 1947, p. 29.
36. Verdi's letter to Vincenzo Torelli, September 13, 1872.
37. Even more than by the famous magazines (such as in its time the celebrated *Biblioteca italiana* favorable to Austria and the soon suppressed *Il conciliatore*) influence was exerted by newspapers such as *La gazzetta privilegiata, L'eco, I teatri, Corriere delle dame, Il censore universale* and *Il Figaro* which were mainly literary, and the various Almanacs, among which the Almanac of La Scala that appeared in 1828, a guide to opera, and later on such newspapers as *La perseveranza, Il pungolo, Il trovatore* and others.
38. In a verse letter to his brother: *"Florence | plus ennuyeuse que Milan, | où, du moins, quatre ou cinq fois l'an | Cerrito danse."* "Florence | more boring than Milan, | where at least four or five times a year | Cerrito dances."
39. A. Levinson, *Meister des Balletts*, 1914 (translated into German by Reinhold von Walter, Potsdam, 1923).
40. That is, the quartet of string instruments.
41. The composer was seated with the orchestra during the first three performances, in accordance with an Italian custom of the time which insisted that he must appear before the audience.
42. *Op. cit.*, pp. 95-96.
43. In AA. VV., *Mascagni* (Milan, 1964).
44. *Op. cit.*, p. 119.
45. With E. Gara's memories and letters, Milan, 1972.
46. In *Nuovi orientamenti della scenografia*, Görlich, Milan, 1965, II, p. 57.
47. Anecdote taken from G. Gavazzeni *Le campane di Bergamo*, Milan, 1963, pp. 106-108.
48. In *Voci parallele*, Milan, 1955, pp. 179-180.

# ILLUSTRATIONS

*Abbreviations:* L.T.S. = Library of La Scala Theatrical Museum; T.M.S. = Theatrical Museum of La Scala.

175. *Giacomo Puccini. Bertarelli Print Collection.*

176. *Birgit Nilsson in Puccini's "Turandot," costume by Nicola Benois and Chou-Ling, 1962.*

177. *Sketch by Chini of first performance of Puccini's "Turandot."*

178. *Poster by Metlicovitz for Puccini's "Madama Butterfly." Ricordi. L.T.S.*

179-181. *Eugenia Burzio in Ponchielli's "La Gioconda." L.T.S.*

182. *Salomea Krusceniski in Strauss's "Salomé." L.T.S.*

183. *Maria Labia in Strauss's "Salomé." L.T.S.*

184. *A scene from "Otello," drawing by A. Bonamore in special number of* Illustrazione Italiana *to mark first performance of Verdi's "Otello." L.T.S.*

185. *Clara Petrella and Tito Gobbi in Puccini's "Il Tabarro," directed by Carlo Maestrini, sets by Giovanni Miglioli, 1959.*

186. *Maria Labia as Mimì in Puccini's "La Bohème." L.T.S.*

187. *Renata Scotto as Mimì in Puccini's "La Bohème." L.T.S.*

188. *Rosetta Pampanini as Mimì in Puccini's "La Bohème." L.T.S.*

189. *Gabriella Tucci as Mimì in Puccini's "La Bohème." L.T.S.*

190. *Mirella Freni as Mimì in Puccini's "La Bohème." L.T.S.*

191. *Gemma Bellincioni and Roberto Stagno in Mascagni's "Cavalleria Rusticana." L.T.S.*

192. *Enrico Caruso as Don José in Bizet's "Carmen." L.T.S.*

193. *Giulietta Simionato and Gian Giacomo Guelfi with the director Franco Enriquez during the rehearsals of Mascagni's "Cavalleria Rusticana," sets by Polidori, 1963.*

194. *Gino Bechi in Mascagni's "Cavalleria Rusticana," 1952.*

195. *Fiorenza Cossotto and Gian Giacomo Guelfi in Mascagni's "Cavalleria Rusticana," sets by Luciano Damiani.*

196. *La Scala in an end-of-the-century photograph. Bertarelli Print Collection.*

197. *The interior of La Scala from* Illustrazione Italiana, *1901-1902, special number dedicated to La Scala.*

198. *The workroom in the loft where stage sets are made, from* Illustrazione Italiana, *1901-1902.*

199. *Drawing by Beltrame for the cover of* Illustrazione Italiana, *1901-1902.*

200. *Drawing by F. Matania from* Illustrazione Italiana, *1901-1902.*

201. *The stage technicians' platform during a performance, drawing by Ferraguti, from* Illustrazione Italiana, *1901-1902.*

202, 205. *The lobby of La Scala, drawings by Ferraguti, from* Illustrazione Italiana, *1901-1902.*

203. *The crowd of curious onlookers at the entrance to La Scala on the evening of a performance, drawing by Ferraguti from* Illustrazione Italiana, *1901-1902.*

204. *Announcement of the tourney of the Nice Cavalry Regiment held at La Scala on May 23, 1890. Bertarelli Print Collection.*

206. *Inside La Scala during the journey of the Nice Cavalry Regiment. Bertarelli Print Collection.*

207. *Crowd coming out of La Scala after a première,* Illustrazione Italiana, *1901-1902.*

208. *Invitation to the ball given at La Scala on the night of January 21, 1857. Bertarelli Print Collection.*

209. *Small calendar for the year 1858. A. Vallardi Edition. Bertarelli Print Collection.*

210, 211. *Small calendar for the year 1873. Bertarelli Print Collection.*

212. *A page from* Il Tempo *of January 20, 1899, with the review of the first performance at La Scala of Mascagni's "Iris."*

213. *A page from* Il Tempo *of March 18, 1900, with the review of the first performance at La Scala of Puccini's "Tosca."*

214. *Poster for the ballet "Excelsior," choreography by Luigi Manzotti, 1881. Treviso, Civic Museum.*

215. *Cover for* Illustrazione Italiana *of February 21, 1886, with a drawing by Dalbono of the ballet "Amor," choreography by Luigi Manzotti.*

216-219. *The dancers at La Scala in drawings by Ferraguti from* Illustrazione Italiana, *1901-1902, special number dedicated to La Scala.*

220. *Arturo Toscanini.*

221. *Franco Faccio in a drawing by Dovera. L.T.S.*

222. *Cleofante Campanini in 1910. L.T.S.*

223. *Leopoldo Mugnone. L.T.S.*

224. *Tullio Serafin in 1905. L.T.S.*

225. *Ettore Panizza. L.T.S.*

226. *Gino Marinuzzi. L.T.S.*

227. *Nazareno De Angelis. L.T.S.*

228. *Ranieri Tenti: Claudia Muzio in Verdi's "La Traviata." L.T.S.*

229. *Inauguration of monument to Giuseppe Verdi at Busseto.*

230. *Claudia Muzio in Bellini's "Norma."*

231. *Rosina Storchio in Verdi's "La Traviata."*

232. *Mariano Stabile in "Falstaff" in 1936, photograph with dedication in singer's hand. L.T.S.*

233. *Gabriella Besanzoni in Bizet's "Carmen."*

234. *Tina Poli Randaccio in Ponchielli's "La Gioconda."*

235. *Salomea Krusceniski in Strauss's "Salomé."*

236. *Maria Gay in Bizet's "Carmen" and Saint-Saens's "Samson et Dalila."*

237. *Giuseppe Borgatti in Giordano's "Andrea Chénier."*

238. *Benvenuto Franci in Verdi's "Aida."*

239. *Aureliano Pertile in Donizetti's "Lucia di Lammermoor."*

240. *Arturo Toscanini (at the right) with friends.*

241. *Arturo Toscanini surrounded by friends.*

242. *Arturo Toscanini leaving for a tour with La Scala's orchestra.*

243. *Drawing of Arturo Toscanini.*

244-246. *Arturo Toscanini conducts the concert on May 11, 1946, for the reopening of La Scala after the war.*

247. *Arturo Toscanini.*

248. *Enrico Caruso in Verdi's "Rigoletto." L.T.S.*

249. *Beniamino Gigli in Puccini's "Tosca." L.T.S.*

250. *Giacomo Lauri Volpi in Puccini's "Manon Lescaut."*

251. *Carlo Galeffi as Barnaba.*

252. *Toti Dal Monte in Verdi's "Rigoletto."*

253. *Melchiorre Luise in Rossini's "Il Barbiere di Siviglia," 1955-1956.*

254. *Mafalda Favero in Verdi's "Falstaff."*

255. *Luigi Alva and Tito Gobbi in Rossini's "Il Barbiere di Siviglia."*

256. *Ebe Stignani and Gino Bechi in Donizetti's "La Favorita."*

257. *Gianna Pederzini in Bizet's "Carmen."*

258. *Victor De Sabata and Arturo Toscanini.*

259, 260, 262, 264, 266, 267. *Victor De Sabata, drawings by Tabet.*

261, 263, 268. *Victor De Sabata conducts the orchestra at La Scala.*

265. *Victor De Sabata and Maria Callas in 1954.*

269, 270. *Hermann Scherchen.*

271. *Wilhelm Furtwängler.*

272. *André Cluytens.*

273. *Karl Boehm.*

274. *Francesco Molinari Pradelli.*

275-278. *Guido Cantelli during a rehearsal.*

279-281. *Guido Cantelli during a performance.*

282, 284. *Herbert von Karajan.*

283, 285, 286. *Herbert von Karajan with Jon Vickers, Peter Glossop and Raina Kabaivanska during the rehearsals of Leoncavallo's "I Pagliacci," 1965.*

287, 288. *Herbert von Karajan and the chorus master Roberto Benaglio during the rehearsals of Verdi's* Requiem Mass, *1963.*

289. *Herbert von Karajan during the rehearsals of Donizetti's "Lucia di Lammermoor," 1954.*

290. *Herbert von Karajan.*

291. *Gianandrea Gavazzeni.*

292-297. *Gianandrea Gavazzeni and the stage director Giorgio De Lullo during the rehearsals for Verdi's "Trovatore" with Fiorenza Cossotto, 1962.*

298-303. *Claudio Abbado.*

304. *Carlo Maria Giulini.*

305. *Zubin Mehta.*

306. *Leonard Bernstein.*

307. *Sergiu Celibidache.*

308, 309. *Georges Prêtre.*

310. Stravinsky's "Rake's Progress" with Mirto Picchi and Elisabeth Schwarzkopf, 1951.

311, 312. Alban Berg's "Lulu," directed by Günther Rennert, sets and costumes by Teo Otto, 1962-1963.

313. Sketch by Jean-Denis Malclès for Ravel's "L'Heure Espagnole," 1958.

314. Poulenc's "Dialogues des Carmélites," director Margherita Wallmann, sets and costumes by Georges Wakhevitch, 1958.

315, 316. Pizzetti's "Murder in the Cathedral," director Margherita Wallmann, sets and costumes by Piero Zuffi, 1958.

317, 318. Gershwin's "Porgy and Bess," director Robert Breen, sets and costumes by Ann Roth and Mace, 1955.

319. Stravinsky's "Oedipus Rex," director Giorgio De Lullo, sets and costumes by Pier Luigi Pizzi.

320. Prokofiev's "Flaming Angel," director Virginio Puecher, sets and costumes by Luciano Damiano, 1956.

321. Berg's "Wozzeck", director Ernek Karel, sets and costumes by Josef Svoboda, 1971.

322. Shostakovich's "The Nose," director Eduardo De Filippo, sets and costumes by Mino Maccari, 1972.

323. Schönberg's "Moses und Aaron," director Gustav Rudolf Sellner, sets and costumes by Michele Raffaelli, 1961.

324-326. Sketches by Pier Luigi Pizzi for Wagner's "Die Walküre," 1973.

327. Dimitri Mitropoulos.

328-331. Dimitri Mitropoulos with the cast of Berg's "Wozzeck," June 5, 1952.

332. Maria Callas in Verdi's "La Traviata," director Luchino Visconti, sets and costumes by Lila De Nobili, 1955.

333, 336. Maria Callas with Ettore Bastianini in Verdi's "La Traviata," 1955.

334, 335. Maria Callas in Verdi's "La Traviata," 1955.

337, 338. Maria Callas with Giuseppe Di Stefano in Verdi's "La Traviata," 1955.

339, 340. Maria Callas in Verdi's "La Traviata," 1955.

341. Maria Callas and Gianni Raimondi in Donizetti's "Anna Bolena," director Luchino Visconti, sets and costumes by Nicola Benois, 1957.

342-346. Maria Callas in Donizetti's "Anna Bolena," 1957.

347. Maria Callas with Mario Del Monaco in Giordano's "Andrea Chénier," director Mario Frigerio, sets and costumes by Alexandre Benois, 1955.

348-352. Maria Callas in Giordano's "Andrea Chénier," 1955.

353-361. Maria Callas and Franco Corelli in Giordano's "Fedora," director Tatiana Pavlova, sets and costumes by Nicola Benois, 1956.

362. Maria Callas and Giuseppe Di Stefano in Verdi's "Un ballo in maschera," director Margherita Wallmann, sets and costumes by Nicola Benois, 1957.

363. Maria Callas in Gluck's "Alceste," director Margherita Wallmann, sets and costumes by Piero Zuffi, 1954.

364-366. Maria Callas in Donizetti's "Lucia di Lammermoor," director Herbert von Karajan, sets and costumes by Gianni Ratto, 1954.

367-369. Maria Callas in Cherubini's "Medea," director Alexis Minotis, sets and costumes by John Tsarouchis, 1961.

370. Maria Callas in Bellini's "Norma," director Margherita Wallmann, sets and costumes by Salvatore Fiume, 1955.

371. A scene from Bellini's "Norma," with Maria Callas and Nicola Zaccaria, 1955.

372. Giulietta Simionato and Leyla Gencer in Bellini's "Norma," director Margherita Wallmann, sets and costumes by Salvatore Fiume, 1964.

373. Leyla Gencer in Bellini's "Norma," 1964.

374, 375. Montserrat Caballé and Gianni Raimondi in Bellini's "Norma," director Mauro Bolognini, sets by Mario Ceroli, costumes by Gabriella Pescucci, 1973.

376. Renata Scotto in Gounod's "Faust," director Carlo Maestrini, sets and costumes by Alexandre Benois, 1962.

377. Mirella Freni in Gounod's "Faust," director Jean-Louis Barrault, sets and costumes by Jacques Dupont, 1967.

378. Placido Domingo in Puccini's "Tosca," director Piero Faggioni, sets and costumes by Nicola Benois, 1974.

379. Renata Tebaldi in Puccini's "Tosca," director Margherita Wallmann, sets and costumes by Pier Luigi Pizzi, 1962.

380. Franco Corelli in Verdi's "Il Trovatore," director Giorgio De Lullo, sets and costumes by Pier Luigi Pizzi, 1962.

381. Mario Del Monaco in Verdi's "Otello," costume by Nicola Benois, 1954.

382. Giulietta Simionato in Rossini's "Cenerentola," costume by Pier Luigi Pizzi, 1964.

383. Lucia Valentini in Rossini's "Cenerentola," costume by Jean-Pierre Ponnelle, 1971.

384. Giulietta Simionato and Ettore Bastianini in Donizetti's "La Favorita," director Margherita Wallmann, sets and costumes by Nicola Benois, 1962.

385. Fiorenza Cossotto in Verdi's "Il Trovatore," costume by Pier Luigi Pizzi, 1962.

386. Nicolai Ghiaurov in Verdi's "Don Carlos," sets and costumes by Jean-Pierre Ponnelle, 1968.

387. The chief prompter, Vasco Naldini.

388. Gianni Raimondi and Renata Scotto in Donizetti's "Lucia di Lammermoor," director Giorgio De Lullo, sets and costumes by Pier Luigi Pizzi, 1967.

389. Leyla Gencer in Gluck's "Alceste," costume by Pier Luigi Pizzi, 1973.

390. Leyla Gencer in Verdi's "Don Carlos," costume by Waklevitch, 1960.

391. A pause in the rehearsals of "Aida," 1951.

392-394. Rehearsal of Rimsky-Korsakov's "The Legend of the Invisible City of Kitesh," 1951.

395. Gian Giacomo Guelfi during the rehearsals of Jacopo Napoli's "Masaniello," 1953.

396. Ferruccio Tagliavini and Elena Rizzieri during rehearsals of Massenet's "Manon," directed by Mario Frigerio, 1953.

397. Carlo Bergonzi during the rehearsals of Jacopo Napoli's "Masaniello," 1953.

398. Triumphal scene from Verdi's "Aida," director Franco Zeffirelli, sets and costumes by Lila De Nobili, 1963.

399. The second act of Puccini's "La Bohème," direction and sets by Franco Zeffirelli, costumes by Marcel Escoffier, 1963.

400. A rehearsal of Verdi's "Il Trovatore," director Giorgio De Lullo, sets and costumes by Pier Luigi Pizzi, conductor Gianandrea Gavazzeni, 1962.

401, 403. Luchino Visconti at rehearsals of Spontini's "Vestale," 1954.

402. Luchino Visconti and Maria Callas at a rehearsal of Spontini's "Vestale," 1954.

404-407. The director Giorgio Strehler, Mirella Freni, Piero Cappuccilli, and Gianni Raimondi at rehearsals for Verdi's "Simone Boccanegra," 1972.

408. Mirelle Freni in Verdi's "Simone Boccanegra," director Giorgio Strehler, sets and costumes by Ezio Frigerio, 1974.

409-412. Scenes from Verdi's "Simone Boccanegra," 1974.

413. Piero Cappuccilli in Verdi's "Simone Boccanegra," 1974.

414. Group of singers at a rehearsal of Verdi's "Simone Boccanegra," 1974.

415. Piero Cappuccilli (far left), Ruggero Raimondi, Mirella Freni, Gianfranco Cecchele and the set designer Ezio Frigerio during a rehearsal of Verdi's "Simone Boccanegra," 1974.

416. A chorus member during a rehearsal of Verdi's "Simone Boccanegra," 1974.

417. Ruggero Raimondi with his wife, Vittoria, during a rehearsal of "Simone Boccanegra," 1974.

418. Maestro Claudio Abbado, the assistant stage director Lamberto Puggelli and Giorgio Strehler at a rehearsal of "Simone Boccanegra," 1974.

419. Mirella Freni and Gianfranco Cecchele during a rehearsal of Verdi's "Simone Boccanegra," 1974.

420. Mirella Freni taking a curtain call at the end of Verdi's "Simone Boccanegra," 1974.

421. Luigi Alva, Graziella Sciutti, conductor Nino Sanzogno, Eugenia Ratti, Carlo Badioli, Giulietta Simionato, Franco Calabrese, after a performance of Cimarosa's "Il Matrimonio Segreto," at the Piccola Scala, director Giorgio Strehler, sets by Luciano Damiani, costumes by Ezio Frigerio, 1955.

# PHOTO CREDITS